FAMILY LAW REFORM

AUSTRALIA
Law Book Co.
Sydney

CANADA and USA
Carswell
Toronto

HONG KONG
Sweet & Maxwell Asia

NEW ZEALAND
Brookers
Wellington

SINGAPORE and MALAYSIA
Sweet & Maxwell Asia
Singapore and Kuala Lumpur

FAMILY LAW REFORM

Annotations to
Family Law (Scotland) Act 2006

by

Joe Thomson

THOMSON

™

W. GREEN

Published in 2006 by
W. Green & Son Ltd
21 Alva Street
Edinburgh EH2 4PS

www.wgreen.thomson.com

Typeset by YHT Ltd, Hillingdon
Printed and bound in Great Britain by
Athenaeum Press Ltd, Gateshead, Tyne & Wear

No natural forests were destroyed to make this product;
only farmed timber was used and replanted

A CIP catalogue record for this book is available from
the British Library.

ISBN-10 0414 01659 9
ISBN-13 9780 414 01659 0

W. Green & Son Ltd 2006

CONTENTS

FAMILY LAW (SCOTLAND) ACT 2006*

(2006 asp 2)

CONTENTS

Family Law Reform

An Act of the Scottish Parliament to amend the law in relation to marriage, divorce and the jurisdiction of the courts in certain consistorial actions; to amend the Matrimonial Homes (Family Protection) (Scotland) Act 1981; to amend the law relating to the domicile of persons who are under 16 years of age; to make further provision as respects responsibilities and rights in relation to children; to make provision conferring rights in relation to property, succession and claims in damages for persons living, or having lived, together as if husband and wife or civil partners; to amend Part 3 of the Civil Partnership Act 2004; to make further provision in relation to persons entitled to damages under the Damages (Scotland) Act 1976; to make provision in relation to certain rules of private international law relating to family law; to make incompetent actions for declarator of freedom and putting to silence; and for connected purposes.   The Bill for this Act of the Scottish Parliament was passed by the Parliament on 15th December 2005 and received Royal Assent on 20th January 2006

PROGRESS OF THE BILL
Introduced on February 7, 2005 by Cathy Jamieson.
Preliminary discussion: Finance Committee on March 8, 2005; Subordinate Legislation Committee on March 8, 2005; Justice 1 Committee on March 9, 2005.
Stage 1 Committees: Subordinate Legislation Committee on March 15, 2005; Justice 1 Committee on March 16, 2005, April 20, 2005, May 4, 11, 18, 25, 2005, June 1, 8, 15, 22, 27, 29, 30, June 2005; September 14, 2005; Finance Committee on May 10, 24, 2005.
Stage 1 Report (Justice 1 Committee) published on July 7, 2005. Parliament: September 15, 2005.
Pre-Stage 2: Justice 1 Committee on September 21, 28, 2005.
Stage 2 Committees: Justice 1 Committee on October 5, 2005, November 2, 9, 16, 23, 30, 2005.
After Stage 2: Subordinate Legislation Committee on December 13, 2005; Report on the Bill as amended at Stage 2 (Subordinate Legislation Committee) published on December 15, 2005.
Stage 3: Parliament: December 15, 2005. Bill passed on December 15, 2005. Royal Assent on January 20, 2006.

INTRODUCTION AND GENERAL NOTE
The Family Law (Scotland) Act 2006 (asp 2) ("the Act") implements the Scottish Executive's commitment to modernise family law in Scotland. In particular, for the first time it gives cohabitants the right to obtain financial provision on the termination of a relationship and the right to apply for financial provision from a deceased cohabitant's intestate estate. It also reduces the periods of separation for the purposes of divorce from two years to one year (with agreement) and five years to two years (without agreement). But the opportunity was, rightly, taken to introduce a myriad of changes over the whole spectrum of the law. While each is important in itself, like the former Law Reform (Miscellaneous Provisions) (Scotland) Acts, the statute lacks a coherent underlying policy: it is simply a device to bring in a miscellany of reforms. Many of these emanated from the proposals of the Scottish Law Commission: *Report on the Ground for Divorce* (Scot Law Com No 116) (April 27, 1989) and *Report on Family Law* (Scot Law Com No 135) (May 6, 1992) ("Family Law Report"). The disparate nature of the statute is reflected in its long title.

COMMENCEMENT
The Act received Royal Assent on January 20, 2006.

ABBREVIATIONS
"the Act": Family Law (Scotland) Act 2006 (asp 2)
"the 1968 Act": Law Reform (Miscellaneous Provisions) (Scotland) Act 1968 (c.70)
"the 1976 Act": Divorce (Scotland) Act 1976 (c.39)
"the 1981 Act": Matrimonial Homes (Family Protection) (Scotland) Act 1981 (c.59)
"the 1985 Act": Family Law (Scotland) Act 1985 (c.37)
"the 1986 Act": Law Reform (Parent and Child) (Scotland) Act 1986 (c.9)
"the 2004 Act": Pensions Act 2004 (c.35)
"Family Law Report": *Report on Family Law* (Scot Law Com No 135) (May 6, 1992)

Marriage

1. Marriage to parent of former spouse: removal of special requirements

In the Marriage (Scotland) Act 1977 (c.15)-
(a) in section 2 (marriage of related persons)-
   (i) in subsection (1), for "subsections (1A) and (1B)" there shall be substituted "subsection (1A)"; and
   (ii) subsection (1B) shall be repealed; and
(b) in Schedule 1 (relationships by affinity referred to in section 2(1B)), paragraph 2A shall be repealed.

GENERAL NOTE

By s.2(1B) and para.2A of Sch.1 to the Marriage (Scotland) Act 1977 (c.15) (i) a man could only marry his mother-in-law or his daughter-in-law if both parties were over the age of 21 and after the deaths of his former wife and her father or the deaths of his son and the son's mother; and (ii) a woman could only marry her father-in-law or her son-in-law if both parties were over the age of 21 and after the deaths of her former husband and his mother or the deaths of her daughter and the daughter's father. The prohibition on parents and children-in-law to marry unless these restrictive criteria are satisfied has been held to amount to a breach of Arts 8 (right to respect for private and family life) and 12 (right to marry) of the European Convention of Human Rights: *B and L v United Kingdom* (2004) 39 E.H.R.R. SE19. Section 1 removes the prohibition so that a man can marry his former wife's mother or his son's former wife and a woman can marry her former husband's father or daughter's former husband when both parties are 16 or over and have otherwise the legal capacity to do so. In so doing, s.1 implements Family Law Report, recommendation 46.

2. Void marriages

After section 20 of the Marriage (Scotland) Act 1977 (c.15) there shall be inserted-

"Void marriages

20A Grounds on which marriage void
(1) Where subsection (2) or (3) applies in relation to a marriage solemnised in Scotland, the marriage shall be void.
(2) This subsection applies if at the time of the marriage ceremony a party to the marriage who was capable of consenting to the marriage purported to give consent but did so by reason only of duress or error.

(3) This subsection applies if at the time of the marriage ceremony a party to the marriage was incapable of-

    (a) understanding the nature of marriage; and

    (b) consenting to the marriage.

(4) If a party to a marriage purported to give consent to the marriage other than by reason only of duress or error, the marriage shall not be void by reason only of that party's having tacitly withheld consent to the marriage at the time when it was solemnised.

(5) In this section "error" means-

    (a) error as to the nature of the ceremony; or

    (b) a mistaken belief held by a person ("A") that the other party at the ceremony with whom A purported to enter into a marriage was the person whom A had agreed to marry.".

GENERAL NOTE

At common law a marriage is null if the parties did not truly consent to take each other as husband and wife. Defective consent for these purposes can arise when one or both parties lack the mental capacity to consent or apparent consent has been obtained as a result of force and fear (*Mahmood v Mahmood* 1993 S.L.T. 589; *Mahmud v Mahmud* 1994 S.L.T. 599) or consent is vitiated by error as to the nature of the ceremony or the identity of the parties (*McLeod v Adams* 1920 1 S.L.T. 229). Scots law also recognised that marriages were null if it could be established that one or both parties had, for religious or other reasons, intended not to become married at the time of the ceremony (*Orlandi v Castelli* 1961 S.C. 113; *H v H* 2005 S.L.T. 1025). This is known as the sham marriage doctrine. It has become controversial because parties can go through a ceremony of marriage in order to obtain certain rights deriving from the status of matrimony, for example in relation to immigration, and later obtain a decree of declarator of nullity on the basis that the marriage was a sham.

The purpose of s.2 is to put the grounds of nullity arising from defective consent on a statutory basis by adding a new s.20A to the Marriage (Scotland) Act 1977 and to abolish the sham marriage doctrine. In so doing it implements Family Law Report, recommendation 48.

Section 20A(1). It should be noticed that these grounds of nullity only apply when a marriage is solemnised in Scotland. On the applicable law when the marriage is solemnised abroad, see beyond s.38(2).

Section 20A(2). This states that a marriage is null if at the time of the marriage ceremony one-or both-of the parties gave consent by reason only of duress or error. Duress is not defined. At common law the test was subjective and it is hoped that the courts will use a similar test in applying the statute. Section 20A(5) provides that in order to be operative an error must be in relation to the nature of the ceremony or the identity of the party to the marriage-as opposed to his or her personal qualities: this reflects the position at common law (Stair *Institutes* 9.9).

Section 20A(3). This states that a marriage is null if at the time of the ceremony a party to the marriage lacked the mental capacity (i) to understand the nature of the ceremony and (ii) consent to the marriage. It is not clear whether the grounds are alternative or cumulative. But it is unlikely that a person who did not understand the nature of the ceremony would have capacity to consent and vice versa. The lack of mental capacity could arise from mental illness, mental impairment or abuse of alcohol or other drugs. If a person is capable of understanding the nature of the ceremony and consenting to the marriage, it is not a ground of nullity that she was facile and had been subject to circumvention before the ceremony took place: *Scott v Kelly* 1992 S.L.T. 915. Such a marriage can only be annulled if it could be established that the consent had been obtained by duress when s.20A(2) would apply.

Section 20A(4). This section purports to abolish the sham marriage doctrine. It does so by stating that in the absence of duress or error, a marriage is not null merely because at the time of the ceremony one or both parties tacitly withheld consent i.e. while giving apparent consent, real or true consent was being withheld. While such a marriage can be regarded as a sham, there is also the situation where rather than tacitly withholding their consent the parties positively intend not to be married by the ceremony. On a strict construction of the words of s.20A(4) such marriages would not be included and would therefore remain null at common law. However, the mischief of the subsection is clear and it is thought that the courts would not favour a construction that kept alive any remnant of the sham marriage doctrine.

3. Abolition of marriage by cohabitation with habit and repute

(1) The rule of law by which marriage may be constituted by cohabitation with habit and repute shall cease to have effect.

(2) Nothing in subsection (1) shall affect the application of the rule in relation to cohabitation with habit and repute where the cohabitation with habit and repute-

   (a) ended before the commencement of this section ("commencement");
   (b) began before, but ended after, commencement; or
   (c) began before, and continues after, commencement.

(3) Nothing in subsection (1) shall affect the application of the rule in relation to cohabitation with habit and repute where-

   (a) the cohabitation with habit and repute began after commencement; and
   (b) the conditions in subsection (4) are met.

(4) Those conditions are-

   (a) that the cohabitation with habit and repute was between two persons, one of whom, ("A"), is domiciled in Scotland;
   (b) that the person with whom A was cohabiting, ("B"), died domiciled in Scotland;
   (c) that, before the cohabitation with habit and repute began, A and B purported to enter into a marriage ("the purported marriage") outwith the United Kingdom;
   (d) that, in consequence of the purported marriage, A and B believed themselves to be married to each other and continued in that belief until B's death;
   (e) that the purported marriage was invalid under the law of the place where the purported marriage was entered into; and
   (f) that A became aware of the invalidity of the purported marriage only after B's death.

GENERAL NOTE

Marriage by cohabitation by habit and repute was the last form of irregular marriage in Scots law. The parties had to have the capacity to marry. If they lived together and were generally thought to be husband and wife then they would become married after a period of cohabitation which could be as little as six to nine months. The doctrine did not apply if the parties made it clear that they were not married but merely living together. In other words, the doctrine only applied where the couple pretended to be married, one of the few situations where Scots law recognised rights arising from bad faith. When one (or both) believed they were regularly married but the marriage was void because of a temporary impediment, they could become validly married as a result of cohabitation with habit and repute after the impediment was removed (*Sheik v Sheik* 2005 Fam. L.R. 7).

There is no doubt that the existence of this form of marriage was anomalous. The Scottish Law Commission recommended its abolition; Family Law Report, recommendation 42. Moreover, couples who lived together were often under the impression that they were married by cohabitation with habit and repute when the doctrine was inapplicable either because they lacked capacity to marry or, more commonly, because they made no pretence of being married and therefore lacked the requisite repute that they were husband and wife. In these circumstances, it was thought that the doctrine should be abolished.

Section 3(1). This provides that after the commencement of the Act, the common law rule that a couple can become married by cohabitation with habit and repute shall cease to exist. However,

s.3(2) provides that a couple may still become married by cohabitation with habit and repute (i) if the cohabitation began and ended before the commencement of the Act i.e. where they have already become married by cohabitation with habit and repute and (ii) if the cohabitation began before but continues after the commencement of the Act. In other words, a couple can still become married by cohabitation with habit and repute even although post Act cohabitation as well as pre Act cohabitation has to be used to infer that they have done so.

There is to be an exceptional situation when a couple can still become married by cohabitation with habit and repute even though their cohabitation began after the commencement of the Act. This is when A and B go through a ceremony of marriage abroad i.e. outside the United Kingdom. They believe that they are validly married but the marriage is in fact invalid under the *lex loci celebrationis*. A is or becomes domiciled in Scotland. The couple cohabit in Scotland with habit and repute that they are married. If B dies domiciled in Scotland, a declarator that they were married by cohabitation with habit and repute can be obtained if A became aware that the purported marriage was invalid only after B had died: ss.3(3) and (4). It should be noticed that the doctrine only applies to foreign marriages. If A and B went through a marriage ceremony in Scotland which unknown to them was void, they cannot become married by post commencement cohabitation with habit and repute. Moreover even if they went through the marriage ceremony abroad, a declarator that they had become married by cohabitation with habit and repute cannot be granted unless B is dead. If B was alive when it was discovered that their marriage was invalid, A and B would have to go through a new ceremony of marriage in order to become married. This is odd since if B had died it is open to obtain a declarator that they had become married by cohabitation and with habit and repute long before B had died!

4. Extension of jurisdiction of sheriff

In subsection (1) of section 5 of the Sheriff Courts (Scotland) Act 1907 (c.51) (extension of jurisdiction), the words "(except declarators of marriage or nullity of marriage)" shall be repealed.

GENERAL NOTE

Jurisdiction to grant declarator of marriage and declarator of nullity of marriage was privative to the Court of Session. This section extends the jurisdiction to the sheriff courts by repealing the provisions of s.5 of the Sheriff Courts (Scotland) Act 1907 (c.51) which exclude such declarators from the jurisdiction of the sheriff court. It implements Family Law Report, recommendation 51.

Matrimonial homes

5. Occupancy rights: duration

In section 1 of the 1981 Act (right of spouse without title to occupy matrimonial home), after subsection (6) there shall be added-
"(7) Subject to subsection (5), if-
(a) there has been no cohabitation between an entitled spouse and a non-entitled spouse during a continuous period of two years; and
(b) during that period the non-entitled spouse has not occupied the matrimonial home,
the non-entitled spouse shall, on the expiry of that period, cease to have occupancy rights in the matrimonial home.
(8) A non-entitled spouse who has ceased to have occupancy rights by virtue of subsection (7) may not apply to the court for an order under section 3(1).".

GENERAL NOTE

By s.1 of the Matrimonial Homes (Family Protection) (Scotland) Act 1981 (c.59) ("the 1981 Act"), a non-entitled spouse has a statutory right to occupy the matrimonial home along with any child of the family (who includes a grandchild). The amendment to s.1, adding new subss.(7) and (8), provides that if the non-entitled spouse has not lived with the entitled spouse for a continuous period of two years and during that period the non-entitled spouse has not occupied the matrimonial home then the non-entitled spouse's statutory right of occupation comes to an end at the expiry of the two year period. In other words, a non-entitled spouse who has separated from her husband will lose her statutory right of occupation if she does not live in the matrimonial home for a continuous period of two years; for example if she left the matrimonial home in order to live with a new lover or because she was imprisoned or moved to a new job. If she loses her statutory right in this way, the non-entitled spouse also loses the right to seek an order under s.3 of the 1981 Act declaring her statutory rights. This means that if the right is lost it does not revive again if the couple became reconciled and the non-entitled spouse returned to the matrimonial home. It implements Family Law Report, recommendation 56.

6. Occupancy rights: dealings with third parties

(1) Section 6 of the 1981 Act (continued exercise of occupancy rights after dealing) shall be amended in accordance with subsections (2) and (3).

(2) After subsection (1), there shall be inserted-

"(1A) The occupancy rights of a non-entitled spouse in relation to a matrimonial home shall not be exercisable in relation to the home where, following a dealing of the entitled spouse relating to the home-

(a) a person acquires the home, or an interest in it, in good faith and for value from a person other than the person who is or, as the case may be, was the entitled spouse; or

(b) a person derives title to the home from a person who acquired title as mentioned in paragraph (a).".

(3) In subsection (3)-

(a) in paragraph (e)-

(i) for "sale", where it first occurs, there shall be substituted "transfer for value"; and

(ii) for the words from "seller", where it first occurs, to the end of the paragraph there shall be substituted

"transferor-

(i) a written declaration signed by the transferor, or a person acting on behalf of the transferor under a power of attorney or as a guardian (within the meaning of the Adults with Incapacity (Scotland) Act 2000 (asp 4)), that the subjects of the transfer are not, or were not at the time of the dealing, a matrimonial home in relation to which a spouse of the transferor has or had occupancy rights; or

(ii) a renunciation of occupancy rights or consent to the dealing which bears to have been properly made or given by the non-entitled spouse or a person acting on behalf of the non-entitled spouse under a power of attorney or as a guardian (within the meaning of the Adults with Incapacity (Scotland) Act 2000 (asp 4))."; and

(b) in paragraph (f), for "5" there shall be substituted "2".

GENERAL NOTE

By s.6(1) of the 1981 Act, unless she has consented to the dealing, a non-entitled spouse's statutory right to occupy the matrimonial home is not to be prejudiced by reason only of any dealing of the entitled spouse in relation to the property: and by reason only of such a dealing, a third party is not entitled to occupy the matrimonial home or any part of it. Put shortly, in any competition between a non-entitled spouse and a third party who has obtained rights in respect of the property as a consequence of a dealing with the entitled spouse, the non-entitled spouse's statutory right of occupation will prevail.

Section 6(2). This adds a new subs.(1A) to s.6 of the 1981 Act. Section 6(1A)(a) states that where a third party in good faith and for value acquires a real right in respect of the home from a person other than the entitled spouse, then the third party's right will prevail against the non-entitled spouse's statutory right. For example, if H, an entitled spouse, gifts a matrimonial home to his mistress, M, M's right as owner of the property cannot prevail against W's, H's non-entitled wife's statutory right of occupation. But if M was to transfer the ownership of the house to T1, a bona fide transferee for value, then T1's real right in the property will prevail over W's statutory right of occupation. Section 6(1A)(b) provides that if, in our example, T1 in turn transferred the ownership of the house to T2, T2's title will prevail over W's statutory right of occupation, even if T2 is not in good faith or has not given value for the property.

Section 6(3)(a). Section 6(3)(e) of the 1981 Act provided that where the dealing consisted of the sale of the matrimonial home by an entitled spouse to a bona fide third party, then the purchaser's rights will prevail over the non-entitled spouse's statutory right of occupation if (i) there was produced to the purchaser an affidavit sworn or affirmed by the seller that the house he is selling is not or was not at the time of the dealing a matrimonial home in relation to which a spouse of the seller had occupancy rights: or (ii) a renunciation of occupancy rights or consent to the dealing which bears to have been properly made by the non-entitled spouse. It should be noted that even though the seller is lying when he swears or affirms the affidavit, the purchaser's rights will prevail provided he was acting in good faith. If he was in bad faith, the non-entitled spouse's statutory right of occupation will prevail. (Though if in these circumstances, the mala fide purchaser sold on to a bona fide transferee for value, the latter's rights will prevail over the non-entitled spouse's statutory right of occupation by virtue of s.6(1A) of the 1981 Act discussed above). Section 6(3) amends s.6(3)(e) by substituting "transfer for value" for sale. This means that dealings for value which are not technically sales are now included such as, for example a lease of the property or an excambion of the property. A written declaration signed by the transferor replaces an affidavit. The provision is extended to include the situations where a person signs on behalf of the transferor, or purports to renounce or consent on behalf of a non-entitled spouse, under a power of attorney or as a guardian within the meaning of the Adults with Incapacity (Scotland) Act 2000 (asp 4).

Section 6(3)(b). Section 6(8)(f) of the 1981 Act provides that if the entitled spouse has permanently ceased to be entitled to occupy the matrimonial home, for example by having sold it to a third party, the non-entitled spouse's statutory right of occupation ceases to be exercisable against the third party if the non-entitled spouse has, at any time thereafter, not occupied the house for a continuous period of five years. Section 6(3)(b) reduces the period of five years to two years. This is consistent with the new ss.1(7) and (8) of the 1981 Act discussed above.

These provisions implement Family Law Report, recommendation 55.

7. Occupancy rights: proposed dealings with third parties

In section 7 of the 1981 Act (court's power to dispense with spouse's consent to dealing and proposed dealing)-

(a) in subsection (1), at the beginning there shall be inserted "Subject to subsections (1A) to (1D) below,";

(b) after that subsection there shall be inserted-

"(1A) Subsection (1B) applies if, in relation to a proposed sale-

(a) negotiations with a third party have not begun; or

(b) negotiations have begun but a price has not been agreed.

    (1B) An order under subsection (1) dispensing with consent may be made only if-
- (a) the price agreed for the sale is no less than such amount as the court specifies in the order; and
- (b) the contract for the sale is concluded before the expiry of such period as may be so specified.

    (1C) Subsection (1D) applies if the proposed dealing is the grant of a heritable security.

    (1D) An order under subsection (1) dispensing with consent may be made only if-
- (a) the heritable security is granted for a loan of no more than such amount as the court specifies in the order; and
- (b) the security is executed before the expiry of such period as may be so specified."; and

  (c) after subsection (3) there shall be inserted-

    "(3A) If the court refuses an application for an order under subsection (1), it may make an order requiring a non-entitled spouse who is or becomes the occupier of the matrimonial home-
- (a) to make such payments to the owner of the home in respect of that spouse's occupation of it as may be specified in the order;
- (b) to comply with such other conditions relating to that spouse's occupation of the matrimonial home as may be so specified.".

GENERAL NOTE

Section 7(1) of the 1981 Act provides that a court can dispense with the need for a non-entitled spouse's consent to a dealing or a proposed dealing on the ground *inter alia* that the consent is being unreasonably withheld. Before the court can consider this issue any proposed dealing must have reached a stage of negotiations where price and other conditions, for example date of entry, have been discussed. It is not enough that the entitled spouse proposes to put the property up for sale: *Fyfe v Fyfe* 1987 S.L.T. (Sh. Ct.) 38. This effectively prevented the entitled spouse from selling the matrimonial home on the open market without the non-entitled spouse's consent. The amendments to s.7 allow an entitled spouse to obtain an order dispensing with the consent of the non-entitled spouse to a dealing where negotiations with a third party have not begun or negotiations have begun but a price has not been agreed, provided the sale is concluded within a period specified in the order at no less than the price stipulated by the court in the order (ss.7(1A) and (1B) of the 1981 Act). If the proposed dealing is the grant of a standard security over the matrimonial home, the court can only make an order dispensing with the consent of the non-entitled spouse if the security is granted for a loan of not more than the sum stipulated in the order and the security is executed within the period specified in that order (ss.7(1C) and (1D) of the 1981 Act).

Where an order dispensing with the consent of a non-entitled spouse is refused, if the non-entitled spouse continues to occupy the matrimonial home the court is given the power to order her to make payments to the entitled spouse and to comply with other conditions relating to the occupation of the property as may be specified in the order (s.7(3A) of the 1981 Act).

8. Occupancy rights: effect of court action

After section 9 of the 1981 Act (provisions where both spouses have title) there shall be inserted-

"*Reckoning of non-cohabitation periods in sections 1 and 6*

9A Effect of court action under section 3, 4 or 5 on reckoning of periods in sections 1 and 6

(1) Subsection (2) applies where an application is made under section 3(1), 4(1) or 5(1) of this Act.

(2) In calculating the period of two years mentioned in section 1(7)(a) or 6(3)(f) of this Act, no account shall be taken of the period mentioned in subsection (3) below.

(3) The period is the period beginning with the date on which the application is made and-

(a) in the case of an application under section 3(1) or 4(1) of this Act, ending on the date on which-

    (i) an order under section 3(3) or, as the case may be, 4(2) of this Act is made; or

    (ii) the application is otherwise finally determined or abandoned;

(b) in the case of an application under section 5(1) of this Act, ending on the date on which-

    (i) the order under section 3(3) or, as the case may be, 4(2) is varied or recalled; or

    (ii) the application is otherwise finally determined or abandoned.".

GENERAL NOTE

An entitled spouse will lose her statutory right of occupation if (i) she has ceased to cohabit with the entitled spouse for a continuous period of two years during which she has not occupied the matrimonial home (s.1(7) of the 1981 Act as added by s.5 of this Act discussed above) or (ii) the entitled spouse has permanently ceased to be entitled to occupy the matrimonial home and at any time thereafter the non-entitled spouse has not occupied the property for a continuous period of two years (s.6(3)(f) of the 1981 Act as amended by s.6(3) of this Act discussed above). In *Stevenson v Roy* 2003 S.C. 544 it was held that for these purposes a non-entitled spouse should still be regarded as not being in occupation of the matrimonial home during periods when she was seeking to exercise her statutory right by bringing proceedings to enable her to re-occupy the property. The amendments to s.9 of the 1981 Act attempt to alleviate this problem. They provide that in calculating the two year period of non-occupation, the following periods are to be ignored:

(i) the period between the application by the non-entitled spouse under the 1981 Act for an order regulating occupancy rights (s.3) or an exclusion order (s.4) and the granting of such an order or the final determination or abandonment of the application; and

(ii) the period between the application by either spouse under s.5 of the 1981 Act for variation or recall of a s.3 or s.6 order and the variation and recall of such an order or the final determination or abandonment of the application.

While such periods do not count towards the two years, they do not break the continuity of the periods when the non-entitled spouse does not occupy the property.

9.   Amendment of definition of matrimonial home

In section 22 of the 1981 Act (interpretation) (which shall become subsection (1) of that section)-

(a) in the definition of "matrimonial home"-

    (i) after "means" there shall be inserted "subject to subsection (2),"; and

    (ii) for the words "one spouse for that" there shall be substituted "a person for one"; and

  (b) at the end there shall be inserted-

      "(2) If-

        (a) the tenancy of a matrimonial home is transferred from one spouse to the other by agreement or under any enactment; and

        (b) following the transfer, the spouse to whom the tenancy was transferred occupies the home but the other spouse does not,

the home shall, on such transfer, cease to be a matrimonial home.".

GENERAL NOTE

A matrimonial home does not include" a residence provided or made available by one spouse for that spouse to live in, whether with any child of the family or not, separately from the other spouse": s.22 of the 1981 Act. This means that if a spouse acquires a house in which she lives separately from the other spouse this will not constitute a matrimonial home even if children of the family also reside there. Moreover it was held in *McRobbie v McRobbie* (Outer House, unreported, August 3, 1983) that where one spouse provided the other with a house where the other spouse lives separately from him, the house does not constitute a matrimonial home. Section 9(a) amends the definition so that a matrimonial home does not include "a residence provided or made available by a person for one spouse to reside in, whether or not with any child of the family, separately from the other spouse". Accordingly, excluded from the definition of matrimonial property is a house provided by any person for one spouse to reside in separately from the other spouse. Person includes the other spouse, the spouse who is to reside there, as well as third parties. Thus the following are not matrimonial homes:

(i)   H acquires a house in which H will live separately from W (or vice versa);
(ii)   H acquires a house for W in which W will live separately from H (or vice versa); and
(iii) Third party acquires a house for W in which W will live separately from H (or vice versa).

These provisions implement Family Law Report, recommendation 63.

Section 9(b) amends s.22 of the 1981 Act expressly to provide that where a tenancy of a matrimonial home is transferred from spouse A to the other spouse B, if B occupies the house and A does not, the property ceases to be a matrimonial home for the purposes of the 1981 Act when the lease was transferred. This implements Family Law Report, recommendation 65.

Matrimonial interdicts

10. Matrimonial interdicts

  (1) Section 14 of the 1981 Act (matrimonial interdicts) shall be amended in accordance with subsections (2) and (3).

  (2) For paragraph (b) of subsection (2) there shall be substituted-

      "(b) subject to subsection (3), prohibits a spouse from entering or remaining in-

        (i) a matrimonial home;

        (ii) any other residence occupied by the applicant spouse;

        (iii) any place of work of the applicant spouse;

        (iv) any school attended by a child in the permanent or temporary care of the applicant spouse.".

  (3) After subsection (2) there shall be added-

      "(3) Subsection (4) applies if in relation to a matrimonial home the non-applicant spouse-

      (a) is an entitled spouse; or

      (b) has occupancy rights.

  (4) Except where subsection (5) applies, the court may not grant a matrimonial interdict prohibiting the non-applicant spouse from entering or remaining in the matrimonial home.

  (5) This subsection applies if-

      (a) the interdict is ancillary to an exclusion order; or

      (b) by virtue of section 1(3), the court refuses leave to exercise occupancy rights.

  (6) In this section and in sections 15 to 17, "applicant spouse" means the spouse who has applied for the interdict; and "non-applicant spouse" shall be construed accordingly.".

GENERAL NOTE

Section 14(2) of the 1981 Act provides that a matrimonial interdict means an interdict, including an interim interdict, which:

> "(a) restrains or prohibits any conduct of one spouse towards the other spouse or a child of the family, or
>
> (b) prohibits a spouse from entering or remaining in a matrimonial home or in a specified area in the vicinity of the matrimonial home."

It was held in *Tattersall v Tattersall* 1983 S.L.T. 506 that a s.14(2)(b) interdict can not be used to exclude the owner of a matrimonial home from his property. This meant that a s.14(2)(b) interdict could only be granted to an entitled spouse against a non-entitled spouse. If a non-entitled spouse sought to exclude an entitled spouse from the matrimonial home or where both spouses were entitled i.e. common owners of the matrimonial home, resort had to be made to s.4 of the 1981 Act for an exclusion order. A s.4 exclusion order can only be granted when it is necessary to do so: *Colagiacomo v Colagiacomo* 1983 SLT 559. A s.14(2)(b) interdict can be granted on the balance of convenience.

Section 10(2) substitutes a new s.14(2)(b) in the 1981 Act. It implements Family Law Report, recommendation 57. As well as being prohibited from entering or remaining in the matrimonial home (s.14(2)(b)(i)), the defender can now be interdicted from entering or remaining in any other residence occupied by the applicant (s.14(2)(b)(ii)), the applicant's place of work (s.14(2)(b)(iii)) or any school attended by a child in the care of the applicant (s.14(2)(b)(iv)).

Section 10(3) adds three subsections to s.14 of the 1981 Act. They deal with the issue raised by *Tattersall v Tattersall* discussed above. Where the defender is an entitled spouse i.e. an owner of the matrimonial property or a non-entitled spouse with occupancy rights, the court cannot use s.14(2)(b)(i) to prohibit the defender from entering or remaining in the matrimonial home: ss.14(3) and (4) of the 1981 Act. (Of course, the court is free to grant interdicts under ss.14 (2)(b)(ii), (iii) and (iv)). However, s.14 (5) of the 1981 Act goes on to provide that the court can grant an interdict under s.14(2)(b)(i) if:

(i)   it is ancillary to a s.4 exclusion order: then it does not matter if the defender is an entitled spouse or a non-entitled spouse with occupancy rights; or

(ii)   the defender is a non-entitled spouse who has not been granted leave under s.1(3) of the 1981 to exercise her occupation rights

The law has therefore been changed in that where the defender is a non-entitled spouse, an entitled spouse cannot use s.14(2)(b)(i) to prevent the defender from entering or remaining in the matrimonial home without applying for a s.4 exclusion order: but s14(2)(b)(i) can be used to exclude a non-entitled spouse if the non-entitled spouse has not been given leave to exercise her statutory rights of occupation. In practice most matrimonial homes are owned in common by the spouses i.e. both are entitled: accordingly resort must be made to s.4 of the 1981 Act for an exclusion order before a s.14(2)(b)(i) interdict can be granted.

GENERAL NOTE

Under s.1(1) of the Divorce (Scotland) Act 1976 (c.39) ("the 1976 Act") a divorce may be granted if it can be established that the marriage has broken down irretrievably or that after the marriage an interim gender recognition certificate has been issued to either of the spouses. Section 1(2) provides that irretrievable breakdown will be established on proof of (a) the defender's adultery; (b) the defender's unreasonable behaviour; (c) the defender's desertion for two years; (d) the non-cohabitation of the parties for two years and the defender's consent to the divorce; and (e) the non-cohabitation of the parties for five years without the defender's consent to the divorce. Sections 11-15 change the law on divorce. In doing so, they implement the major recommendations of the Scottish Law Commission in its Report on the *Reform of the Ground of Divorce* (Scot Law Com No 116). However adultery remains a separate ground for establishing irretrievable breakdown and is not subsumed under unreasonable behaviour. And with the survival of adultery the defences of *lenocinium* and condonation remain: s.1(3) of the 1976 Act.

11. Divorce: reduction in separation periods

In subsection (2) of section 1 of the 1976 Act (irretrievable breakdown of marriage to be sole ground of divorce)-
  (a) in paragraph (d), for "two years" there shall be substituted "one year"; and
  (b) in paragraph (e), for "five" there shall be substituted "two".

GENERAL NOTE

This reduces the period of non-cohabitation with consent from two years to one and the period of non-cohabitation without consent from five years to two.

12. Irretrievable breakdown of marriage: desertion no longer to be ground

Paragraph (c) of section 1(2) of the 1976 Act (irretrievable breakdown of marriage to be sole ground of divorce) shall be repealed.

GENERAL NOTE

This abolishes desertion as a separate ground for establishing irretrievable breakdown of marriage.

13. Non-cohabitation without consent: removal of bar to divorce

Subsection (5) of section 1 of the 1976 Act (irretrievable breakdown of marriage to be sole ground of divorce) shall be repealed.

GENERAL NOTE

Where irretrievable breakdown of marriage has been established by five years non-cohabitation, s.1(5) of the 1976 Act provided that the court could refuse to grant a decree of divorce if satisfied that the grant of the decree would result in grave financial hardship to the defender. With the introduction of the regime of financial provision on divorce under the Family Law (Scotland) Act 1985 (c.37) ("the 1985 Act"), in particular s.9(1)(e) under which the court can award reasonable financial provision to a spouse who at the time of the divorce seems likely to suffer serious financial hardship as a result of divorce, s.1(5) has become redundant. Section 13 repeals s.1(5) of the 1976 Act. and thereby implements the Family Law Report, recommendation 69.

14. Collusion no longer to be bar to divorce

(1) Any rule of law by which collusion between parties is a bar to their divorce shall cease to have effect.

(2) Section 9 of the 1976 Act (abolition of the oath of calumny) shall be repealed.

GENERAL NOTE

In modern divorce practice, parties are encouraged to ease the stresses of the process as much as possible. In particular this is done when children of the family are involved. So for example a party may be advised not to put up a relevant defence. At common law this could constitute collusion and could operate as a bar to divorce as would an agreement to put up a false case. To avoid such outcomes s.14(1) provides that collusion is no longer to operate as a bar to divorce. This implements the Family Law Report, recommendation 68(b). Section 14(2) repeals s.9 of the 1976 Act which abolished the oath of calumny but expressly stated that it did not affect "any rule of law relating to collusion". The repeal of s.9 is therefore consequential on the abolition of collusion as a bar to divorce by s.14(1). The repeal of s.9 does not, of course, revive the oath of calumny: Interpretation Act 1978 (c.30), s.16.

15. Postponement of decree of divorce where religious impediment to remarry exists

After section 3 of the 1976 Act (action for divorce following on decree of separation) there shall be inserted-

"**3A Postponement of decree of divorce where religious impediment to remarry exists**

—(1) Notwithstanding that irretrievable breakdown of a marriage has been established in an action for divorce, the court may-

   (a) on the application of a party ("the applicant"); and
   (b) if satisfied-
       (i) that subsection (2) applies; and
       (ii) that it is just and reasonable to do so,

   postpone the grant of decree in the action until it is satisfied that the other party has complied with subsection (3).

(2) This subsection applies where-

   (a) the applicant is prevented from entering into a religious marriage by virtue of a requirement of the religion of that marriage; and
   (b) the other party can act so as to remove, or enable or contribute to the removal of, the impediment which prevents that marriage.

(3) A party complies with this subsection by acting in the way described in subsection (2)(b).

(4) The court may, whether or not on the application of a party and notwithstanding that subsection (2) applies, recall a postponement under subsection (1).

(5) The court may, before recalling a postponement under subsection (1), order the other party to produce a certificate from a relevant religious body confirming that the other party has acted in the way described in subsection 2(b).

(6) For the purposes of subsection (5), a religious body is "relevant" if the applicant considers the body competent to provide the confirmation referred to in that subsection.

(7) In this section-

"religious marriage" means a marriage solemnised by a marriage celebrant of a prescribed religious body, and "religion of that marriage" shall be construed accordingly;

"prescribed" means prescribed by regulations made by the Scottish Ministers.

(8) Any reference in this section to a marriage celebrant of a prescribed religious body is a reference to-

(a) a minister, clergyman, pastor or priest of such a body;

(b) a person who has, on the nomination of such a body, been registered under section 9 of the Marriage (Scotland) Act 1977 (c.15) as empowered to solemnise marriages; or

(c) any person who is recognised by such a body as entitled to solemnise marriages on its behalf.

(9) Regulations under subsection (7) shall be made by statutory instrument; and any such instrument shall be subject to annulment in pursuance of a resolution of the Scottish Parliament.".

GENERAL NOTE

In certain religions, for example Judaism, a woman who has been divorced under Scots law is not allowed to enter a religious marriage unless she has also been divorced under the law of her religion. This may involve her husband divorcing her by delivering to her a document of divorce (in Judaism, for example, this is known as a get). If he refuses to do so, not only will she be unable to marry again in accordance with her religion but she may also be ostracised by her family. The new s.3A of the 1976 Act gives the court power on the application of either of the parties to postpone the grant of a decree of divorce until a religious divorce has taken place. So for example if H is seeking a divorce from W, W can apply under s.3A to have the grant of the decree of divorce postponed until H divorces her under the law of their religion by for example delivering a document of divorce so that she will have no impediment to having a religious marriage later.

The power to postpone grant of decree arises "Notwithstanding that irretrievable breakdown of a marriage has been established in an action of divorce": s.3A(1). It is clear that the pursuer is being denied a remedy to which he would otherwise be entitled under Scots law. This is done for religious reasons i.e. because "(a) the applicant is prevented from entering into a religious marriage by virtue of a requirement of the religion of that marriage; and (b) the other party can act so as to remove, or enable or contribute to the removal of, the impediment which prevents the marriage": s.3A(2). In addition to s.3A(2) being applicable, the court must also be satisfied that it is just and reasonable to postpone the grant of decree: s.3A(1)(b)(ii). The court can recall the postponement when it has received a certificate from the relevant religious body that the other party has acted to remove the impediment. But the court can recall the postponement even though this has not occurred: s.3A(4). Where W is seeking a divorce from H, however, postponing decree of divorce will not help W to obtain a religious divorce from H if H does not want to divorce her. It should also be noted that no power to postpone grant of decree arises when the divorce is based on the issue of an interim gender recognition certificate to either of the parties: it only applies if the divorce is based on irretrievable breakdown of marriage.

Financial provision

16. Financial provision: valuation of matrimonial property

In section 10 of the Family Law (Scotland) Act 1985 (c.37) (which provides for the sharing of the value of matrimonial property and fixes the date of its valuation)-

(a) in subsection (2), at the beginning there shall be inserted "Subject to subsection (3A) below,"; and

(b) after subsection (3), there shall be inserted-

"(3A) In its application to property transferred by virtue of an order under section 8(1)(aa) of this Act this section shall have effect as if-

(a) in subsection (2) above, for "relevant date" there were substituted "appropriate valuation date";

(b) after that subsection there were inserted-

"(2A) Subject to subsection (2B), in this section the "appropriate valuation date" means-

(a) where the parties to the marriage or, as the case may be, the partners agree on a date, that date;

(b) where there is no such agreement, the date of the making of the order under section 8(1)(aa).

(2B) If the court considers that, because of the exceptional circumstances of the case, subsection (2A)(b) should not apply, the appropriate valuation date shall be such other date (being a date as near as may be to the date referred to in subsection (2A)(b)) as the court may determine."; and

(c) subsection (3) did not apply.".

GENERAL NOTE

In *Wallis v Wallis* 1993 S.L.T. 1348, the House of Lords held that for the purposes of fair sharing of matrimonial property under s.9(1)(a) of the 1985 Act, the net value of the matrimonial property is its net value at the relevant date - usually the date when the couple ceased to cohabit. Any increase in value of the couple's assets between the relevant date and the date of divorce was to be ignored. This meant that if the court made a property transfer order under s.8(aa) of the 1985 Act, the transferee could obtain a windfall if the property transferred had risen in value between the relevant date and the date of divorce. This was particularly likely to arise in relation to heritable property. For example, H and W are common owners of the family home. The net value of the house at the relevant date is £200k. At the time of the divorce, the net value of the house has risen to £300k. Under s.9(1)(a), each spouse is entitled to fair division of the net value of the matrimonial property at the relevant date: *prima facie* fair sharing is equal sharing. Thus in so far as the matrimonial home is concerned H is entitled to £100k and W is entitled to £100k. But if the court orders H to transfer his one half *pro indiviso* share of the property to W, she will receive at the time of the transfer i.e. at the date of the divorce, an asset which is worth £150k giving her a windfall of £50k. In spite of the injustice inherent in the decision, *Wallis v Wallis* has been consistently followed: see for example, *Dible v Dible* 1997 S.L.T. 787; *Kennedy v Kennedy* 2004 Fam. L.R. 70; *Christie v Christie* 2004 S.L.T. (Sh Ct) 95. Where the house was owned in common, instead of a property transfer order, the court could order division and sale of the property enabling both spouses to benefit from any increase in value since the relevant date: *McCaskill v McCaskill* 2004 Fam. L.R. 123.

Section 16 amends s.10 of the 1985 Act to avoid the *Wallis v Wallis* problem. The date for the valuation of matrimonial property for the purposes of fair division under s.9(1)(a) remains the relevant date: ss.10(2) and (3) of the 1985 Act. However a new s.10(3A) is added. This provides that when a property transfer order is made, the date when the property being transferred is to be valued is no longer to be the relevant date but the "appropriate valuation date". The appropriate valuation date is to be a date agreed by the parties to the marriage or civil partnership or, in the absence of such an agreement, the date on which the property transfer order is made: this will usually be the date of divorce or dissolution. In exceptional circumstances, the appropriate valuation date can be such date as the court shall determine, being a date as near as maybe to the date on which the property transfer order is made.

Given that s.10(3A) is only triggered when the court intends to make a property transfer order under s.8(aa), the provision makes the smallest possible inroad into the fundamental principle that for the purpose of fair sharing of matrimonial property under s.9(1)(a) the property is valued at the relevant date. But such an inroad was inevitable if the injustice inherent in *Wallis v Wallis* was to be avoided. It also seems sensible that in the absence of a date agreed between the parties, the appropriate valuation date should *prima facie* be the date on which the property transfer order is made.

It will be interesting to see what the court will regard as exceptional circumstances. If in our example above above, H's other assets had risen in value between the relevant date and the date of divorce while W's had not, is it fair that she should have to pay him the date of divorce value of his *pro indiviso* share? Is this a case where a court could decide that there are exceptional circumstances and that the relevant date value of the house should still be used?

17. Financial provision on divorce and dissolution of civil partnership: Pension Protection Fund

(1) The Family Law (Scotland) Act 1985 (c.37) shall be amended in accordance with subsections (2) to (5).

(2) In section 8 (orders for financial provision), after subsection (4) there shall be inserted-

"(4A) The court shall not make a pension sharing order, or an order under section 12A(2) or (3) of this Act, in relation to matrimonial property, or partnership property, consisting of compensation such as is mentioned in section 10(5A).".

(3) In section 10 (sharing of value of property)-

(a) in each of subsections (4) and (4A), for "subsection (5)" there shall be substituted "subsections (5) and (5A)";

(b) in subsection (5), after "(4)(b)" there shall be inserted "or (4A)(b)";

(c) after subsection (5) there shall be inserted-

"(5A) Where either person is entitled to compensation payable under Chapter 3 of Part 2 of the Pensions Act 2004 (c.35) or any provision in force in Northern Ireland corresponding to that Chapter, the proportion of the compensation which is referable to the period to which subsection (4)(b) or (4A)(b) above refers shall be taken to form part of the matrimonial property or partnership property.";

(d) after subsection (8A) there shall be inserted-

"(8B) The Scottish Ministers may by regulations make provision for or in connection with the verification, or apportionment, of compensation such as is mentioned in subsection (5A).”; and

(e) in subsection (9), after "(8)" there shall be inserted "or (8B)".

(4) In section 12A (orders for payment of capital sum: pensions lump sum)-

(a) after subsection (7) there shall be inserted-

"(7A) Where-

(a) the court makes an order under subsection (3); and

(b) after the making of the order the Board gives the trustees or managers of the scheme a notice under section 160 of the Pensions Act 2004 (c.35) ("the 2004 Act"), or the Northern Ireland provision, in relation to the scheme,

the order shall, on the giving of such notice, be recalled.

(7B) Subsection (7C) applies where-

(a) the court makes an order under subsection (2) imposing requirements on the trustees or managers of an occupational pension scheme; and

(b) after the making of the order the Board gives the trustees or managers of the scheme a notice under section 160 of the 2004 Act, or the Northern Ireland provision, in relation to the scheme.

(7C) The order shall have effect from the time when the notice is given-

   (a) as if-

      (i) references to the trustees or managers of the scheme were references to the Board; and

      (ii) references to any lump sum to which the person with benefits under a pension arrangement is or might become entitled under the scheme were references to the amount of any compensation payable under that Chapter of the 2004 Act, or the Northern Ireland provision, to which that person is or might become entitled in respect of the lump sum; and

   (b) subject to such other modifications as may be prescribed by regulations by the Scottish Ministers.";

(b) in subsection (9), for "subsection" there shall be substituted "subsections (7C)(b) and"; and

(c) after subsection (10) there shall be added-

"(11) In subsections (7A) to (7C) "the Northern Ireland provision", in relation to a provision of the 2004 Act, means any provision in force in Northern Ireland corresponding to the provision of that Act.".

(5) In section 16 (agreements on financial provision), after subsection (2A) there shall be inserted-

"(2B) Subsection (2C) applies where-

   (a) the parties to a marriage or the partners in a civil partnership have entered into an agreement as to financial provision to be made on divorce or on dissolution of the civil partnership; and

   (b) the agreement includes provision in respect of a person's rights or interests or benefits under an occupational pension scheme.

(2C) The Board of the Pension Protection Fund's subsequently assuming responsibility for the occupational pension scheme in accordance with Chapter 3 of Part 2 of the Pension Act 2004 (c.35) or any provision in force in Northern Ireland corresponding to that Chapter shall not affect-

   (a) the power of the court under subsection (1)(b) to make an order setting aside or varying the agreement or any term of it;

   (b) on an appeal, the powers of the appeal court in relation to the order.".

GENERAL NOTE

This provision makes amendments to the 1985 Act to take account of compensation payable under the Pensions Act 2004 (c.35) ("the 2004 Act") to which spouses or civil partners may become entitled. Section 17(2) adds a new s.8(4A) to the 1985 Act under which a court is disempowered from making a pension order or a pension lump sum order out of any such compensation which is due to a spouse or civil partner. A new s.10(5A) is added by s.17(3). This provides that compensation due under the 2004 Act which is referable to the period of the marriage or civil partnership before the relevant date, is to be treated as matrimonial property and partnership property respectively. Thus it would appear that on divorce or dissolution such compensation is subject to fair division under s.9(1)(a) and is subject to all the orders available under s.8 except pension sharing orders and pension lump sum orders.

If a pension lump sum order has been made in respect of a spouse or civil partner's benefits under a pension fund, then if the Board of the Pension Protection Fund gives notice to the trustees or managers of the pension scheme, then the order shall have effect as if references to the trustees and managers were references to the Board and references to the lump sum was a reference to the compensation payable under the 2004 Act; and any order made under s.12A(3) (requirements relating to the payment of the lump sum) shall be recalled: s.17(4) adding ss.12A(7A), (7B) and (7C). Where the parties have made an agreement in respect of financial provision on divorce or dissolution and there are provisions in respect of pension rights, the court is to retain jurisdiction to set aside or vary the agreement even if the Board of the Pension Protection Fund assumes responsibility for the pension scheme: s.17(5) adding ss.16(2B) and (2C) to the 1985 Act.

18.   Financial provision: incidental orders

In subsection (2) of section 14 of the Family Law (Scotland) Act 1985 (c.37) (incidental orders), after paragraph (j) there shall be inserted-
> "(ja) in relation to a deed relating to moveable property, an order dispensing with the execution of the deed by the grantor and directing the sheriff clerk to execute the deed;".

GENERAL NOTE

In respect of a deed relating to heritable property, the court can make an order dispensing with the execution of the deed by the grantor and directing the sheriff clerk to execute the deed: Sheriff Courts (Scotland) Act 1907, s.5A. This new incidental order gives the court the power to make such an order in respect of deeds relating to moveable property, for example share certificates.

Special destinations: revocation on divorce or annulment

19.   Special destinations: revocation on divorce or annulment

(1) Subsections (2) and (3) apply where-
  (a) heritable property is held in the name of-
    (i) a person ("A") and A's spouse ("B") and the survivor of them;
    (ii) A, B and another person and the survivor or survivors of them;
    (iii) A with a special destination on A's death, in favour of B;
  (b) A and B's marriage is terminated by divorce or annulment; and
  (c) after the divorce or annulment A dies.
(2) In relation to the succession to A's heritable property (or part of it) under the destination, B shall be deemed to have failed to survive A.
(3) If a person has in good faith and for value (whether by purchase or otherwise) acquired title to the heritable property, the title so acquired shall not be challengeable on the ground that, by virtue of subsection (2), the property falls to the estate of A.
(4) Subsection (2) shall not apply if the destination specifies that B is to take under the destination despite the termination of A and B's marriage by divorce or annulment.

GENERAL NOTE

The analogous provision for civil partnerships is s.124A of the Civil Partnership Act 2004 (c.33), to be found in para.11 of Sch.1 to this Act.

Where title to property is taken in the joint names of spouses or civil partners, the property is common property. This means that while the property is possessed undivided, each spouse or civil partner has his or her own separate title to half the property i.e. each spouse or civil partner owns a one half *pro indiviso* share of the whole undivided property. During his or her lifetime, each is entitled to dispose of their share by selling or donating it to a third party. There is no need to have the consent of the other co-owner. Similarly, each co-owner is free to dispose of her or his share by will. Complications arise if the title has been taken in the names of the spouses or civil partners and the survivor. This is known as a special destination. Where for example, title to a house is taken in the names of husband and wife and the survivor, on the death of the husband his *pro indiviso* share of the property will automatically pass to his wife. Even if there is a special destination, a *pro indiviso* owner can always dispose of his share during his lifetime. However, where both co owners have contributed to the purchase of the property, the courts will readily infer from a special destination to the survivor that there is a contractual relationship between them that neither will revoke the arrangement by testamentary deed: in other words, on death the deceased's share will still pass under the special destination even it has been bequeathed to a third party. Moreover, problems arise if the couple divorce or their civil partnership is dissolved. For example, title to a family home is taken in the names of A and B and the survivor. A and B are civil partners. When their civil partnership is dissolved, they agree that B should have the former family home. If A conveys her one half *pro indiviso* share to B, B becomes the sole owner of the house. But the survivorship destination of B's original one half *pro indiviso* share in favour of A has not been evacuated. If B dies, a one half *pro indiviso* share of the property will automatically be transferred to A: see for example, *Gardner's Exors v Raeburn* 1996 S.L.T. 745. And if both A and B contributed to the purchase of the family home, there will be an implied agreement that B cannot defeat the destination by her will. Therefore A will still obtain a one half *pro indiviso* share even if B had bequeathed the family home to her new civil partner, C. To avoid this result, at the time of the dissolution both A and B must convey their one half *pro indiviso* shares to B thereby evacuating the special destination of B's share to A. Alternatively, A and B could expressly agree to renounce all rights of succession to each other's property thereby evacuating the special destination.

It will be clear that the law was complex and contained pitfalls for the unwary or badly advised. In its *Report on Succession* (Scot Law Com No 124, recommendation 30(a)) the Scottish Law Commission recommended that a special destination should automatically be revoked by divorce or annulment: recommendations 17(b) and (d). This recommendation is implemented in relation to divorce or annulment of marriage by s.19: s.124A of the Civil Partnership Act 2004 (as added by para.11 of Sch.1 to this Act) provides the same solution on the dissolution of a civil partnership.

Where title to heritable property is taken by A with a special destination to B or by A and B with a special destination to the survivor, then if A and B divorce or have their civil partnership dissolved, if A subsequently dies, for the purpose of inheriting under the special destination, B is deemed to have failed to survive A: ss.19(1) and (2); ss.124A(1) and (2). Accordingly, B does not acquire the property or A's *pro indiviso* share of the property from A's estate. For example, property is taken in the name of A and B and the survivor. On divorce (or dissolution) B's one half *pro indiviso* share is transferred to A without A evacuating the special destination in favour of B. A dies. B is deemed not to have survived A and the whole of the property remains in A's estate. Of course, if A transfers the property to a third party before he dies, this automatically evacuates the special destination to B.

The new rule means that if the criteria are satisfied, the title to the property may become inaccurate. For example, A may have acquired property in his own name with a destination in favour of B. The couple divorce or the civil partnership is dissolved and A subsequently dies. As a result of ss.19(1) and (2) or ss.124A (1) or (2) the property will now remain in A's estate as B is deemed not to have survived A. But as far as the title is concerned, it remains subject to the special destination and it will not be evident from the Register that there has been a divorce or dissolution. Consequently, B may appear to be the owner because of the special destination. In ignorance of the law or in bad faith, B may transfer the property to a third party who will attempt to acquire title through the special destination to B. Section 19(3) and s.124A(3) provide that when the third party has acquired title in good faith and for value in such circumstances, his title is not challengeable on the ground that the special destination was revoked on divorce or dissolution and the property remains in the estate of A. A's estate can attempt to recover the value that B received from the transfer under the law of unjustified enrichment. A's estate is not entitled to any indemnity from the keeper in respect of the loss of the property as a consequence of s.19(3) and s.124A(3): ss.12(3)(r) and (s) of the Land Registration (Scotland) Act 1979 (c.33) as added by para.3 of Sch.2 to this Act.

It is open to A and B to specify in the destination that B is to take under the destination despite the termination of their marriage or civil partnership: s.19(4) and s.124A(4).

This provision provides a remarkable example of the continued use of legal fictions.

Aliment

20. Variations of agreements on aliment: powers of court

(1) Section 7 of the Family Law (Scotland) Act 1985 (c.37) (agreements on aliment) shall be amended as follows.

(2) After subsection (2) there shall be inserted-

"(2ZA) On an application under subsection (2) above, the court may-

(a) pending determination of the application, make such interim order as it thinks fit;

(b) make an order backdating a variation of the amount payable under the agreement to-

(i) the date of the application or such later date as the court thinks fit; or

(ii) on special cause shown, a date prior to the date of the application.

(2ZB) Where the court makes an order under subsection (2ZA)(b) above, it may order any sums paid under the agreement to be repaid on such terms (including terms relating to repayment by instalments) as the court thinks fit.

(2ZC) Nothing in subsection (2ZA) shall empower the court to substitute a lump sum for a periodical payment..

(3) In subsection (4), for "subsection (2) above" there shall be substituted "this section".

GENERAL NOTE

Where a person has made an agreement to pay aliment to or for the benefit of another person, on a material change of circumstances, application can be made to the court by either party for a variation of the amount payable under the agreement or termination of the agreement: s.7(2) of the 1985 Act. Section 20 amends s.7 to give the court the following powers when an application is made under s.7(2):

(i) to make an interim order;
(ii) to backdate a variation of the amount payable to the date of the application or a later date or in exceptional circumstances a date before the date of the application: but the court cannot substitute a lump sum for a periodical allowance; and
(iii) where a variation has been backdated, to order any sums paid under the agreement to be repaid on such terms as the court thinks fit.

21. Abolition of status of illegitimacy

(1) The Law Reform (Parent and Child) (Scotland) Act 1986 (c.9) shall be amended in accordance with subsections (2) to (4).

(2) In section 1 (legal equality of children)-

(a) for subsection (1) there shall be substituted-

"(1) No person whose status is governed by Scots law shall be illegitimate; and accordingly the fact that a person's parents are not or have not been married to each other shall be left out of account in-

(a) determining the person's legal status; or

(b) establishing the legal relationship between the person and any other person.";

(b) in subsection (4), in paragraph (a), for the words from "this", where it first occurs, to the end of that paragraph there shall be substituted "section 21 of the Family Law (Scotland) Act 2006 (asp 2)"; and

(c) after that subsection there shall be added-

"(5) In subsection (4), "enactment" includes an Act of the Scottish Parliament.

(6) It shall no longer be competent to bring an action for declarator of legitimacy, legitimation or illegitimacy.".

(3) The title of section 1 shall become "Abolition of status of illegitimacy".

(4) In subsection (1) of section 9 (savings and supplementary provisions)-

(a) in paragraph (c), at the end, there shall be inserted "(including, in particular, the competence of bringing an action of declarator of legitimacy, legitimation or illegitimacy in connection with such succession or devolution)"; and

(b) after that paragraph, there shall be inserted-

"(ca) affect the functions of the Lord Lyon King of Arms so far as relating to the granting of arms;".

GENERAL NOTE

The Law Reform (Parent and Child) (Scotland) Act 1986 (c.9) ("the 1986 Act") removed the legal disabilities of children whose parents were not married to each other at the date of conception or subsequently. This was done by enacting that "the fact that a person's parents are not and have not been married to one another shall be left out of account in establishing the legal relationship between the person and any other person; and accordingly any such relationship shall have effect as if the parents were or had been married": s.1(1). The effect of this provision is that children have legal equality regardless of the status of their parents at the time of their birth. Nevertheless, resort still had to be made to the concepts of legitimacy and ilegitimacy for certain limited purposes, for example the rule that an illegitimate child takes the domicile of her mother as her domicile of origin and dependence: s.9(1)(a) of the 1986 Act. Since 1986, children born to unmarried parents have become fully accepted as part of contemporary family structures and any legal discrimination is difficult to justify. Twenty years on from the 1986 Act, the opportunity has now been taken finally to abolish the status of illegitimacy: see s.21(3). This implements the Family Law Report, recommendation 88.

Section 21(2)(a) substitutes a new s.1(1) of the 1986 Act which begins by declaring that "no person whose status is governed by Scots law shall be illegitimate". It goes on to state that "the fact that a person's parents are not or have not been married to each other shall be left out of account in (a) determining the person's legal status; or (b) establishing the legal relationship between the person and any other person." Because the status of illegitimacy no longer exists i.e. everyone is legitimate, there is no need for the doctrine of legitimation. Therefore the Legitimation (Scotland) Act 1968 (c.22) is repealed: s.45(2) and Sch.3 to this Act.

Section 1(4)(a) of the 1986 Act provided that nothing in the Act was to affect the construction and effect of any enactment passed or made before its commencement unless the enactments were amended by the 1986 Act itself. Section 21(2)(b) amends s.1(4) so that s.21 does not have retrospective effect in relation to the construction or effect of any earlier enactments. An enactment includes an Act of the Scottish Parliament: s.21(2)(c) adding a new s.1(5) to the 1986 Act. However, by s.1(2) of the 1986 Act (as amended) a reference to a child or any other person in future enactments will be construed in accordance with s.21: s.45(2) and Sch.3 to this Act repealing the words, "subject to subsection (4) below", in s.1(2) of the 1986 Act.

In relation to deeds, the 1986 Act was not retrospective: s.1(4)(b). Thus a reference to a child or children in a deed executed before the commencement of the Law Reform (Miscellaneous Provisions) (Scotland) Act 1968 (c.70) ("the 1968 Act") does not include, unless the contrary intention appears, illegitimate relationships. If a deed was executed after the commencement of the 1968 Act any reference to a relative includes, unless the contrary intention appears, an illegitimate relationship. But even in relation to a deed executed after the commencement of the 1986 Act, the Act did not affect express references to legitimate or illegitimate persons or relationships: s.1(4)(c). Thus for example, even after the commencement of the 1986 Act a testator was free expressly to make a bequest to A's legitimate children with the effect that A's illegitimate children would be excluded. If the bequest was simply to A's children then, of course, both illegitimate and legitimate children would be included.

Section 1(4)(c) is now repealed: s.45(2) and Sch.3 to this Act. After the commencement of s.21, illegitimacy will not exist. Accordingly it would appear that a reference in a post commencement deed to A's legitimate or lawful children will be construed as any child of A: s.1(2) of the 1986 Act (as amended as discussed above).

Actions for declarator of legitimacy, legitimation and illegitimacy are no longer to be competent: s.21(2)(c) adding s.1(6) to the 1986 Act and s.45(1) and para.6(2) of Sch.2 to this Act amending s.7 of the 1986 Act. The 1986 Act did not affect the succession or devolution of any title, coat of arms, honour or dignity transmissible on the death of the holder: s.9(1)(c) of the 1986 Act. This exception remains and declarators of legitimacy, legitimation and illegitimacy remain competent in respect of such matters: s.21(4)(a) amending s.9(1)(c) of the 1986 Act. In addition, s.21(4)(b) amends s.9(1) of the 1986 Act by adding a s.9(1)(ca) where it is expressly provided that the 1986 Act does not "affect the functions of the Lord Lyon King of Arms so far as relating to the granting of arms".

Domicile of persons under 16

22. Domicile of persons under 16

(1) Subsection (2) applies where-
   (a) the parents of a child are domiciled in the same country as each other; and
   (b) the child has a home with a parent or a home (or homes) with both of them.
(2) The child shall be domiciled in the same country as the child's parents.
(3) Where subsection (2) does not apply, the child shall be domiciled in the country with which the child has for the time being the closest connection.
(4) In this section, "child" means a person under 16 years of age.

GENERAL NOTE

A child's domicile of origin depended on whether or not he was legitimate. If he was legitimate, his domicile of origin was that of his father at the date of the birth: if he was illegitimate, his domicile of origin was that of his mother at the date of the birth. Until the child reaches the age of 16 when he can acquire his own domicile of choice (s.7 of the Age of Legal Capacity (Scotland) Act 1991 (c.50)), a child's domicile is dependent on that of his parent. This means that in the case of an illegitimate child his domicile changed if and when his mother's domicile changed: in the case of a legitimate child his domicile changed if and when his father's domicile changed. However, a legitimate child's domicile followed that of his mother if his father was dead or the child had his home with his mother and no home with his father: Domicile and Matrimonial Proceedings Act 1973 (c.45), s.4. These rules could not survive the abolition of the status of illegitimacy by s.21 of this Act, discussed above. Section 22 provides new rules which do not involve a distinction between legitimate and illegitimate children: to that extent it implements the Family Law Report, recommendation 89.

A child shall be domiciled in the same country as her parents if the parents are domiciled in the same country as each other and the child has her home(s) with a parent or both of them: ss.22(1) and (2). This rule would appear to apply both to the acquisition of a domicile of origin and a child's domicile of dependence. Thus for example, if a child is born and her parents have the same domicile X and the child is living with her father or mother or both of them, her domicile of origin will be X. It doesn't matter if at the time of her birth her parents while domiciled in X are living in Y: the child's domicile of origin will be X. Once a child's domicile of origin is established it cannot be changed. But it can be displaced if the child acquires a different domicile by dependency on his parents. So if in our example, after her birth the child's parents both acquire a domicile of choice in Y, the child's domicile of dependence will become that of her parents i.e. Y, provided the child continues to have a home with her parent(s).

Where ss.22(1) and (2) do not apply, the child shall be domiciled in the country with which the child has for the time being the closest connection. Again this would appear to apply to the acquisition of a domicile of origin. Thus if a child is born whose parents have different domiciles, ss.21(1) and (2) do not apply and the child's domicile is the country with which she has the closest connection at the time of her birth. This is likely to be the country where the child was born and lives: and will often, although not necessarily, be the country of the mother's domicile. Similarly, if the father is dead when the child is born, the child's domicile of origin will be the country with which she has the closest connection which will often, although again not necessarily, be the country of the domicile of the child's mother. Once the child's domicile of origin is established, it cannot be changed. However, the child's domicile of origin can be displaced if the child obtains a domicile of dependency by virtue of ss.22(1) and (2) or comes to have a closer connection with a different country. So for example if a child is born to parents who have different domiciles, ss.21(1) and (2) do not apply and the child's domicile of origin is the country with which she has closest connection: let us assume this is X where she lives with her mother who is domiciled in X. The mother and father later move to Y where they both acquire a domicile of choice. If the child has her home with her parent(s), ss.22(1) and (2) apply and the child's domicile of dependency is Y. On the other hand, if only the mother moved to Y and acquired a domicile of choice there, ss.22(1) and (2) would not apply even if the child had a home with her mother because the parents do not have the same domiciles. But the child's domicile of origin, X, may be displaced for the time being if the child has a home with her mother and she now has a closer connection with Y than with X.

Because of the rule in ss.22(1) and (2), a child's domicile may have little, if any, connection with the country where she resides. For instance a child is born in Scotland. She lives in Scotland with her parents who are domiciled in Canada and have come to Scotland to work here for a Canadian company. The parents have no intention to live permanently in Scotland. Accordingly, they do not acquire a domicile of choice here. The child's domicile of origin is therefore Canadian and she remains a Canadian domiciliary for as long as she lives with her parents even though the family have never left Scotland since she was born.

23. Parental responsibilities and parental rights of unmarried fathers

(1) Section 3 of the Children (Scotland) Act 1995 (c.36) (provisions relating both to parental responsibilities and parental rights) shall be amended in accordance with subsections (2) and (3).

(2) In paragraph (b) of subsection (1) (cases in which parents have parental responsibilities and parental rights)-

    (a) the words from "married" to the end shall become sub-paragraph (i) of that paragraph; and

    (b) at the end there shall be added "or

        (ii) where not married to the mother at that time or subsequently, the father is registered as the child's father under any of the enactments mentioned in subsection (1A).".

(3) After subsection (1) there shall be inserted-

    "(1A) Those enactments are-

        (a) section 18(1)(a), (b)(i) and (c) and (2)(b) of the Registration of Births, Deaths and Marriages (Scotland) Act 1965 (c.49);

        (b) sections 10(1)(a) to (e) and 10A(1)(a) to (e) of the Births and Deaths Registration Act 1953 (c.20); and

        (c) article 14(3)(a) to (e) of the Births and Deaths Registration (Northern Ireland) Order 1976 (S.I. 1976/ 1041).".

(4) Paragraph (b)(ii) of subsection (1) of section 3 of the Children (Scotland) Act 1995 (c.36) (which is inserted by subsection (2)(b)) shall not confer parental responsibilities or parental rights on a man who, before the coming into force of subsections (2) and (3), was registered under any of the enactments mentioned in subsection (1A) of that section (which is inserted by subsection (3)).

GENERAL NOTE

A woman who gives birth to a child and no other woman is to be treated as the child's mother: Human Fertilisation and Embryology Act 1990 (c.37), s.27. The mother of a child automatically has parental responsibilities in relation to her child: s.3(1)(a) of the Children (Scotland) Act 1995 (c.36).

A man is presumed to be the father of a child if he was married to the mother of the child at any time during the period beginning with the conception and ending with the birth of the child: s.5(1)(a) of the 1986 Act. If he is in fact the child's father, he will automatically acquire parental responsibilities and rights if he was married to the child's mother at the date of conception or any time thereafter: Children (Scotland) Act 1995, s.3(1)(b). This means that (i) a man who is presumed to be the child's father by virtue of s.5(1)(a) of the 1986 Act automatically acquires parental responsibilities and rights if he is in fact the child's father; and (ii) a man who is not presumed to be the child's father by virtue of s.5(1)(a) of the 1986 Act automatically acquires parental responsibilities and rights if and when he marries the child's mother and is in fact the child's father.

Accordingly, a man who is in fact the child's father does not automatically acquire parental responsibilities and rights if he has never been married to and does not marry the child's mother. It is irrelevant that as the child's father, he owes the child an obligation of aliment: 1985 Act, s.1(1)(c). However, he can obtain parental responsibilities and rights if the mother agrees that he may have them: s.4 of the 1995 Act. Alternatively, he can apply to court under s.11 of the 1995 Act for an order giving him parental responsibilities and rights but the welfare of the child is the paramount consideration and the court will only make such an order if it is in the child's interests to do so.

However, under s.5(1)(b) of the 1986 Act a man is also presumed to be the father of a child if both he and the mother of the child have acknowledged that he is the father and the child has been registered as such. Sections 23(2) and (3) amend s.3(1)(b) of the 1995 Act so that a man who is presumed to be the father of a child by virtue of s.5(1)(b) of the 1986 Act will automatically have parental responsibilities and rights: to that extent it implements Family Law Report, recommendation 5.

It is only a man who is presumed to be the father of the child by virtue of s.5(1)(b) of the 1986 Act who will automatically have parental responsibilities and rights. Thus a man who obtains a declarator of paternity by establishing that he is the father of the child does not automatically obtain parental responsibilities and rights and must continue to seek either a s.4 agreement from the mother or an order under s.11 of the 1995 Act giving him parental responsibilities and rights.

Section 23(4) provides that these amendments are not to have retrospective effect. This means that a man who is presumed to be the child's father under s.5(1)(b) of the 1986 Act will not obtain parental responsibilities and rights if the birth was registered before the commencement of s.23. It will be important to let a father in this position know that he still does not have parental responsibilities and rights in spite of the enactment of s.23 and that he will still have to seek a s.4 agreement or a court order under s.11 of the 1995 Act if he wishes to obtain them.

Protection of children from abuse

24. Orders under section 11 of Children (Scotland) Act 1995: protection from abuse

After subsection (7) of section 11 of the Children (Scotland) Act 1995 (c.36) (court orders relating to parental responsibilities etc.) there shall be inserted-

"(7A) In carrying out the duties imposed by subsection (7)(a) above, the court shall have regard in particular to the matters mentioned in subsection (7B) below.

(7B) Those matters are-

(a) the need to protect the child from-

(i) any abuse; or

(ii) the risk of any abuse,

which affects, or might affect, the child;

(b) the effect such abuse, or the risk of such abuse, might have on the child;

(c) the ability of a person-

(i) who has carried out abuse which affects or might affect the child; or

(ii) who might carry out such abuse,

to care for, or otherwise meet the needs of, the child; and

(d) the effect any abuse, or the risk of any abuse, might have on the carrying out of responsibilities in connection with the welfare of the child by a person who has (or, by virtue of an order under subsection (1), would have) those responsibilities.

(7C) In subsection (7B) above-

"abuse" includes-

(a) violence, harassment, threatening conduct and any other conduct giving rise, or likely to give rise, to physical or mental injury, fear, alarm or distress;

(b) abuse of a person other than the child; and

(c) domestic abuse;

"conduct" includes-

(a) speech; and

(b) presence in a specified place or area.

(7D) Where-
    (a) the court is considering making an order under subsection (1) above; and
    (b) in pursuance of the order two or more relevant persons would have to co-operate with one another as respects matters affecting the child,
the court shall consider whether it would be appropriate to make the order.

    (7E) In subsection (7D) above, "relevant person", in relation to a child, means-
    (a) a person having parental responsibilities or parental rights in respect of the child; or
    (b) where a parent of the child does not have parental responsibilities or parental rights in respect of the child, a parent of the child.".

GENERAL NOTE

In actions relating to parental responsibilities and rights brought under s.11(1) of the Children (Scotland) Act 1995, the three overarching principles which determine every case are articulated in s.11(7):

"... in considering whether or not to make an order under subsection (1) above and what order to make, the court:

(a)shall regard the welfare of the child concerned as its paramount consideration and shall not make any such order unless it considers that it would be better for the child that the order be made than that none should be made at all: and

(b)taking account of the child's age and maturity, shall so far as practicable:

(i)give him the opportunity to indicate whether he wishes to express his views;

(ii)if he does so wish, give him an opportunity to express them; and

(iii)have regard to such views as he may express."

As the welfare of the child is the paramount consideration, it might be thought that evidence that a child had been the object of physical or mental abuse by one of the parties would be an important factor to be taken into account in any application under s.11(1) of the 1995 Act. Section 24 amends s.11(7) of the 1995 Act. A new s.11(7A) provides that in carrying out its duties under s.11(7)(a) the court should have regard to the following matters listed in a new s.11(7B):

(a) the need to protect the child from abuse or the threat of abuse which might affect the child;

(b)the effect such abuse or the risk of such abuse may have on the child;

(c)the ability of the abuser to care for or otherwise meet the needs of the child; and

(d)the effect of such abuse or the risk of such abuse on a person with parental responsibilities (or who would have parental responsibilities by virtue of an order under s.11(1)) from carrying out these responsibilities.

Abuse is defined to include violence, harassment, threatening conduct and any other conduct giving rise to physical or mental injury, fear, alarm or distress: s.11(7C)(a). Conduct includes speech and being present at a particular place or area: ss.11(7C)(a) and (b). Importantly, abuse includes abuse directed at a person other than the child: s.11(7C)(b). Thus the court must take into account the fact that for example the child's mother has been abused even if the abuser has not abused the child. Also included in abuse is "domestic abuse": s.11(7C)(c).

These provisions focus on abuse or the risk of abuse the person who has care of a child as well as the direct abuse or the possibility of direct abuse of the child herself. Because abuse of the person who has care of the child may affect the quality of that care, it is a matter which indirectly affects the welfare of the child which must always remain the paramount consideration. More controversial, perhaps, is the consideration of an abuser's ability to care for a child. It is, of course, clearly a relevant factor when the person has directly abused the child in the past but is the fact that he may have abused a partner in itself relevant to his ability to care for the child? This is particularly pertinent given the width of the definition of abuse which includes any language which could give rise to distress and the mere presence of a person in a particular place or area. Once again it has to be remembered that the welfare of the child is the paramount consideration and that the child's views are relevant. Where adults have had a tempestuous, even violent, relationship, it does not mean that continued contact with a child is necessarily against the child's interests.

The effect of the new ss.11(7D) and (7E) is to oblige the court to consider whether it should make an order where the result of so doing is that two or more persons-usually the child's parents-would have to co-operate with each other. The inference is that if co-operation is likely to be difficult, a court should not make the order and that the status quo should continue. It is thought that these provisions are potentially problematic. If it is in the child's best interests that the order should be made, the fact that the parents will share parental responsibilities and rights and have to co-operate should not inhibit the court from making the order which ex-hypothesi is in the best interests of the child.

Cohabitation

25. Meaning of cohabitant in sections 26 to 29

(1) In sections 26 to 29, "cohabitant" means either member of a couple consisting of-
  (a) a man and a woman who are (or were) living together as if they were husband and wife; or
  (b) two persons of the same sex who are (or were) living together as if they were civil partners.
(2) In determining for the purposes of any of sections 26 to 29 whether a person ("A") is a cohabitant of another person ("B"), the court shall have regard to-
  (a) the length of the period during which A and B have been living together (or lived together);
  (b) the nature of their relationship during that period; and
  (c) the nature and extent of any financial arrangements subsisting, or which subsisted, during that period.
(3) In subsection (2) and section 28, "court" means Court of Session or sheriff.

GENERAL NOTE

Subsection (1)

This section defines cohabitant for the purposes of ss.26-29 of the Act which give cohabitants important new rights. In so doing they implement the Family Law Report, recommendations 80-83.

An opposite sex cohabitant is defined as either member of a couple consisting of a man and a woman who are (or were) living together as if they were husband and wife. The concept of living together as husband and wife is familiar. It involves a couple who live together in a relationship which exhibits the characteristics of marriage including sexual relations, emotional commitment, shared finances, social acceptance as a couple and stability. A same sex cohabitant is defined as either member of a couple who are (or were) living together as if they were civil partners. While a civil partnership is a new legal institution it is clearly analogous to marriage apart from the fact that civil partners are persons of the same, as opposed to the opposite, sex. Accordingly the concept of living together as if they were civil partners involves similar characteristics as living together as though they were husband and wife namely sexual relations, emotional commitment, shared finances, social acceptance as a couple and stability.

Subsection (2)

This provision is problematic. It does not make sense. Having defined cohabitant in s.25(1), s.25(2) now provides that in determining whether a person is a cohabitant for the purposes of ss.26-29, the court shall have regard to (a) the length of the period during which the couple have been living together (or lived together) (b) the nature of their relationship during that period and (c) the nature and extent of any financial arrangements subsisting or which subsisted during the relationship. But to give a definition of cohabitant in s.25(1) and then redefine cohabitant in the following subsection is intellectually incoherent. The provision would have made sense if it had stated that the factors in s.25(2) were to be considered in determining under s.25(1) whether or not a couple were living together as husband and wife or civil partners: if the couple were not, then they are not cohabitants for the purposes of ss.26-29. Alternatively, having determined that the couple were living together as husband and wife or civil partners, the provision could have stated that in exercising its discretion i.e. in deciding what order, if any, it should make for financial provision on separation (s.28) or death (s.29) a court should consider the length and nature of the parties' relationship and the nature and extent of any financial arrangements subsisting or which subsisted during the relationship.

It should be noted, however, that there is no minimum period of cohabitation before the cohabitants obtain their rights under ss.26-29.

26. Rights in certain household goods

(1) Subsection (2) applies where any question arises (whether during or after the cohabitation) as to the respective rights of ownership of cohabitants in any household goods.

(2) It shall be presumed that each cohabitant has a right to an equal share in household goods acquired (other than by gift or succession from a third party) during the period of cohabitation.

(3) The presumption in subsection (2) shall be rebuttable.

(4) In this section, "household goods" means any goods (including decorative or ornamental goods) kept or used at any time during the cohabitation in any residence in which the cohabitants are (or were) cohabiting for their joint domestic purposes; but does not include-

(a) money;

(b) securities;

(c) any motor car, caravan or other road vehicle; or

(d) any domestic animal.

GENERAL NOTE

This section provides that in any question as to the respective rights of ownership of cohabitants in household goods, there shall be a rebuttable presumption that each cohabitant has an equal share in any household goods acquired during the period of cohabitation. The presumption does not apply to household goods acquired by gift or succession from a third party. Household goods are defined in s.26(4) as any goods including decorative or ornamental goods kept or used at any time during the cohabitation in any residence in which the couple are or were cohabiting for joint domestic purposes. These would include for example household furniture, a cooker, white goods and kitchen utensils, appliances, television, CD player and a radio. Because the goods must be kept for joint domestic purposes it would not, for example, include a wrist watch or jewellery. Money and securities, road vehicles and pets are expressly excluded. Because the presumption only applies to goods i.e. moveable property, there is no presumption of equal shares in heritable property, in particular the house where the couple live. Unlike the analogous provision for spouses and civil partners in s.25 of the 1985 Act, there is no equivalent to s.25(2). This provides that the presumption of equal shares shall not be rebutted "by reason only that ... the goods in question were purchased from a third party by either party alone or by both in unequal shares". It would appear therefore that in relation to cohabitants such evidence could in itself rebut the presumption.

It is thought that "an equal share in household goods" means that the parties are common owners of the property.

It is difficult to see why a couple who are living together as husband and wife or civil partners should not be treated as cohabitants for the purpose of this section because of the length and nature of their relationship or the nature and extent of their financial arrangements i.e. s.25(2) is not applicable: though the latter factor might constitute evidence to rebut the statutory presumption of common ownership.

27. Rights in certain money and property

(1) Subsection (2) applies where, in relation to cohabitants, any question arises (whether during or after the cohabitation) as to the right of a cohabitant to-

    (a) money derived from any allowance made by either cohabitant for their joint household expenses or for similar purposes; or

    (b) any property acquired out of such money.

(2) Subject to any agreement between the cohabitants to the contrary, the money or property shall be treated as belonging to each cohabitant in equal shares.

(3) In this section "property" does not include a residence used by the cohabitants as the sole or main residence in which they live (or lived) together.

GENERAL NOTE

A transfers money to B for a specific purpose. B does not use all the money for that purpose. At common law, A remained owner of the money and of any property bought out of it. This was considered to be unfair where the money was a housekeeping allowance and the savings were made by a thrifty housewife. This led to the Married Women's Property Act 1964 (c.19) which provided that subject to any agreement to the contrary such savings and any property bought with such money should be owned by both spouses in equal shares. The current provision which applies to allowances made by a spouse to a spouse and civil partner to civil partner is to be found in s.26 of the 1985 Act.

This section provides that a similar rule should apply to savings made from housekeeping allowances by cohabitants and any property bought out of such money. The rule that the savings and any property derived from such money is owned in common is subject to any agreement to the contrary. Unlike s.26 of the 1985 Act, s.27(3) expressly provides that property does not include the house which the cohabitants used as their sole or principal residence.

It is difficult to see why a couple who are living together as husband and wife or civil partners should not be treated as cohabitants for the purpose of this section because of the length and nature of their relationship or the nature and extent of any financial arrangements between them i.e. s.25(2) is not applicable. The parties' financial arrangements could, of course, include an agreement that any savings from an allowance or any property bought from such money should not be owned in equal shares.

28. Financial provision where cohabitation ends otherwise than by death

(1) Subsection (2) applies where cohabitants cease to cohabit otherwise than by reason of the death of one (or both) of them.

(2) On the application of a cohabitant (the "applicant"), the appropriate court may, after having regard to the matters mentioned in subsection (3)-

    (a) make an order requiring the other cohabitant (the "defender") to pay a capital sum of an amount specified in the order to the applicant;

    (b) make an order requiring the defender to pay such amount as may be specified in the order in respect of any economic burden of caring, after the end of the cohabitation, for a child of whom the cohabitants are the parents;

    (c) make such interim order as it thinks fit.

(3) Those matters are-

    (a) whether (and, if so, to what extent) the defender has derived economic advantage from contributions made by the applicant; and

    (b) whether (and, if so, to what extent) the applicant has suffered economic disadvantage in the interests of-

        (i) the defender; or

        (ii) any relevant child.

(4) In considering whether to make an order under subsection (2)(a), the appropriate court shall have regard to the matters mentioned in sub-sections (5) and (6).

(5) The first matter is the extent to which any economic advantage derived by the defender from contributions made by the applicant is offset by any economic disadvantage suffered by the defender in the interests of-

    (a) the applicant; or

    (b) any relevant child.

(6) The second matter is the extent to which any economic disadvantage suffered by the applicant in the interests of-

    (a) the defender; or

    (b) any relevant child,

is offset by any economic advantage the applicant has derived from contributions made by the defender.

(7) In making an order under paragraph (a) or (b) of subsection (2), the appropriate court may specify that the amount shall be payable-

    (a) on such date as may be specified;

    (b) in instalments.

(8) Any application under this section shall be made not later than one year after the day on which the cohabitants cease to cohabit.

(9) In this section-

"appropriate court" means-

        (a) where the cohabitants are a man and a woman, the court which would have jurisdiction to hear an action of divorce in relation to them if they were married to each other;

        (b) where the cohabitants are of the same sex, the court which would have jurisdiction to hear an action for the dissolution of the civil partnership if they were civil partners of each other;

"child" means a person under 16 years of age;

"contributions" includes indirect and non-financial contributions (and, in particular, any such contribution made by looking after any relevant child or any house in which they cohabited); and

"economic advantage" includes gains in-

        (a) capital;

        (b) income; and

        (c) earning capacity;

and "economic disadvantage" shall be construed accordingly.

    (10) For the purposes of this section, a child is "relevant" if the child is-

        (a) a child of whom the cohabitants are the parents;

        (b) a child who is or was accepted by the cohabitants as a child of the family.

GENERAL NOTE

    This section provides that a cohabitant can apply to a court for financial provision when the cohabitation has ended otherwise than by the death of one (or both) cohabitants.

Subsection (1)

    The right to apply for financial provision arises when the couple "cease to cohabit". This is ultimately a question of fact. While "hard" cases can be envisaged, for example where one cohabitant is in jail or hospital, in practice it is unlikely that many difficulties will arise. For the purpose of fair division of matrimonial property under s.9(1)(a) of the 1985 Act, the relevant date is defined as "the date on which the parties ceased to cohabit": s.10(3) of the 1985 Act. The application of this definition has caused surprisingly little difficulty (but see, for example, *Banks v Banks* [2005] CSOH 144).

Subsection (2)

    This subsection lists the orders which are available to the court on an application for financial provision. These are (a) an order for the payment to the applicant of a capital sum of an amount to be specified in the order; (b) an order to pay to the applicant such amount as may be specified in the order "in respect of any economic burden of caring, after the end of the cohabitation, for a child of whom the cohabitants are parents": and (c) such interim order as the court thinks fit. For the purposes of s.28(2)(b) a child is a person under the age of 16 (s.28(9)) of whom the cohabitants are the parents. It therefore does not include a child who has been accepted or treated by the applicant or the defender (or both) as a child of the family. Thus a s.28(2)(b) order cannot be made when the cohabitants have been living together as if they were civil partners as any child living with them cannot be the biological child of *both* cohabitants as each is the same sex: yet such cohabitants may sustain economic loss after the cohabitation has ended from caring for a child who has lived with them, in the same way as opposite sex cohabitants who are the parents of a child.

    In considering whether to make any of these orders the court must consider the matters mentioned in s.28(3) namely (a) whether and if so to what extent the defender has derived economic advantage from contributions made by the applicant and (b) whether and if so to what extent the applicant has suffered economic disadvantage in the interests of the defender and any relevant child. While it can be readily seen how fair account of the economic advantages received by the defender and economic disadvantages sustained by the applicant can form the basis of an order under s.28(2)(a) it is difficult to see why it is applicable in relation to an order under s.28(2)(b) which expressly stipulates that its purpose is to compensate the applicant for the economic burden of caring for a child of the cohabitants after the cohabitation has ended.

    Only a capital sum payment can be ordered under s.28(2)(a) but it appears that both a capital sum or periodical payments can be ordered under s.28(2)(b). A court can specify the date on which payments must be paid and that a capital sum payment should be payable in instalments: s.28(7).

Subsection (3)

    As we have seen this section sets out the matters which a court has to consider in a claim for financial provision under s.28(2)(a) (and incoherently s.28(2)(b)). These are economic advantages received by the defender from contributions made by the applicant and economic disadvantages sustained by the applicant in the interests of the defender and a relevant child. For this purpose, in contrast to s.28(2)(b), a relevant child is a person under the age of 16 who is either a child of whom the cohabitants are the parents or who is or was accepted by the cohabitants as a child of the family: ss.28(9) and (10). The acceptance criterion appears to be the same as creates liability to aliment a child under s.1(1)(d) of the 1985 Act.

    Contributions include indirect and non-financial contributions and in particular the contribution made by looking after any relevant child or any house in which the couple cohabited:

s.28(9). Economic advantage includes gains in capital, income and earning capacity: *ibid*. Economic disadvantage is to be construed accordingly viz losses in capital, income and earning capacity. Unlike the analogous principle which applies in relation to financial provision on divorce or dissolution of a civil partnership, s.9(1)(b) of the 1985 Act, s.28(3) does not apply to economic advantages obtained or economic disadvantages sustained before the cohabitation began.

Subsections (5) and (6)

However in deciding to make an order under s.28(2)(a), s.28(4) provides that the court has to consider the matters in ss.28(5) and (6). First the court must consider the extent to which any economic advantage derived by the defender from the applicant's contributions is offset by any economic disadvantage sustained by the defender in the interests of the applicant or a relevant child: s.28(5). Secondly the court must consider the extent to which any economic disadvantage sustained by the applicant in the interests of the defender or any relevant child is offset by any economic advantage the applicant has derived from the defender's contributions: s.28(6). It is only if after this balancing exercise there is an economic imbalance in favour of the applicant that an award of financial provision can be made. Although cohabitants do not owe an obligation of aliment to each other during the cohabitation, it would be strange if there were not some economic advantages and economic disadvantages to offset in most relationships.

It is also important to remember that a court might not treat the applicant as a cohabitant for the purpose of a claim for financial provision because of the length and nature of the relationship and the nature and extent of any financial arrangements which subsisted during the relationship i.e. s.25(2) could be applicable. This is likely to be the case where the couple were both earning and there was no financial dependency between the parties.

Section 9(1)(b) of the 1985 Act, the analogous principle applicable on divorce or dissolution of a civil partnership, has not been used as much as might have been anticipated. This has been for several reasons. There is no doubt that it is difficult to quantify economic advantages and disadvantages. When this has been done it is then necessary to engage in the balancing process: because spouses and civil partners are under an obligation to aliment each other, there is often little imbalance in favour of the claimant. Sometimes resort is not made to s.9(1)(b) because the parties are content with their share of the matrimonial or partnership property under s.9(1)(a). When this is not the case, a claim under s.9(1)(b) will often take the form of an increased share of the matrimonial property so that, for example, if the claimant is going to look after the children she can remain in the family home: s.11(2)(b). Where s.9(1)(b) has been used is when a couple have no or very little matrimonial or partnership property which is subject to fair sharing under s.9(1)(a) of the 1985 Act but nevertheless have significant resources: for example if H has inherited a farm or has been successful in a business which he founded before he was married. In these circumstances, the courts have been prepared to award quite substantial sums under s.9(1)(b), taking a somewhat cavalier approach to the balancing process: see for example *Randali v Randali* 1994 S.L.T. (SH Ct) 25; *Wilson v Wilson* 1999 S.L.T. 249; *R v R* 2000 Fam. L.R. 43. There is no equivalent to s.9(1)(a) for cohabitants. It will therefore be interesting to see whether the courts will adopt the same approach to claims under s.28(2)(a) as they have done in respect of claims under s.9(1)(b) when there is no matrimonial or partnership property which is subject to fair division under s.9(1)(a). On the other hand if the balancing process is taken seriously it will reduce substantially the amount of the award. The problems of valuing economic advantages and economic disadvantage remain.

Subsection (8)

A claim for financial provision has to be made within a year from when the parties ceased to cohabit.

29. Application to court by survivor for provision on intestacy

(1) This section applies where-
    (a) a cohabitant (the "deceased") dies intestate; and
    (b) immediately before the death the deceased was-
        (i) domiciled in Scotland; and
        (ii) cohabiting with another cohabitant (the survivor).

(2) Subject to subsection (4), on the application of the survivor, the court may-

    (a) after having regard to the matters mentioned in subsection (3), make an order-

        (i) for payment to the survivor out of the deceased's net intestate estate of a capital sum of such amount as may be specified in the order;

        (ii) for transfer to the survivor of such property (whether heritable or moveable) from that estate as may be so specified;

    (b) make such interim order as it thinks fit.

(3) Those matters are-

    (a) the size and nature of the deceased's net intestate estate;

    (b) any benefit received, or to be received, by the survivor-

        (i) on, or in consequence of, the deceased's death; and

        (ii) from somewhere other than the deceased's net intestate estate;

    (c) the nature and extent of any other rights against, or claims on, the deceased's net intestate estate; and

    (d) any other matter the court considers appropriate.

(4) An order or interim order under subsection (2) shall not have the effect of awarding to the survivor an amount which would exceed the amount to which the survivor would have been entitled had the survivor been the spouse or civil partner of the deceased.

(5) An application under this section may be made to-

    (a) the Court of Session;

    (b) a sheriff in the sheriffdom in which the deceased was habitually resident at the date of death;

    (c) if at the date of death it is uncertain in which sheriffdom the deceased was habitually resident, the sheriff at Edinburgh.

(6) Any application under this section shall be made before the expiry of the period of 6 months beginning with the day on which the deceased died.

(7) In making an order under paragraph (a)(i) of subsection (2), the court may specify that the capital sum shall be payable-

    (a) on such date as may be specified;

    (b) in instalments.

(8) In making an order under paragraph (a)(ii) of subsection (2), the court may specify that the transfer shall be effective on such date as may be specified.

(9) If the court makes an order in accordance with subsection (7), it may, on an application by any party having an interest, vary the date or method of payment of the capital sum.

(10) In this section-

    "intestate" shall be construed in accordance with section 36(1) of the Succession (Scotland) Act 1964 (c.41);

    "legal rights" has the meaning given by section 36(1) of the Succession (Scotland) Act 1964 (c.41);

    "net intestate estate" means so much of the intestate estate as remains after provision for the satisfaction of-

        (a) inheritance tax;

        (b) other liabilities of the estate having priority over legal rights and the prior rights of a surviving spouse or surviving civil partner; and

(c) the legal rights, and the prior rights, of any surviving spouse or surviving civil partner; and

"prior rights" has the meaning given by section 36(1) of the Succession (Scotland) Act 1964 (c.41).

GENERAL NOTE

When cohabitation ends as a result of the death of one of the parties, under the Succession (Scotland) Act 1964 (c.41) a surviving cohabitant has no right of succession in relation to her deceased cohabitant's intestate estate i.e. when the deceased died without a will. As around seventy five per cent of Scots die intestate, a surviving cohabitant can find herself without any capital. Where the deceased owned the house in which they lived together, the surviving cohabitant can be evicted by the deceased's heirs- usually his children or grandchildren. Section 29 now gives a surviving cohabitant the right to apply for a share of her deceased cohabitant's property where the deceased died intestate.

Section 29(1)(a)

The right to apply for a share of the deceased's estate only arises if the deceased cohabitant died intestate. Unlike a surviving spouse or civil partner, a surviving cohabitant has no legal rights. A cohabitant is therefore free to make a will in which he makes no provision for a surviving cohabitant: and because he died testate, the surviving cohabitant has no rights under s.29.

Section 29(1)(b)

The deceased must have been domiciled in Scotland immediately before he died. He must also have been cohabiting with the surviving cohabitant immediately before his death. The policy appears clear. A former cohabitant is to have no rights under s.29. However the use of "immediately" is unfortunate. Would a surviving cohabitant still have a claim if the deceased had been in hospital or a nursing home for several months before he died? The answer must surely be yes. To achieve this result the provision will have to be construed purposively.

It should also be noted that under the Succession (Scotland) Act 1964 a surviving spouse or civil partner does not have to be living with the deceased before they have prior rights on the deceased's estate. The surviving spouse or civil partner has a prior right to the dwelling house (owned by the deceased) in which the survivor was ordinarily resident at the date of the deceased's death: but the survivor does not have to have been living there with the deceased immediately before he died. A surviving cohabitant's right under s.29 is dependent on living with the deceased at the time of his death.

Section 29(2)

On an application by the surviving cohabitant, the court can make an order (i) for payment of a capital sum to the applicant out of the deceased's net intestate estate and (ii) for heritable or moveable property to be transferred from the deceased's net intestate estate to the applicant. The court can specify the date on which the capital sum should be paid, that the capital sum can be paid in instalments and the date when any property should be transferred: ss.29(7) and (8). The application must be made within six months beginning with the day on which the deceased died: s.29(6).

Net intestate estate is defined in s.29(10). It is so much of the intestate estate as remains after provision has been made for the satisfaction of (a) inheritance tax; (b) other liabilities of the estate having priority over the prior rights and legal rights of a surviving spouse or civil partner; and (c) the prior and legal rights of a surviving spouse or civil partner. The last point is important. Where the deceased has died with a surviving spouse or civil partner as well as a surviving cohabitant, then the surviving cohabitant's claim under s.29(2) only applies to what remains of the estate after the prior rights and legal rights of the surviving spouse or civil partner are satisfied. Often the prior rights and legal rights of a surviving spouse or civil partner will exhaust the estate and therefore the surviving cohabitant's right under s.20(2) will be valueless. On the other hand, in many cases there will not be a surviving spouse or civil partner and the net intestate estate could be considerable. For it should be noticed that in calculating the net intestate estate, no provision has to be made for the satisfaction of the legal rights (*legitim*) of the deceased's children (and their issue). In other words, a surviving cohabitant's claim under s.29(2) must be considered *before* the succession rights of the deceased's children are addressed.

Section 29(3)

In considering a claim by a surviving cohabitant under s.29(2), the court has to consider the following:

(i)   the size and nature of the net intestate estate;
(ii)   any benefit received by the surviving cohabitant as a result of the death, for example a pension or life insurance;
(iii) the nature and extent of any other rights against, or claims on the deceased's net intestate estate. It is at this stage that the court can take into account that the deceased's children (and their issue) have legal rights and are the heirs on intestacy; and
(iv) any other matter the court considers appropriate.

It should also be remembered that the court could take the view that in the light of the length and nature of the relationship and the degree and extent of any financial arrangements which subsisted during the relationship, the applicant should not be treated as a cohabitant for the purpose of a claim under s.29(2) i.e. s.25(2) may be applicable.

Section 29(4)

This section provides that an order under s.29(2) must not have the effect of awarding a surviving cohabitant an amount which is more than that to which she or he would have been entitled if she or he had been a surviving spouse or civil partner of the deceased. In other words the maximum order that a surviving cohabitant can receive is the equivalent of the prior rights and legal rights that he or she would have received out of the deceased's intestate estate if the survivor had been the deceased's spouse or civil partner. (Theoretically, at least, this must include the amount that a surviving spouse or civil partner would obtain in the unusual circumstances when a surviving spouse or civil partner is the deceased's heir on intestacy).

While s.29(4) lays down the maximum that a surviving cohabitant can obtain, the statute gives the court little or no guidance on how it should exercise its discretion under s.29(2). Is the purpose to recognise the surviving cohabitant's economic contribution to the relationship or to compensate for any economic disadvantages she has sustained? Or is it to help a surviving spouse who was financially dependent on the deceased by providing her with reasonable financial provision from the estate? Or should a surviving cohabitant be treated as a surviving spouse or civil partner unless there are compelling reasons not to do so? These are serious issues which the legislation does nothing to address leaving the courts to find for themselves the principles which should govern the wide discretion given in s.29(2).

30. Administration of Justice Act 1982: extension of definition of relative

In section 13 of the Administration of Justice Act 1982 (c.53) (supplementary provisions and definitions in relation to Part 2), in the definition of relative, after paragraph (b) insert-

> "(ba) any person, not being the civil partner of the injured person, who was, at the time of the act or omission giving rise to liability in the responsible person, living with the injured person as the civil partner of the injured person;".

GENERAL NOTE

Under s.8 of the Administration of Justice Act 1982 (c.53), where a person has sustained personal injuries, the injured person can recover damages which amount to reasonable remuneration for necessary services rendered to him or her by a relative. Section 9 of the Administration of Justice Act 1982 provides that an injured person who has been providing unpaid personal services to a relative can sue for damages if as a result of the injuries he or she is unable to continue to do so. This section provides that an injured person's same sex cohabitant is to be treated as a relative for the purposes of the Act.

Cohabitation: domestic interdicts

31. Domestic interdicts

(1) The 1981 Act shall be amended in accordance with subsections (2) and (3).

(2) In subsection (3) of section 18 (cohabiting couples: occupancy rights and application of certain provisions of Act), for the words from "sections", where it first occurs, to "17" there shall be substituted section 13.

(3) After section 18 there shall be inserted-

"Domestic interdicts

18A Meaning of "domestic interdict"

(1) In section 18B, "domestic interdict" means-

  (a) an interdict granted on the application of a person ("A") who is (or was) living with another person ("B") as if they were husband and wife against B for any of the purposes mentioned in subsection (2); or

  (b) an interdict granted on the application of a person ("C") who is (or was) living with another person ("D") as if they were civil partners against D for any of the purposes mentioned in subsection (2).

(2) Those purposes are-

  (a) restraining or prohibiting such conduct of the defender towards-

    (i) the pursuer; or

    (ii) any child in the permanent or temporary care of the pursuer,

  as the court may specify;

  (b) prohibiting the defender from entering or remaining in-

    (i) a family home occupied by the pursuer and the defender;

    (ii) any other residence occupied by the pursuer;

    (iii) any place of work of the pursuer;

    (iv) any school attended by a child in the permanent or temporary care of the pursuer.

(3) In this section and in section 18B-

  "family home" means, subject to subsection (4), any house, caravan, houseboat or other structure which has been provided or has been made available by the pursuer or the defender (or both of them) as (or has become) a family residence for them and includes any garden or other ground or building usually occupied with, or otherwise required for the amenity or convenience of, the house, caravan, houseboat or other structure; but does not include a residence provided or made available by any person for the pursuer or, as the case may be, the defender to reside in (whether or not with any child of the pursuer and the defender) separately from the defender or, as the case may be, the pursuer; and

"interdict" includes interim interdict.

(4) If the tenancy of a family home is transferred from a pursuer to a defender (or, as the case may be, from a defender to a pursuer) by agreement or under any enactment, the home shall, on such transfer, cease to be a family home.

(5) In subsection (3), "child of the pursuer and the defender" includes any child or grandchild of the pursuer or the defender, and any person who has been brought up or treated by the pursuer or the defender as if the person were a child of the pursuer or, as the case may be, the defender, whatever the age of such a child, grandchild or person.

18B   Domestic interdicts: further provision

(1) Subsection (2) applies if the defender-

   (a) is entitled to occupy a family home;

   (b) is permitted by a third party to occupy it; or

   (c) has, by virtue of section 18(1), occupancy rights in it.

(2) Except where subsection (3) applies, the court may not grant a domestic interdict prohibiting the defender from entering or remaining in the family home.

(3) This subsection applies if-

   (a) the interdict is ancillary to an exclusion order; or

   (b) an order under section 18(1) granting or extending occupancy rights is recalled.".

GENERAL NOTE

Section 18(1) of the 1981 Act gives opposite sex cohabitants statutory rights of occupation similar to those enjoyed by spouses and civil partners. By s.34 of this Act, s.18 has been amended to give statutory rights of occupation to same sex cohabitants. This section adds a new s.18A under which an opposite sex or a same sex cohabitant can obtain a domestic interdict against the other cohabitant (a) restraining or prohibiting the defender's conduct towards the pursuer or any child in the pursuer's permanent or temporary care: ss.18A(1) and (2)(a); and (b) prohibiting the defender from entering or remaining in (i) a family home occupied by the pursuer and the defender; (ii) any other residence occupied by the pursuer; (iii) the pursuer's place of work; and any school attended by a child in the pursuer's care: ss.18A(1) and (2)(b). Where the defender is an entitled partner or has statutory occupancy rights under s.18(1) a domestic interdict prohibiting the defender from entering or remaining in the family home occupied by the pursuer cannot be made unless it is ancillary to an exclusion order under s.4 or an order under s.18(1) granting or extending occupancy rights is recalled: s.18B.

Section 18(3) provides the definition of a family home for this purpose. This is familiar from the definition of matrimonial home in s.22 of the 1981 Act.

Amendment of Protection from Abuse (Scotland) Act 2001: powers of arrest

32.   Amendment of Protection from Abuse (Scotland) Act 2001: powers of arrest

(1) Section 1 of the Protection from Abuse (Scotland) Act 2001 (asp 14) (attachment of power of arrest to interdict) shall be amended as follows.

(2) After subsection (1) there shall be inserted-

"(1A) In the case of an interdict which is-

    (a) a matrimonial interdict (as defined by section 14(2) of the Matrimonial Homes (Family Protection) (Scotland) Act 1981 (c.59)) which is ancillary to-

        (i) an exclusion order within the meaning of section 4(1) of that Act; or

        (ii) an interim order under section 4(6) of that Act; or

    (b) a relevant interdict (as defined by section 113(2) of the Civil Partnership Act 2004 (c.33)) which is ancillary to-

        (i) an exclusion order within the meaning of section 104(1) of that Act; or

        (ii) an interim order under section 104(6) of that Act,

the court must, on an application under subsection (1), attach a power of arrest to the interdict.".

(3) In subsection (2), at the beginning there shall be inserted "In the case of any other interdict,".

GENERAL NOTE

This amends the Protection from Abuse (Scotland) Act 2001 (asp 14) so that the attachment of a power of arrest to all types of interdict is now governed by the provisions of that Act. A distinction remains: powers of arrest must be attached to matrimonial interdicts (spouses) and relevant interdicts (civil partners) which are ancillary to exclusion orders, s.1(1A) of the 2001 Act, while others such as domestic interdicts are dealt with under the general provisions of s.1(2) of the Protection from Abuse (Scotland) Act 2001.

Amendments of Civil Partnership Act 2004

33. Amendments of Civil Partnership Act 2004

Schedule 1, which contains amendments of the Civil Partnership Act 2004 (c.33), shall have effect.

Application of 1981 Act to cohabiting couples of same sex

34. Application of 1981 Act to cohabiting couples of same sex

(1) Section 18 of the 1981 Act (occupancy rights of cohabiting couples) shall be amended in accordance with subsections (2) and (3).

(2) In subsection (1)-

    (a) after "wife" there shall be inserted "or two persons of the same sex are living together as if they were civil partners";

    (b) after "wife (", there shall be inserted "in either case"; and

    (c) for "man and the woman" there shall be substituted "entitled partner and the non-entitled partner".

(3) In subsection (2)-

    (a) for "a man and a woman there shall be substituted "two persons"; and

    (b) in paragraph (b), for the words from "are" to the end of that paragraph there shall be substituted

        "is any child-

            (i) of whom they are the parents; or

            (ii) who they have treated as a child of theirs.".

GENERAL NOTE

This extends the right to obtain statutory rights of occupation under s.18(1) of the 1981 Act to same sex as well as opposite sex cohabitants. A child for the purpose of ss.18 and 18A of the 1981 Act is a child or any grandchild of the cohabitants or any person who has been treated by them as their child: the age of the child so defined is irrelevant.

Amendments of Damages (Scotland) Act 1976

35. Amendments of Damages (Scotland) Act 1976

(1) The Damages (Scotland) Act 1976 (c.13) shall be amended in accordance with subsections (2) to (5).

(2) In subsection (4) of section 1 (rights of relatives of deceased person), at the beginning there shall be inserted "Subject to subsection (4A),".

(3) After that subsection, there shall be inserted-

"(4A) Notwithstanding section 10(2) of, and Schedule 1 to, this Act, no award of damages under subsection (4) above shall be made to a person related by affinity to the deceased.

(4B) In subsection (4A), a "person related by affinity to the deceased" includes-

(a) a stepchild, step-parent, stepbrother or stepsister of the deceased; and

(b) any person who was an ascendant or descendant of any of the step-relatives mentioned in paragraph (a).".

(4) In subsection (2) of section 10 (interpretation), for the words from "sub-paragraph" to "or (c)", there shall be substituted "any of sub-paragraphs (a) to (cc)".

(5) In paragraph 1 of Schedule 1 (definition of relative)-

(a) in sub-paragraph (c), for "paragraph" there shall be substituted "sub-paragraph";

(b) after that sub-paragraph, there shall be inserted-

"(ca) any person not falling within sub-paragraph (b) above who accepted the deceased as a child of the person's family;

(cb) any person who-

(i) was the brother or sister of the deceased; or

(ii) was brought up in the same household as the deceased and who was accepted as a child of the family in which the deceased was a child;

(cc) any person who was a grandparent or grandchild of the deceased;";

(c) in sub-paragraph (d), after "person" there shall be inserted "not falling within sub-paragraph (b) or (cc) above"; and

(d) in sub-paragraph (e), after "person" there shall be inserted "not falling within sub-paragraph (cb)(i) above".

GENERAL NOTE

Under the Damages (Scotland) Act 1976 (c.13) members of the deceased's immediate family have title to sue for damages for non-patrimonial loss arising from his death from personal injuries sustained as a consequence of the defender's fault. These amendments change the membership of the deceased's immediate family. The Damages (Scotland) Act 1976 has also been amended by para.2 of Sch.2 to this Act to include a deceased's civil partner and a person who was, immediately before the deceased's death, living with the deceased in a relationship which had the characteristics of the relationship between civil partners. As a consequence a deceased's immediate family now consists of the following: surviving spouse, surviving civil partner, surviving opposite sex cohabitant, surviving same sex cohabitant, biological parent and child, adoptive parent and child, parent and child by virtue of a parental order, any person accepted by the deceased as a child of the family, any person who accepted the deceased as a child of the family, brother and sister, de facto brother and sister, grandparent and grandchild. Persons who are only related to the deceased by affinity are not included and have no title to sue for non-patrimonial loss. Thus, for example, a step parent who has not accepted his step child as a child of the family is excluded: but a step parent who has accepted his step child would be included. The latter is not excluded by s.1(4A) of the 1976 Act which must be construed puposively, namely, "related by affinity" means "*only* related by affinity to the deceased". These amendments implement the recommendations of the Scottish Law Commission in their Report on *Title to Sue for Non-Patrimonial Loss* (Scot Law Com No 187) (August 2002).

Amendments of Adults with Incapacity (Scotland) Act 2000

36. Amendments of Adults with Incapacity (Scotland) Act 2000

Section 24 of the Adults with Incapacity (Scotland) Act 2000 (asp 4) (termination of continuing or welfare power of attorney) shall be amended as follows-

    (a) after subsection (1), there shall be inserted-

          "(1A) If the granter and the continuing or welfare attorney are in civil partnership with each other the power of attorney shall, unless the document conferring it provides otherwise, come to an end on the granting of-

              (a) a decree of separation of the partners in the civil partnership;

              (b) a decree of dissolution of the civil partnership;

              (c) a declarator of nullity of the civil partnership."

    (b) in subsection (4), after "(1)" there shall be inserted "or subsection (1A)".

GENERAL NOTE

This amends the Adults with Incapacity (Scotland) Act 2000 so that where the granter and the continuing or welfare attorney are in a civil partnership with each other, the power of attorney shall come to an end on the granting of a decree of separation, dissolution or declarator of nullity of the civil partnership. However the attorney will not be terminated in these circumstances if the document conferring it states otherwise. This section follows the analogous provision for spouses in s.24(1) of the Adults with Incapacity (Scotland) Act 2000.

Jurisdiction

37. Jurisdiction: actions for declarator of recognition of certain foreign decrees

    (1) The Domicile and Matrimonial Proceedings Act 1973 (c.45) shall be amended in accordance with subsections (2) and (3).

    (2) In section 7 (jurisdiction of Court of Session in certain consistorial causes)-

      (a) in subsection (1)-

         (i) for "(2) to (8)" there shall be substituted "(2A) to (10)"; and

         (ii) at the end there shall be inserted-

             "(aa) an action for declarator of recognition, or non-recognition, of a relevant foreign decree.";

(b) in subsection (3A), after "marriage", where it first occurs, there shall be inserted "or for declarator of recognition, or non-recognition, of a relevant foreign decree"; and

(c) after subsection (8) there shall be added-

"(9) In this section, "relevant foreign decree" means a decree of divorce, nullity or separation granted outwith a member state of the European Union.

(10) References in subsection (3A) to a marriage shall, in the case of an action for declarator of recognition, or non-recognition, of a relevant foreign decree, be construed as references to the marriage to which the relevant foreign decree relates.".

(3) In section 8 (jurisdiction of sheriff court in certain consistorial causes)-

(a) in subsection (1)-

(i) for "(4)" there shall be substituted "(6)";

(ii) the words from "an" to the end shall become paragraph (a) of that subsection; and

(iii) at the end there shall be added "and

(b) an action for declarator of recognition, or non-recognition, of a relevant foreign decree."

(b) in subsection (2), after divorce there shall be inserted or for declarator of recognition, or non-recognition, of a relevant foreign decree; and

(c) after subsection (4) there shall be added-

"(5) In this section, "relevant foreign decree" has the meaning given by section 7(9).

(6) References in subsection (2) to a marriage shall, in the case of an action for declarator of recognition, or non-recognition, of a relevant foreign decree, be construed as references to the marriage to which the relevant foreign decree relates.".

GENERAL NOTE

This provision amends the Domicile and Matrimonial Proceedings Act 1973 so that both the Court of Session and the sheriff court have jurisdiction to grant a declarator of recognition or non-recognition of a relevant foreign decree. A relevant foreign decree is defined as a decree of divorce, nullity or separation granted by a non European Union court. This implements the Family Law Report, recommendation 53.

Private international law

38. Validity of marriages

(1) Subject to the Foreign Marriage Act 1892 (c.23), the question whether a marriage is formally valid shall be determined by the law of the place where the marriage was celebrated.

(2) The question whether a person who enters into a marriage-

(a) had capacity; or

(b) consented,

to enter into it shall, subject to subsections (3) and (4) and to section 50 of the Family Law Act 1986 (c.55) (non-recognition of divorce or annulment in another jurisdiction no bar to remarriage), be determined by the law of the place where, immediately before the marriage, that person was domiciled.

    (3) If a marriage entered into in Scotland is void under a rule of Scots internal law, then, notwithstanding subsection (2), that rule shall prevail over any law under which the marriage would be valid.

    (4) The capacity of the person to enter into the marriage shall not be determined under the law of the place where, immediately before the marriage, the person was domiciled in so far as it would be contrary to public policy in Scotland for such capacity to be so determined.

    (5) If the law of the place in which a person is domiciled requires a person under a certain age to obtain parental consent before entering into a marriage, that requirement shall not be taken to affect the capacity of a person to enter into a marriage in Scotland unless failure to obtain such consent would render invalid any marriage that the person purported to enter into in any form anywhere in the world.

GENERAL NOTE

This provision puts into statutory form the rules of private international law in respect of validity of marriages. It implements the Family Law Report, recommendations 70–75.

Subsection (1)

This provides that the question of the formal validity of a marriage shall be determined by the law of the place where the marriage was celebrated. The Foreign Marriage Act 1892 (c.23) deals with marriages performed abroad by British consuls etc.

Subsection (2) (a)

This provides that a person's capacity to marry is to be determined by the law of the place where immediately before the marriage the person was domiciled. There are three exceptions to this rule:

(i)   Where the marriage is celebrated in Scotland, a person must also have capacity under Scots internal law; s.38(3). Thus, for example, the marriage of a person under the age of 16 will be void if celebrated in Scotland even though that person had capacity to marry under the law of her domicile. No one can marry in Scotland if she is under 16: Marriage (Scotland) Act 1977, s.1(2).

(ii)   Capacity will not be determined by the law of a person's domicile if it would be contrary to public policy in Scotland to do so: for example, if the law of the person's domicile would not allow her to marry another person if she had been widowed or divorced: s.38(4).

(iii)   If a person has been married and she has been divorced by a UK court or her divorce is recognised by a UK court, the fact that the law of her domicile does not recognise her divorce will not be regarded as rendering her remarriage invalid in the UK: Family Law Act 1986 (c.55), s.50.

Subsection (2) (b)

This provides that the question of whether a person has given legally effective consent to be married is to be determined by the law of the place where immediately before the marriage the person was domiciled. At common law the rule on the applicable law to govern defective consent was uncertain: *Singh v Singh* 2005 S.L.T. 749; *Di Rollo v Di Rollo* 1959 S.C. 75. It is now clear that it is the law of the domicile of the person claiming lack of consent.

If a person domiciled in Scotland claims that she married abroad under error or duress, it would appear that the relevant law to determine whether or not her consent was defective is Scots law. However, s.20A of the Marriage (Scotland) Act 1977 (section 2 of this Act) is not applicable since it only applies to marriages solemnised in Scotland. It is assumed that the common law on defective consent arising from error or duress will still govern if Scots law is the relevant law by virtue of s.38(2)(b).

This provides that any requirement under the law of a person's domicile that parental consent is necessary before she can marry under a certain age is not to be characterised as a rule that affects her capacity to marry unless under that law failure to obtain parental consent would render invalid any marriage she entered into anywhere in the world.

39. Matrimonial property

(1) Any question in relation to the rights of spouses to each other's immoveable property arising by virtue of the marriage shall be determined by the law of the place in which the property is situated.

(2) Subject to subsections (4) and (5), if spouses are domiciled in the same country, any question in relation to the rights of the spouses to each other's moveable property arising by virtue of the marriage shall be determined by the law of that country.

(3) Subject to subsections (4) and (5), if spouses are domiciled in different countries then, for the purposes of any question in relation to the rights of the spouses to each other's moveable property arising by virtue of the marriage, the spouses shall be taken to have the same rights to such property as they had immediately before the marriage.

(4) Any question in relation to-

  (a) the use or occupation of a matrimonial home which is moveable; or

  (b) the use of the contents of a matrimonial home (whether the home is moveable or immoveable),

shall be determined by the law of the country in which the home is situated.

(5) A change of domicile by a spouse (or both spouses) shall not affect a right in moveable property which, immediately before the change, has vested in either spouse.

(6) This section shall not apply-

  (a) in relation to the law on aliment, financial provision on divorce, transfer of property on divorce or succession;

  (b) to the extent that spouses agree otherwise.

(7) In this section, "matrimonial home" has the same meaning as in section 22 of the 1981 Act.

GENERAL NOTE

This section implements the Family Law Report, recommendations 77-79. Section 39(1) provides that any question in relation to the rights of spouses to each other's immoveable property (land) arising by virtue of marriage is to be determined by the law of the place where the land was situated. If the couple have the same domicile, any question between them in relation to moveable property arising by virtue of marriage is to be determined by the law of the country of their domicile; s.39(2). If they have different domiciles, they are to have the same rights to their moveable property as they had immediately before they were married: s.39(3). A change of domicile is not to affect a right in moveable property which has vested immediately before the change. It should be noted that the scope of these provision is narrow as they only apply to property questions which arise by virtue of the parties' marriage i.e. issues of matrimonial property.

Section 39(4) provides an exception in respect of any question in relation to (a) the use or occupation of a matrimonial home which is moveable as opposed to immoveable property, for example a caravan or a barge; and (b) the use of the contents of a (moveable or immoveable) matrimonial home. Here any question is to be determined by the law of the place where the home is situated.

Importantly, this section does not apply to family law matters i.e. the law on aliment, financial provision on divorce, transfer of property on divorce or succession: s.39(6)(a). The parties can also agree to "contract out" of the rules: s.39(6)(b).

40. Aliment

Subject to the Maintenance Orders (Reciprocal Enforcement) Act 1972 (c.18), a court in Scotland shall apply Scots internal law in any action for aliment which comes before it.

GENERAL NOTE

This implements the Family Law Report, recommendation 91.

41. Effect of parents' marriage in determining status to depend on law of domicile

Any question arising as to the effect on a person's status of-
  (a) the person's parents being, or having been, married to each other; or
  (b) the person's parents not being, or not having been, married to each other,
shall be determined by the law of the country in which the person is domiciled at the time at which the question arises.

GENERAL NOTE

Although s.21 of this Act has abolished the status of illegitimacy for the purpose of Scots internal law, that status may still arise in questions which have a foreign element. Section 41 provides a new rule of Scots private international law that the effect on a person's status of his parents' marital status is to be determined by the law of his domicile at the time the question arises. This is most likely to arise as an incidental question. For example, A dies domiciled in X. His property includes moveables situated in Scotland. Under his will he leaves all his property to his child, B. Under the law of X only legitimate children can inherit. A was never married to B's mother. Succession to moveable property is governed by the law of the deceased's domicile at the time of his death i.e. the law of X. Under that law B can only inherit if he is legitimate. As a matter of Scots private international law, that incidental question is to be governed by the law of B's domicile. If B was domiciled in X and was illegitimate under that law, he could not inherit. But if B was domiciled in Scotland, his parents' marital status is irrelevant i.e. he is legitimate and he can inherit-at least in so far as the moveable estate in Scotland is concerned!

Declarator of freedom and putting to silence: action no longer competent

42. Action for declarator of freedom and putting to silence to cease to be competent

It shall not be competent to raise an action for declarator of freedom and putting to silence.

GENERAL NOTE

The Court of Session had jurisdiction to grant a declarator that a pursuer is not married and to restrain the defender from ascertaining that he is. This was known as an action for declarator of freedom and putting to silence. It was rarely, if ever, used in modern times. Section 42 provides that such actions are no longer competent. This implements the Family Law Report, recommendation 52(a).

43. Interpretation

In this Act-
"the 1976 Act" means the Divorce (Scotland) Act 1976 (c.39); and
"the 1981 Act" means the Matrimonial Homes (Family Protection) (Scotland) Act 1981 (c.59).

44. Ancillary provision

(1) The Scottish Ministers may by order made by statutory instrument make such consequential, transitional or saving provision as they consider appropriate for the purposes of, in consequence of or for giving full effect to this Act or any provision of it.
(2) An order under subsection (1) may modify any enactment (including this Act).
(3) The power conferred by subsection (1) on the Scottish Ministers to make orders may be exercised so as to make different provision for different purposes.
(4) A statutory instrument containing an order under subsection (1) shall, subject to subsection (5), be subject to annulment in pursuance of a resolution of the Scottish Parliament.
(5) A statutory instrument containing an order under subsection (1) which includes provision modifying an Act or an Act of the Scottish Parliament shall not be made unless a draft of the instrument has been laid before, and approved by resolution of, the Scottish Parliament.

45. Minor and consequential amendments and repeals

(1) Schedule 2 (which contains minor amendments and amendments consequential on the provisions of this Act) shall have effect.
(2) The enactments mentioned in the first column in schedule 3 (which include enactments that are spent) are repealed to the extent set out in the second column.

46. Short title and commencement

(1) This Act may be cited as the Family Law (Scotland) Act 2006.
(2) The provisions of this Act (except this section) shall come into force on such day as the Scottish Ministers may by order made by statutory instrument appoint.
(3) An order under subsection (2) may-
  (a) appoint different days for different purposes; and
  (b) include such transitional or saving provision as the Scottish Ministers consider necessary or expedient in connection with the coming into force of the provisions brought into force.

GENERAL NOTE
This Act will commence on May 4, 2006.

SCHEDULE 1

AMENDMENTS OF THE CIVIL PARTNERSHIP ACT 2004

(introduced by section 33)

1. The Civil Partnership Act 2004 (c.33) shall be amended in accordance with this schedule.

2. In section 86 (eligibility to register in Scotland as civil partners)-
    (a) in subsection (2), for "subsections (3) and (4) there shall be substituted "subsection (3)"; and
    (b) for subsections (4) and (5) there shall be substituted-
        "(4) Paragraph 2 of Schedule 10 has effect subject to the modifications specified in subsection (5) in the case of a person (here the relevant person) whose gender has become the acquired gender under the Gender Recognition Act 2004 (c. 7).
        (5) The reference in that paragraph to-
            (a) a former wife of the relevant person includes any former husband of the relevant person, and
            (b) a former husband of the relevant person includes any former wife of the relevant person.".

3. In section 101 (right of civil partner without title to occupy family home)-
    (a) after subsection (6) there shall be inserted-
        "(6A) Subject to subsection (5), if-
            (a) there has been no cohabitation between an entitled partner and a non-entitled partner during a continuous period of two years, and
            (b) during that period the non-entitled partner has not occupied the family home,
      the non-entitled partner shall, on the expiry of that period, cease to have occupancy rights in the family home.
        (6B) A non-entitled partner who has ceased to have occupancy rights by virtue of subsection (6A) may not apply to the court for an order under section 103(1).": and
    (b) in subsection (7)-
        (i) in the definition of "child of the family", for the words from "a", where it first occurs, to "family", there shall be substituted "any child or grandchild of either civil partner, and any person who has been brought up or treated by either civil partner as if the person were a child of that partner, whatever the age of such a child, grandchild or person"; and
        (ii) in the definition of "family", for "so accepted", there shall be substituted ", grandchild or person so treated".

4. In subsection (1) of section 103 (regulation by court of rights of occupancy of family home), at the beginning there shall be inserted "Subject to section 101(6A),".

5. In section 106 (continued exercise of occupancy rights after dealing)-
    (a) after subsection (1) there shall be inserted-
        "(1A) The occupancy rights of a non-entitled partner in relation to a family home shall not be exercisable in relation to the home where, following a dealing of the entitled partner relating to the home"
        (a) a person acquires the home, or an interest in it, in good faith and for value from a person other than the person who is or, as the case may be, was the entitled partner, or
        (b) a person derives title to the home from a person who acquired title as mentioned in paragraph (a)."; and
    (b) in subsection (3)-
        (i) in paragraph (e), for "sale", where it first occurs, there shall be substituted "transfer for value";
        (ii) in paragraph (e), for the words from "seller", where it first occurs, to the end of the paragraph there shall be substituted "transferor-

            (i) a written declaration signed by the transferor, or a person acting on behalf of the transferor under a power of attorney or as a guardian (within the meaning of the Adults with Incapacity (Scotland) Act 2000 (asp 4)), that the subjects of the transfer are not, or were not at the time of the dealing, a family home in relation to which a civil partner of the transferor has or had occupancy rights, or

(ii) a renunciation of occupancy rights or consent to the dealing which bears to have been properly made or given by the non-entitled partner or a person acting on behalf of the non-entitled partner under a power of attorney or as a guardian (within the meaning of the Adults with Incapacity (Scotland) Act 2000 (asp 4)).”; and

(iii) in paragraph (f), for “5” there shall be substitued “2”.

6. In section 107 (dispensation with civil partner's consent to dealing)-

(a) in subsection (1), at the beginning there shall be inserted Subject to subsections (1A) and (1C),”;

(b) after that subsection there shall be inserted-

“(1A) Subsection (1B) applies if, in relation to a proposed sale-

(a) negotiations with a third party have not begun, or

(b) negotiations have begun but a price has not been agreed.

(1B) An order under subsection (1) dispensing with consent may be made only if-

(a) the price agreed for the sale is no less than such amount as the court specifies in the order, and

(b) the contract for the sale is concluded before the expiry of such period as may be so specified.

(1C) Subsection (1D) applies if the proposed dealing is the grant of a heritable security.

(1D) An order under subsection (1) dispensing with consent may be made only if-

(a) the heritable security is granted for a loan of no more than such amount as the court specifies in the order, and

(b) the security is executed before the expiry of such period as may be so specified.”; and

(c) after subsection (3) there shall be inserted-

“(3A) If the court refuses an application for an order under subsection (1), it may make an order requiring a non-entitled partner who is or becomes the occupier of the family home-

(a) to make such payments to the owner of the home in respect of that partner's occupation of it as may be specified in the order,

(b) to comply with such other conditions relating to that partner's occupation of the family home as may be so specified.”.

7. After section 111 there shall be inserted-

“111A Effect of court action under section 103, 104 or 105 on reckoning of periods in sections 101 and 106

(1) Subsection (2) applies where an application is made under section 103(1), 104(1) or 105(1).

(2) In calculating the period of two years mentioned in section 101(6A)(a) or 106(3)(f), no account shall be taken of the period mentioned in subsection (3).

(3) The period is the period beginning with the date on which the application is made and-

(a) in the case of an application under section 103(1) or 104(1), ending on the date on which”

(i) an order under section 103(3) or, as the case may be, 104(2) is made, or

(ii) the application is otherwise finally determined or abandoned,

(b) in the case of an application under section 105(1), ending on the date on which-

(i) the order under section 103(3) or, as the case may be, 104(2) is varied or recalled, or

(ii) the application is otherwise finally determined or abandoned. Effect of court action under section 103, 104 or 105 on reckoning of periods in sections 101 and 106.

8. In section 113 (civil partnerships: competency of interdict)-

    (a) in subsection (2), for paragraph (b) there shall be substituted-

> "(b) subject to subsection (3), prohibits a civil partner from entering or remaining in-
>
>> (i) a family home,
>>
>> (ii) any other residence occupied by the applicant civil partner,
>>
>> (iii) any place of work of the applicant civil partner,
>>
>> (iv) any school attended by a child in the permanent or temporary care of the applicant civil partner"; and

    (b) after that subsection, there shall be added-

> "(3) Subsection (4) applies if in relation to a family home the non-applicant civil partner-
>
>> (a) is an entitled partner, or
>>
>> (b) has occupancy rights.
>
> (4) Except where subsection (5) applies, the court may not grant a relevant interdict prohibiting the non-applicant civil partner from entering or remaining in the family home.
>
> (5) This subsection applies if-
>
>> (a) the interdict is ancillary to an exclusion order, or
>>
>> (b) by virtue of section 101(4), the court refuses leave to exercise occupancy rights.
>
> (6) In this section and in sections 114 to 116, "applicant civil partner" means the civil partner who has applied for the interdict; and "non-applicant civil partner" is to be construed accordingly.".

9. In subsection (3) of section 117 (dissolution of civil partnerships)-

    (a) in paragraph (c), for "two years" there shall be substituted "one year"; and

    (b) in paragraph (d), for 5" there shall be substituted "two".

10. In section 123 (nullity) (which shall become subsection (1) of that section)-

    (a) the word "or", which occurs immediately after paragraph (a), shall be repealed;

    (b) the word "validly" in paragraph (b) shall be repealed;

    (c) at the end of paragraph (b) there shall be inserted", or

> (c) at the time of registration one of them who was capable of consenting to the formation of the civil partnership purported to give consent but did so by reason only of duress or error."; and

    (d) at the end, there shall be added-

> (2) In this section "error" means-
>
>> (a) error as to the nature of civil partnership, or
>>
>> (b) a mistaken belief held by a person ("A") that the other person with whom A purported to register a civil partnership was the person with whom A had agreed to register a civil partnership.".

11. After section 124 there shall be inserted-

"Special destinations: revocation on dissolution or annulment

124A Special destination: revocation on dissolution or annulment

  (1) Subsections (2) and (3) apply where-

    (a) heritable property is held in the name of-

>> (i) a person ("A") and A's civil partner ("B") and the survivor of them,
>>
>> (ii) A, B and another person and the survivor or survivors of them,
>>
>> (iii) A with a special destination on A's death, in favour of B,

    (b) A and B's civil partnership is terminated by dissolution or annulment, and

    (c) after the dissolution or annulment A dies.

  (2) In relation to the succession to A's heritable property (or part of it) under the destination, B shall be deemed to have failed to survive A.

  (3) If a person has in good faith and for value (whether by purchase or otherwise) acquired title to the heritable property, the title so acquired shall not be challengeable on the ground that, by virtue of subsection (2), the property falls to the estate of A.

  (4) Subsection (2) shall not apply if the destination specifies that B is to take under the destination despite the termination of A and B's civil partnership by dissolution or annulment.".

12. Section 135 (interpretation of Part 3) shall become subsection (1) of that section and-

    (a) in the definition of "family home"-
        (i) after "means" there shall be inserted ", subject to subsection (2),"; and
        (ii) for the words "one civil partner for that" there shall be substituted "a person for one"; and
    (b) at the end there shall be inserted-
        "(2) If-
           (a) the tenancy of a family home is transferred from one civil partner to the other by agreement or under any enactment, and
           (b) following the transfer, the civil partner to whom the tenancy was transferred occupies the home but the other civil partner does not,
the home shall, on such transfer, cease to be a family home.".

GENERAL NOTE

Paragraph (2)

This removes the restrictions on persons related by affinity from entering a civil partnership. The analogous provisions in relation to marriage were removed by s.1 of this Act discussed above.

Paragraphs (3)-(8)

These amend s.101 of the Civil Partnership Act 2004 to make analogous amendments as those made to the 1981 Act by ss.5-9 of this Act discussed above. The amendment to s.101(7) has the effect that the definition of child is now the same as that under the 1981 Act i.e. any child or grandchild of either civil partner or any person brought up or treated by either civil partner as if that person was a child of the civil partner: the age of the child or grandchild is irrelevant.

Paragraph (9)

For the purpose of dissolution of a civil partnership, the period of non cohabitation with agreement is reduced from two years to one and of non cohabitation without agreement from five years to two.

Paragraph (10)

These amendments are analogous to those in relation to nullity of marriage in s.2 of this Act discussed above.

Paragraph (11)

These provisions are analogous to those in s.19 of this Act discussed above.

SCHEDULE 2

MINOR AND CONSEQUENTIAL AMENDMENTS

(introduced by section 45(1))

1. The Domicile and Matrimonial Proceedings Act 1973 (c.45)

In section 7 of the Domicile and Matrimonial Proceedings Act 1973 (jurisdiction of Court of Session)-
    (a) in paragraph (a) of subsection (1)-
        (i) after "marriage", where it first occurs, there shall be inserted "or"; and
        (ii) the words "declarator of freedom and putting to silence" shall be repealed;
    (b) subsection (2) shall be repealed; and
    (c) in subsection (5)-
        (i) after "marriage", where it secondly occurs, there shall be inserted "or"; and
        (ii) "or declarator of freedom and putting to silence" shall be repealed.

2. The Damages (Scotland) Act 1976 (c.13)

In paragraph 1 of Schedule 1 to the Damages (Scotland) Act 1976 (definition of "relative")-
    (a) in sub-paragraph (a), after "spouse there shall be inserted "or civil partner";
    (b) in sub-paragraph (aa)-

     (i) after "spouse" there shall be inserted "or civil partner"; and

     (ii) at the end there shall be added "or in a relationship which had the characteristics of the relationship between civil partners";

    (c) after sub-paragraph (e), the word "and" shall be repealed; and

    (d) after sub-paragraph (f), there shall be added "and

> (g) any person who, having been a civil partner of the deceased, had ceased to be so by virtue of the dissolution of the civil partnership.".

3. The Land Registration (Scotland) Act 1979 (c.33)

In subsection (3) of section 12 of the Land Registration (Scotland) Act 1979 (Keeper's indemnity in respect of loss), at the end there shall be added-

> "(r) the loss is suffered by the estate of a deceased former spouse in respect of heritable property falling to it where the title to the property or to any interest in the property has been acquired by another person and is unchallengeable by virtue of section 19 of the Family Law (Scotland) Act 2006 (asp 2);
>
> (s) the loss is suffered by the estate of a deceased former civil partner in respect of heritable property falling to it where the title to the property or to any interest in the property has been acquired by another person and is unchallengeable by virtue of section 124A of the Civil Partnership Act 2004 (c.33)."

4. The Matrimonial Homes (Family Protection) (Scotland) Act 1981 (c.59)

(1) The Matrimonial Homes (Family Protection) (Scotland) Act 1981 shall be amended as follows.

(2) In subsection (1) of section 3 (regulation by court of rights of occupancy of matrimonial home), at the beginning there shall be inserted "Subject to section 1(7) of this Act,".

(3) In the proviso to section 17(2), for "10" there shall be substituted "8".

5. The Family Law (Scotland) Act 1985 (c.37)

(1) The Family Law (Scotland) Act 1985 shall be amended as follows.

(2) In subsection (2) of section 12A (orders for payment of capital sum: pensions lump sum), for "party", where it first occurs, there shall be substituted "person".

(3) In subsection (2) of section 16 (agreements on financial provision), after "divorce", wherever it occurs, there shall be inserted "or of dissolution of the civil partnership".

(4) In subsection (1) of section 27 (interpretation), in the definition of "partner", for "has", where it first occurs, there shall be substituted "was".

6. The Law Reform (Parent and Child) (Scotland) Act 1986 (c.9)

(1) The Law Reform (Parent and Child) (Scotland) Act 1986 shall be amended as follows.

(2) In subsections (1) and (5) of section 7 (actions for declarator), for the words "non-parentage, legitimacy, legitimation or illegitimacy", in each place where they occur there shall be substituted "or non-parentage".

(3) In section 9 (savings and supplementary provisions)-

    (a) in paragraph (b) of subsection (1), at the beginning there shall be inserted subject to subsection (1A) below,"; and

    (b) after that subsection, there shall be inserted-

> "1A) Subsections (1) and (2) of section 1 of this Act shall apply in relation to adopted children.".

7. The Civil Evidence (Family Mediation) (Scotland) Act 1995 (c.6)

In subsection (7) of section 1 of the Civil Evidence (Family Mediation) (Scotland) Act 1995 (inadmissibility in civil proceedings of information as to what occurred during family mediation)-

    (a) the words from "a" to "wife" shall form paragraph (a) of that subsection; and

    (b) after "wife" there shall be added"; or

> (b) two persons who are not civil partners of each other but are living together as if they were civil partners.".

8. The Children (Scotland) Act 1995 (c.36)

In subsection (4) of section 12 of the Children (Scotland) Act 1995 (restrictions on decrees for divorce, separation or annulment affecting children)"

    (a) the existing words from the parties to the end shall become paragraph (a) (with the existing paragraphs (a) and (b) becoming sub-paragraphs (i) and (ii)); and

    (b) after the new paragraph (a), there shall be added

        ; or

            (b) the partners in a civil partnership, means a child who has been treated by both partners as a child of the family which their partnership constitutes..

GENERAL NOTE

Paragraph (2)

This amends the Damages (Scotland) Act 1976 so that the deceased's immediate family include the deceased's civil partner or a person who was, immediately before the deceased's death, living with the deceased in a relationship which had the characteristics of the relationship between civil partners. A former civil partner is not a member of the deceased's immediate family. See also s.35 of this Act discussed above.

Paragraph (3)

This was discussed above at s.19 of this Act.

Paragraph (7)

The 1995 Act is amended to include same sex partners

Paragraph (8)

In an action for divorce the court must consider whether it is necessary to exercise its powers in relation to any children of the family. If not satisfied that arrangements have been made which are in the children's best interests, the court can postpone granting decree. As a result of this amendment, in an action for dissolution of a civil partnership the court will have the same duty and powers in respect of any child of the family.

SCHEDULE 3 section 45(2)

REPEALS

(introduced by)

Enactment	Extent of repeal
The Conjugal Rights (Scotland) Amendment Act 1861 (c.86)	The whole Act.
The Married Women's Policies of Assurance (Scotland) Act 1880 (c.26)	In section 2, in the definition of "children", the words illegitimate or.
The Sheriff Courts (Scotland) Act 1907 (c.51)	Section 38B.
The Law Reform (Husband and Wife) Act 1962 (c.48)	The whole Act.
The Industrial and Provident Societies Act 1965 (c.12)	In section 25, in subsection (1), the words "subject to subsection (2) of this section," and subsection (2).
The Legitimation (Scotland) Act 1968 (c.22)	The whole Act.
The Domicile and Matrimonial Proceedings Act 1973 (c.45)	Section 4.

Family Law Reform

Enactment	Extent of repeal
The Friendly Societies Act 1974 (c.46)	In section 68, subsection (2) and, in subsection (3), the words from "and" to the end.
The Damages (Scotland) Act 1976 (c.13)	In Schedule 1, in paragraph 1(d), the words "(other than a parent or child)".
The Divorce (Scotland) Act 1976 (c.39)	In section 2, subsection (3) and, in subsection (4), the word "(c)".
The Adoption (Scotland) Act 1978 (c.28)	In section 39, in subsections (1) and (2), the word "legitimate", wherever it occurs.
	In section 65, in the definition of "relative", the words ", where the child is illegitimate,".
The Matrimonial Homes (Family Protection) (Scotland) Act 1981 (c.59)	In section 14(2), the words "and section 15".
	Sections 15 to 17.
	Section 21.
	In section 22, in the definition of "matrimonial home", the words "attached to, and".
The Law Reform (Parent and Child) (Scotland) Act 1986 (c.9)	In section 1, in subsection (2), the words "Subject to subsection (4) below,", subsection (3) and, in subsection (4), paragraph (c).
	In section 9(1), paragraph (a).
The Civil Evidence (Scotland) Act 1988 (c.32)	In section 8, in subsection (2), the words "legitimacy, legitimation, illegitimacy,".
The Court of Session Act 1988 (c.36)	Section 19.
The Age of Legal Capacity (Scotland) Act 1991 (c.50)	Section 7.
The Protection from Abuse (Scotland) Act 2001 (asp 14)	In section 1(2), paragraph (b).
	Section 6.
The Civil Partnership Act 2004 (c.33)	Section 86(6) and (7).
	In section 113(2), the words "and in section 114".
	Sections 114 to 116.
	In section 117, subsections (3)(b), (6) and (7).
	In section 119, subsections (1) and (2) and, in subsection (3), the word "(b)".
	Section 129.
	In section 135, in the definition of "family home", the words "attached to, and".
	In Schedule 10, paragraph 3.
	In Schedule 28, paragraphs 42 and 60(3).

GENERAL NOTE

The Law Reform (Husband and Wife) Act 1962 (c.48)

At common law, spouses could not sue each other in delict. Section 2(1) of the Law Reform (Husband and Wife) Act 1962 allowed them to do so as if they were not married. However, under s.2(2) of the Act the court had a discretion to dismiss the proceedings if it appeared that no substantial benefit would accrue to either party. As it was enough that at least some benefit accrued to the pursuer, in practice the discretion was rarely if, ever, exercised. By repealing the Law Reform (Husband and Wife) Act 1962 the discretion is removed. The common law does not revive by virtue of s.16 of the Interpretation Act 1978.

The Age of Legal Capacity (Scotland) Act 1991, s.7

Section 7 of the 1991 Act provides that "The time at which a person first becomes capable of having an independent domicile shall be the date at which he attains the age of 16". Section 22 of this Act, discussed above, provides new rules for ascertaining the domicile of a child. It defines a child as a person under the age of 16. It is therefore implicit in the section that on reaching the age of 16, a person's domicile will be determined by the rules that apply to adults and that accordingly the young person can acquire a domicile of choice. In these circumstances, s.7 of the Age of Legal Capacity (Scotland) Act 1991 can be repealed.

CIVIL PARTNERSHIP ACT 2004

(2004, c.33)

. . .

PART 3

CIVIL PARTNERSHIP: SCOTLAND

Chapters 1 and 2 of this Part deal with the formation and registration of civil partnerships.

Chapters 3 and 4 make provision for civil partners equivalent to that contained for married partners in the Matrimonial Homes (Family Protection) (Scotland) Act 1981.

Chapter 5 provides grounds for dissolution of a civil partnership, separation and nullity on grounds similar to divorce, separation and nullity for married partners with the notable exception of "adultery" as a ground for dissolving a civil partnership.

Chapter 6 deals with "miscellaneous" matters, and interpretation. The "miscellaneous" matters are very important for they include succession rights for civil partners equivalent to those for spouses.

CHAPTER 1

FORMATION AND ELIGIBILITY

Formation of civil partnership by registration

85.—(1) For the purposes of section 1, two people are to be regarded as having registered as civil partners of each other once each of them has signed the civil partnership schedule, in the presence of—

(a) each other,

(b) two witnesses both of whom have attained the age of 16, and

(c) the authorised registrar,

(all being present at a registration office or at a place agreed under section 93).

(2) But the two people must be eligible to be so registered.

(3) Subsection (1) applies regardless of whether subsection (4) is complied with.

(4) After the civil partnership schedule has been signed under subsection (1), it must also be signed, in the presence of the civil partners and each other by—

(a) each of the two witnesses, and

(b) the authorised registrar.

Eligibility

86.—(1) Two people are not eligible to register in Scotland as civil partners of each other if—

(a) they are not of the same sex,

(b) they are related in a forbidden degree,

(c) either has not attained the age of 16,

(d) either is married or already in civil partnership, or

(e) either is incapable of—

(i) understanding the nature of civil partnership, or

(ii) validly consenting to its formation.

[1] (2) Subject to subsection (3), a man is related in a forbidden degree to another man if related to him in a degree specified in column 1 of Schedule 10 and a woman is related in a forbidden degree to another woman if related to her in a degree specified in column 2 of that Schedule.

(3) A man and any man related to him in a degree specified in column 1

of paragraph 2 of Schedule 10, or a woman and any woman related to her in a degree specified in column 2 of that paragraph, are not related in a forbidden degree if—

(a) both persons have attained the age of 21, and

(b) the younger has not at any time before attaining the age of 18 lived in the same household as the elder and been treated by the elder as a child of the elder's family.

[2] (4) Paragraph 2 of Schedule 10 has effect subject to the modifications specified in subsection (5) in the case of a person (here the "relevant person") whose gender has become the acquired gender under the Gender Recognition Act 2004 (c.7).

(5) The reference in that paragraph to-

(a) a former wife of the relevant person includes any former husband of the relevant person, and

(b) a former husband of the relevant person includes any former wife of the relevant person.

(6) [*Repealed by Family Law (Scotland) Act 2006 (asp 2), Sch.3*].

(7) [*Repealed by Family Law (Scotland) Act 2006 (asp 2), Sch.3*].

(8) References in this section and in Schedule 10 to relationships and degrees of relationship are to be construed in accordance with section 1(1) of the Law Reform (Parent and Child) (Scotland) Act 1986 (c.9).

(9) For the purposes of this section, a degree of relationship specified in paragraph 1 of Schedule 10 exists whether it is of the full blood or the half blood.

(10) Amend section 41(1) of the Adoption (Scotland) Act 1978 (c.28) (application to determination of forbidden degrees of provisions of that Act relating to the status conferred by adoption) as follows—

(a) after first "marriage" insert ", to the eligibility of persons to register as civil partners of each other", and

(b) for "and incest" substitute ", to such eligibility and to incest".

NOTE

1. Amended by Family Law (Scotland) Act 2006 (asp 2), s.33, Sch.1.

2. Substituted by Family Law (Scotland) Act 2006 (asp 2), s.33, Sch.1.

CHAPTER 2

REGISTRATION

Appointment of authorised registrars

87.—For the purpose of affording reasonable facilities throughout Scotland for registration as civil partners, the Registrar General—

(a) is to appoint such number of district registrars as he thinks necessary, and

(b) may, in respect of any district for which he has made an appointment under paragraph (a), appoint one or more assistant registrars, as persons who may carry out such registration (in this Part referred to as "authorised registrars").

Notice of proposed civil partnership

88.—(1) In order to register as civil partners, each of the intended civil partners must submit to the district registrar a notice, in the prescribed form and accompanied by the prescribed fee, of intention to enter civil partnership (in this Part referred to as a "notice of proposed civil partnership").

(2) A notice submitted under subsection (1) must also be accompanied by—

(a) the birth certificate of the person submitting it,

(b) if that person has previously been married or in civil partnership and—
   (i) the marriage or civil partnership has been dissolved, a copy of the decree of divorce or dissolution, or
   (ii) the other party to that marriage or civil partnership has died, the death certificate of that other party, and
(c) if that person has previously ostensibly been married or in civil partnership but decree of annulment has been obtained, a copy of that decree.

(3) If a person is unable to submit a certificate or decree required by subsection (2) he may instead make a declaration to that effect, stating what the reasons are; and he must provide the district registrar with such—

(a) information in respect of the matters to which the certificate or document would have related, and
(b) documentary evidence in support of that information,

as the district registrar may require.

(4) If a document submitted under subsection (2) or (3) is in a language other than English, the person submitting it must attach to the document a translation of it in English, certified by the translator as a correct translation.

(5) A person submitting a notice under subsection (1) must make and sign the necessary declaration (the form for which must be included in any form prescribed for the notice).

(6) The necessary declaration is a declaration that the person submitting the notice believes that the intended civil partners are eligible to be in civil partnership with each other.

Civil partnership notice book

89.—(1) On receipt of a notice of proposed civil partnership, the district registrar is to enter in a book (to be known as "the civil partnership book") supplied to him for that purpose by the Registrar General such particulars, extracted from the notice, as may be prescribed and the date of receipt by him of that notice.

(2) The form and content of any page of that book is to be prescribed.

Publicisation

90.—(1) Where notices of a proposed civil partnership are submitted to a district registrar, he must, as soon as practicable after the day on which they are submitted (or, if the two documents are not submitted on the same day, after the day on which the first is submitted), publicise the relevant information and send it to the Registrar General who must also publicise it.

(2) "The relevant information" means—
(a) the names of the intended civil partners, and
(b) the date on which it is intended to register them as civil partners of each other, being a date more than 14 days after publicisation by the district registrar under subsection (1).

(3) Paragraph (b) of subsection (2) is subject to section 91.

(4) The manner in which and means by which relevant information is to be publicised are to be prescribed.

Early registration

91.—An authorised registrar who receives a request in writing from one or both of two intended civil partners that they should be registered as civil partners of each other on a date specified in the request (being a date 14 days or fewer after publicisation by the district registrar under subsection (1) of section 90) may, provided that he is authorised to do so by the Registrar General, fix that date as the date for registration; and if a date is so fixed, paragraph (b) of subsection (2) of that section is to be construed as if it were a reference to that date.

Objections to registration

92.—(1) Any person may at any time before the registration in Scotland of two people as civil partners of each other submit in writing an objection to such registration to the district registrar.

(2) But where the objection is that the intended civil partners are not eligible to be in civil partnership with each other because either is incapable of—

(a) understanding the nature of civil partnership, or

(b) validly consenting to its formation,

it shall be accompanied by a supporting certificate signed by a registered medical practitioner.

(3) A person claiming that he may have reason to submit such an objection may, free of charge and at any time when the registration office at which a notice of proposed civil partnership to which the objection would relate is open for public business, inspect any relevant entry in the civil partnership book.

(4) Where the district registrar receives an objection in accordance with subsection (1) he must—

(a) in any case where he is satisfied that the objection relates to no more than a misdescription or inaccuracy in a notice submitted under section 88(1)—

(i) notify the intended civil partners of the nature of the objection and make such enquiries into the matter mentioned in it as he thinks fit, and

(ii) subject to the approval of the Registrar General, make any necessary correction to any document relating to the proposed civil partnership, or

(b) in any other case—

(i) at once notify the Registrar General of the objection, and

(ii) pending consideration of the objection by the Registrar General, suspend the completion or issue of the civil partnership schedule in respect of the proposed civil partnership.

(5) If the Registrar General is satisfied, on consideration of an objection of which he has received notification under subsection (4)(b)(i) that—

(a) there is a legal impediment to registration, he must direct the district registrar not to register the intended civil partners and to notify them accordingly, or

(b) there is no such impediment, he must inform the district registrar to that effect.

(6) For the purposes of this section and section 94, there is a legal impediment to registration where the intended civil partners are not eligible to be in civil partnership with each other.

Place of registration

93.—(1) Two people may be registered as civil partners of each other at a registration office or any other place which they and the local registration authority agree is to be the place of registration.

(2) The place of registration may, if the approval of the Registrar General is obtained, be outwith the district of the authorised registrar carrying out the registration.

(3) But the place must not be in religious premises, that is to say premises which—

(a) are used solely or mainly for religious purposes, or

(2) Any payment made under subsection (1)(a) or any obligation performed under subsection (1)(b) has effect in relation to the rights of a third party as if the payment were made or the obligation were performed by the entitled partner; and the performance of an obligation which has been enforced under subsection (1)(c) has effect as if it had been enforced by the entitled partner.

(3) Where there is an entitled and a non-entitled partner, the court, on the application of either of them, may, having regard in particular to the respective financial circumstances of the partners, make an order apportioning expenditure incurred or to be incurred by either partner—

(a) without the consent of the other partner, on any of the items mentioned in paragraphs (a) and (d) of subsection (1);

(b) with the consent of the other partner, on anything relating to a family home.

(4) Where both partners are entitled, or permitted by a third party, to occupy a family home—

(a) either partner is entitled, without the consent of the other partner, to carry out such non-essential repairs or improvements as may be authorised by an order of the court, being such repairs or improvements as the court considers to be appropriate for the reasonable enjoyment of the occupancy rights;

(b) the court, on the application of either partner, may, having regard in particular to the respective financial circumstances of the partners, make an order apportioning expenditure incurred or to be incurred by either partner, with or without the consent of the other partner, on anything relating to the family home.

(5) Where one partner ("A") owns or hires, or is acquiring under a hire-purchase or conditional sale agreement, furniture and plenishings in a family home—

(a) the other partner may, without the consent of A—

(i) make any payment due by A which is necessary, or take any other step which A is entitled to take, to secure the possession or use of any such furniture and plenishings (and any such payment is to have effect in relation to the rights of a third party as if it were made by A), or

(ii) carry out such essential repairs to the furniture and plenishings as A is entitled to carry out;

(b) the court, on the application of either partner, may, having regard in particular to the respective financial circumstances of the partners, make an order apportioning expenditure incurred or to be incurred by either partner—

(i) without the consent of the other partner, in making payments under a hire, hire-purchase or conditional sale agreement, or in paying interest charges in respect of the furniture and plenishings, or in carrying out essential repairs to the furniture and plenishings, or

(ii) with the consent of the other partner, on anything relating to the furniture or plenishings.

(6) An order under subsection (3), (4)(b) or (5)(b) may require one partner to make a payment to the other partner in implementation of the apportionment.

(7) Any application under subsection (3), (4)(b) or (5)(b) is to be made within 5 years after the date on which any payment in respect of such incurred expenditure was made.

(8) Where—

(a) the entitled partner is a tenant of a family home,

(b) possession of it is necessary in order to continue the tenancy, and

(c) the entitled partner abandons such possession,

the tenancy is continued by such possession by the non-entitled partner.

(9) In this section "improvements" includes alterations and enlargement.

Regulation by court of rights of occupancy of family home

103.—[1] (1) Subject to section 101(6A), where there is an entitled and a non-entitled partner, or where both partners are entitled, or permitted by a third party, to occupy a family home, either partner may apply to the court for an order—

(a) declaring the occupancy rights of the applicant partner;

(b) enforcing the occupancy rights of the applicant partner;

(c) restricting the occupancy rights of the non-applicant partner;

(d) regulating the exercise by either partner of his or her occupancy rights;

(e) protecting the occupancy rights of the applicant partner in relation to the other partner.

(2) Where one partner owns or hires, or is acquiring under a hire-purchase or conditional sale agreement, furniture and plenishings in a family home and the other partner has occupancy rights in that home, that other person may apply to the court for an order granting to the applicant the possession or use in the family home of any such furniture and plenishings; but, subject to section 102, an order under this subsection does not prejudice the rights of any third party in relation to the non-performance of any obligation under such hire-purchase or conditional sale agreement.

(3) The court is to grant an application under subsection (1)(a) if it appears to the court that the application relates to a family home; and, on an application under any of paragraphs (b) to (e) of subsection (1) or under subsection (2), the court may make such order relating to the application as appears to it to be just and reasonable having regard to all the circumstances of the case including—

(a) the conduct of the partners, whether in relation to each other or otherwise,

(b) the respective needs and financial resources of the partners,

(c) the needs of any child of the family,

(d) the extent (if any) to which—

    (i) the family home, and

    (ii) in relation only to an order under subsection (2), any item of furniture and plenishings referred to in that subsection, is used in connection with a trade, business or profession of either partner, and

(e) whether the entitled partner offers or has offered to make available to the non-entitled partner any suitable alternative accommodation.

(4) Pending the making of an order under subsection (3), the court, on the application of either partner, may make such interim order as it considers necessary or expedient in relation to—

(a) the residence of either partner in the home to which the application relates,

(b) the personal effects of either partner or of any child of the family, or

(c) the furniture and plenishings,

but an interim order may be made only if the non-applicant partner has been afforded an opportunity of being heard by or represented before the court.

(5) The court is not to make an order under subsection (3) or (4) if it appears that the effect of the order would be to exclude the non-applicant partner from the family home.

(6) If the court makes an order under subsection (3) or (4) which requires the delivery to one partner of anything which has been left in or

removed from the family home, it may also grant a warrant authorising a messenger-at-arms or sheriff officer to enter the family home or other premises occupied by the other partner and to search for and take possession of the thing required to be delivered, (if need be by opening shut and lockfast places) and to deliver the thing in accordance with the order.

(7) A warrant granted under subsection (6) is to be executed only after expiry of such period as the court is to specify in the order for delivery.

(8) Where it appears to the court—

(a) on the application of a non-entitled partner, that the applicant has suffered a loss of occupancy rights or that the quality of the applicant's occupation of a family home has been impaired, or

(b) on the application of a partner who has been given the possession or use of furniture and plenishings by virtue of an order under subsection (3), that the applicant has suffered a loss of such possession or use or that the quality of the applicant's possession or use of the furniture and plenishings has been impaired,

in consequence of any act or default on the part of the other partner which was intended to result in such loss or impairment, it may order that other partner to pay to the applicant such compensation as it considers just and reasonable in respect of that loss or impairment.

(9) A partner may renounce in writing the right to apply under subsection (2) for the possession or use of any item of furniture and plenishings.

NOTE
1. Amended by Family Law (Scotland) Act 2006 (asp 2), s.33, Sch.1.

Exclusion orders

104.—(1) Where there is an entitled and non-entitled partner, or where both partners are entitled, or permitted by a third party, to occupy a family home, either partner, whether or not that partner is in occupation at the time of the application, may apply to the court for an order (in this Chapter referred to as "an exclusion order") suspending the occupancy rights of the other partner ("the non-applicant partner") in a family home.

(2) Subject to subsection (3), the court is to make an exclusion order if it appears to it that to do so is necessary for the protection of the applicant or any child of the family from any conduct, or threatened or reasonably apprehended conduct, of the non-applicant partner which is or would be injurious to the physical or mental health of the applicant or child.

(3) The court is not to make an exclusion order if it appears to it that to do so would be unjustified or unreasonable—

(a) having regard to all the circumstances of the case including the matters specified in paragraphs (a) to (e) of section 103(3), and

(b) where the family home—

(i) is, or is part of, an agricultural holding within the meaning of section 1 of the Agricultural Holdings (Scotland) Act 1991 (c.55), or

(ii) is let, or is a home in respect of which possession is given, to the non-applicant partner or to both partners by an employer as an incident of employment,

having regard to any requirement that the non-applicant partner, or, as the case may be, both partners must reside in the family home and to the likely consequences of the exclusion of the non-applicant partner from the family home.

(4) In making an exclusion order the court is, on the application of the applicant partner—

(a) to grant a warrant for the summary ejection of the non-applicant partner from the family home unless the non-applicant partner satisfies the court that it is unnecessary for it to grant such a remedy,

(b) to grant an interdict prohibiting the non-applicant partner from entering the family home without the express permission of the applicant, and

(c) to grant an interdict prohibiting the removal by the non-applicant partner, except with the written consent of the applicant or by a further order of the court, of any furniture and plenishings in the family home unless the non-applicant partner satisfies the court that it is unnecessary for it to grant such a remedy.

(5) In making an exclusion order the court may—

(a) grant an interdict prohibiting the non-applicant partner from entering or remaining in a specified area in the vicinity of the family home;

(b) where the warrant for the summary ejection of the non-applicant partner has been granted in that partner's absence, give directions as to the preservation of that partner's goods and effects which remain in the family home;

(c) on the application of either partner, make the exclusion order or the warrant or interdict mentioned in paragraph (a), (b) or (c) of subsection (4) or paragraph (a) of this subsection subject to such terms and conditions as the court may prescribe;

(d) on the application of either partner, make such other order as it considers necessary for the proper enforcement of an order made under subsection (4) or paragraph (a), (b) or (c).

(6) Pending the making of an exclusion order, the court may, on the application of the applicant partner, make an interim order suspending the occupancy rights of the non-applicant partner in the family home to which the application for the exclusion order relates; and subsections (4) and (5) apply to such an interim order as they apply to an exclusion order.

(7) But an interim order may be made only if the non-applicant partner has been afforded an opportunity of being heard by or represented before the court.

(8) Without prejudice to subsections (1) and (6), where both partners are entitled, or permitted by a third party, to occupy a family home, it is incompetent for one partner to bring an action of ejection from the family home against the other partner.

Duration of orders under sections 103 and 104

105.—(1) The court may, on the application of either partner, vary or recall any order made by it under section 103 or 104.

(2) Subject to subsection (3), any such order, unless previously so varied or recalled, ceases to have effect—

(a) on the dissolution of the civil partnership,

(b) subject to section 106(1), where there is an entitled and non-entitled partner, on the entitled partner ceasing to be an entitled partner in respect of the family home to which the order relates, or

(c) where both partners are entitled, or permitted by a third party, to occupy the family home, on both partners ceasing to be so entitled or permitted.

(3) Without prejudice to the generality of subsection (2), an order under section 103(3) or (4) which grants the possession or use of furniture and plenishings ceases to have effect if the furniture and plenishings cease to be permitted by a third party to be retained in the family home.

(a) an application is made for an order under this section, and
(b) an action is or has been raised by a non-entitled partner to enforce occupancy rights,

the action is to be sisted until the conclusion of the proceedings on the application.

NOTE
1. Amended by Family Law (Scotland) Act 2006 (asp 2), s.33, Sch.1.
2. Inserted by Family Law (Scotland) Act 2006 (asp 2), s.33, Sch.1.

Interests of heritable creditors

108.—(1) The rights of a third party with an interest in the family home as a creditor under a secured loan in relation to the non-performance of any obligation under the loan are not prejudiced by reason only of the occupancy rights of the non-entitled partner; but where a non-entitled partner has or obtains occupation of a family home and—
(a) the entitled partner is not in occupation, and
(b) there is a third party with such an interest in the family home,

the court may, on the application of the third party, make an order requiring the non-entitled partner to make any payment due by the entitled partner in respect of the loan.

(2) This section does not apply to secured loans in respect of which the security was granted prior to the commencement of section 13 of the Law Reform (Miscellaneous Provisions) (Scotland) Act 1985 (c.73) unless the third party in granting the secured loan acted in good faith and there was produced to the third party by the entitled partner—
(a) an affidavit sworn or affirmed by the entitled partner declaring that there is no non-entitled partner, or
(b) a renunciation of occupancy rights or consent to the taking of the loan which bears to have been properly made or given by the non-entitled partner.

(3) This section does not apply to secured loans in respect of which the security was granted after the commencement of section 13 of the Law Reform (Miscellaneous Provisions) (Scotland) Act 1985 (c.73) unless the third party in granting the secured loan acted in good faith and there was produced to the third party by the grantor—
(a) an affidavit sworn or affirmed by the grantor declaring that the security subjects are not or were not at the time of the granting of the security a family home in relation to which a civil partner of the grantor has or had occupancy rights, or
(b) a renunciation of occupancy rights or consent to the granting of the security which bears to have been properly made or given by the non-entitled partner.

(4) For the purposes of subsections (2) and (3), the time of granting a security, in the case of a heritable security, is the date of delivery of the deed creating the security.

Provisions where both civil partners have title

109.—(1) Subject to subsection (2), where, apart from the provisions of this Chapter, both civil partners are entitled to occupy a family home—
(a) the rights in that home of one civil partner are not prejudiced by reason only of any dealing of the other civil partner, and
(b) a third party is not by reason only of such a dealing entitled to occupy that home or any part of it.

(2) Sections 106(3) and 107 and the definition of "dealing" in section 106(2) apply for the purposes of subsection (1) as they apply for the purposes of section 106(1) but subject to the following modifications—

(a) any reference to the entitled partner and to the non-entitled partner is to be construed as a reference to a civil partner who has entered into, or as the case may be proposes to enter into, a dealing and to the other civil partner respectively, and

(b) in paragraph (b) of section 107(4) the reference to occupancy rights is to be construed as a reference to any rights in the family home.

Rights of occupancy in relation to division and sale

110. Where a civil partner brings an action for the division and sale of a family home owned in common with the other civil partner, the court, after having regard to all the circumstances of the case including—

(a) the matters specified in paragraphs (a) to (d) of section 103(3), and

(b) whether the civil partner bringing the action offers or has offered to make available to the other civil partner any suitable alternative accommodation,

may refuse to grant decree in that action or may postpone the granting of decree for such period as it considers reasonable in the circumstances or may grant decree subject to such conditions as it may prescribe.

Adjudication

111.—(1) Where a family home as regards which there is an entitled partner and a non-entitled partner is adjudged, the Court of Session, on the application of the non-entitled partner made within 40 days after the date of the decree of adjudication, may—

(a) order the reduction of the decree, or

(b) make such order as it thinks appropriate to protect the occupancy rights of the non-entitled partner,

if satisfied that the purpose of the diligence was wholly or mainly to defeat the occupancy rights of the non-entitled partner.

(2) Section 106(2) applies in construing "entitled partner" and "non-entitled partner" for the purposes of subsection (1).

Effect of court action under section 103, 104 or 105 on reckoning of periods in sections 101 and 106

[1] **111A.**—(1) Subsection (2) applies where an application is made under section 103(1), 104(1) or 105(1).

(2) In calculating the period of two years mentioned in section 101(6A)(a) or 106(3)(f), no account shall be taken of the period mentioned in subsection (3).

(3) The period is the period beginning with the date on which the application is made and—

(a) in the case of an application under section 103(1) or 104(1), ending on the date on which—

   (i) an order under section 103(3) or, as the case may be, 104(2) is made, or

   (ii) the application is otherwise finally determined or abandoned,

(b) in the case of an application under section 105(1), ending on the date on which—

   (i) the order under section 103(3) or, as the case may be, 104(2) is varied or recalled, or

   (ii) the application is otherwise finally determined or abandoned.

Transfer of tenancy

Transfer of tenancy

112.—(1) The court may, on the application of a non-entitled partner, make an order transferring the tenancy of a family home to that partner

Continued exercise of occupancy rights after dealing

106.—(1) Subject to subsection (3)—

(a) the continued exercise of the rights conferred on a non-entitled partner by the provisions of this Chapter in respect of a family home are not prejudiced by reason only of any dealing of the entitled partner relating to that home, and

(b) a third party is not by reason only of such a dealing entitled to occupy that home or any part of it.

¹(1A) The occupancy rights of a non-entitled partner in relation to a family home shall not be exercisable in relation to the home where, following a dealing of the entitled partner relating to the home—

(a) a person acquires the home, or an interest in it, in good faith and for value from a person other than the person who is or, as the case may be, was the entitled partner, or

(b) a person derives title to the home from a person who acquired title as mentioned in paragraph (a).

(2) In this section and section 107—

"dealing" includes the grant of a heritable security and the creation of a trust but does not include a conveyance under section 80 of the Lands Clauses Consolidation Act 1845 (c.18);

"entitled partner" does not include a civil partner who, apart from the provisions of this Chapter—

(a) is permitted by a third party to occupy a family home, or

(b) is entitled to occupy a family home along with an individual who is not the other civil partner whether or not that individual has waived a right of occupation in favour of the civil partner so entitled,

("non-entitled partner" being construed accordingly).

(3) This section does not apply in any case where—

(a) the non-entitled partner in writing either—

(i) consents or has consented to the dealing (any consent being in such form as the Scottish Ministers may, by regulations made by statutory instrument, prescribe), or

(ii) renounces or has renounced occupancy rights in relation to the family home or property to which the dealing relates,

(b) the court has made an order under section 107 dispensing with the consent of the non-entitled partner to the dealing,

(c) the dealing occurred, or implements a binding obligation entered into by the entitled partner, before the registration of the civil partnership,

(d) the dealing occurred, or implements a binding obligation entered into, before the commencement of this section,

²(e) the dealing comprises a transfer for value to a third party who has acted in good faith, if there is produced to the third party by the transferor—

(i) a written declaration signed by the transferor, or a person acting on behalf of the transferor under a power of attorney or as a guardian (within the meaning of the Adults with Incapacity (Scotland) Act 2000 (asp 4)), that the subjects of the transfer are not, or were not at the time of the dealing, a family home in relation to which a civil partner of the transferor has or had occupancy rights, or

(ii) a renunciation of occupancy rights or consent to the dealing which bears to have been properly made or given by the non-entitled partner or a person acting on behalf of the non-entitled partner under a power of attorney or as a guardian (within the meaning of the Adults with Incapacity (Scotland) Act 2000 (asp 4)).

²(f) the entitled partner has permanently ceased to be entitled to occupy the family home, and at any time after that a continuous

period of 2 years has elapsed during which the non-entitled partner has not occupied the family home.

(4) For the purposes of subsection (3)(e), the time of the dealing, in the case of the sale of an interest in heritable property, is the date of delivery to the purchaser of the deed transferring title to that interest.

NOTE
1. Inserted by Family Law (Scotland) Act 2006 (asp 2), s.33, Sch.1.
2. Amended by Family Law (Scotland) Act 2006 (asp 2), s.33, Sch.1

Dispensation with civil partner's consent to dealing

107.—[1] (1) Subject to subsections (1A) and (1C), the court may, on the application of an entitled partner or any other person having an interest, make an order dispensing with the consent of a non-entitled partner to a dealing which has taken place or a proposed dealing, if—

(a) such consent is unreasonably withheld,

(b) such consent cannot be given by reason of physical or mental disability, or

(c) the non-entitled partner cannot be found after reasonable steps have been taken to trace that partner.

[2] (1A) Subsection (1B) applies if, in relation to a proposed sale—

(a) negotiations with a third party have not begun, or

(b) negotiations have begun but a price has not been agreed.

[2] (1B) An order under subsection (1) dispensing with consent may be made only if—

(a) the price agreed for the sale is no less than such amount as the court specifies in the order, and

(b) the contract for the sale is concluded before the expiry of such period as may be so specified.

[2] (1C) Subsection (1D) applies if the proposed dealing is the grant of a heritable security.

[2] (1D) An order under subsection (1) dispensing with consent may be made only if—

(a) the heritable security is granted for a loan of no more than such amount as the court specifies in the order, and

(b) the security is executed before the expiry of such period as may be so specified.

(2) For the purposes of subsection (1)(a), a non-entitled partner has unreasonably withheld consent to a dealing which has taken place or a proposed dealing, where it appears to the court either—

(a) that the non-entitled partner—

(i) has led the entitled partner to believe that the non-entitled partner would consent to the dealing, and

(ii) would not be prejudiced by any change in the circumstances of the case since the conduct which gave rise to that belief occurred, or

(b) that the entitled partner has, having taken all reasonable steps to do so, been unable to obtain an answer to a request for consent.

(3) The court, in considering whether to make an order under subsection (1), is to have regard to all the circumstances of the case including the matters specified in paragraphs (a) to (e) of section 103(3).

[2] (3A) If the court refuses an application for an order under subsection (1), it may make an order requiring a non-entitled partner who is or becomes the occupier of the family home—

(a) to make such payments to the owner of the home in respect of that partner's occupation of it as may be specified in the order,

(b) to comply with such other conditions relating to that partner's occupation of the family home as may be so specified.

(4) Where—

70

    (a) an application is made for an order under this section, and

    (b) an action is or has been raised by a non-entitled partner to enforce occupancy rights,

the action is to be sisted until the conclusion of the proceedings on the application.

NOTE

    1. Amended by Family Law (Scotland) Act 2006 (asp 2), s.33, Sch.1.

    2. Inserted by Family Law (Scotland) Act 2006 (asp 2), s.33, Sch.1.

Interests of heritable creditors

    108.—(1) The rights of a third party with an interest in the family home as a creditor under a secured loan in relation to the non-performance of any obligation under the loan are not prejudiced by reason only of the occupancy rights of the non-entitled partner; but where a non-entitled partner has or obtains occupation of a family home and—

    (a) the entitled partner is not in occupation, and

    (b) there is a third party with such an interest in the family home,

the court may, on the application of the third party, make an order requiring the non-entitled partner to make any payment due by the entitled partner in respect of the loan.

    (2) This section does not apply to secured loans in respect of which the security was granted prior to the commencement of section 13 of the Law Reform (Miscellaneous Provisions) (Scotland) Act 1985 (c.73) unless the third party in granting the secured loan acted in good faith and there was produced to the third party by the entitled partner—

    (a) an affidavit sworn or affirmed by the entitled partner declaring that there is no non-entitled partner, or

    (b) a renunciation of occupancy rights or consent to the taking of the loan which bears to have been properly made or given by the non-entitled partner.

    (3) This section does not apply to secured loans in respect of which the security was granted after the commencement of section 13 of the Law Reform (Miscellaneous Provisions) (Scotland) Act 1985 (c.73) unless the third party in granting the secured loan acted in good faith and there was produced to the third party by the grantor—

    (a) an affidavit sworn or affirmed by the grantor declaring that the security subjects are not or were not at the time of the granting of the security a family home in relation to which a civil partner of the grantor has or had occupancy rights, or

    (b) a renunciation of occupancy rights or consent to the granting of the security which bears to have been properly made or given by the non-entitled partner.

    (4) For the purposes of subsections (2) and (3), the time of granting a security, in the case of a heritable security, is the date of delivery of the deed creating the security.

Provisions where both civil partners have title

    109.—(1) Subject to subsection (2), where, apart from the provisions of this Chapter, both civil partners are entitled to occupy a family home—

    (a) the rights in that home of one civil partner are not prejudiced by reason only of any dealing of the other civil partner, and

    (b) a third party is not by reason only of such a dealing entitled to occupy that home or any part of it.

    (2) Sections 106(3) and 107 and the definition of "dealing" in section 106(2) apply for the purposes of subsection (1) as they apply for the purposes of section 106(1) but subject to the following modifications—

(a) any reference to the entitled partner and to the non-entitled partner is to be construed as a reference to a civil partner who has entered into, or as the case may be proposes to enter into, a dealing and to the other civil partner respectively, and

(b) in paragraph (b) of section 107(4) the reference to occupancy rights is to be construed as a reference to any rights in the family home.

Rights of occupancy in relation to division and sale

110. Where a civil partner brings an action for the division and sale of a family home owned in common with the other civil partner, the court, after having regard to all the circumstances of the case including—

(a) the matters specified in paragraphs (a) to (d) of section 103(3), and

(b) whether the civil partner bringing the action offers or has offered to make available to the other civil partner any suitable alternative accommodation,

may refuse to grant decree in that action or may postpone the granting of decree for such period as it considers reasonable in the circumstances or may grant decree subject to such conditions as it may prescribe.

Adjudication

111.—(1) Where a family home as regards which there is an entitled partner and a non-entitled partner is adjudged, the Court of Session, on the application of the non-entitled partner made within 40 days after the date of the decree of adjudication, may—

(a) order the reduction of the decree, or

(b) make such order as it thinks appropriate to protect the occupancy rights of the non-entitled partner,

if satisfied that the purpose of the diligence was wholly or mainly to defeat the occupancy rights of the non-entitled partner.

(2) Section 106(2) applies in construing "entitled partner" and "non-entitled partner" for the purposes of subsection (1).

Effect of court action under section 103, 104 or 105 on reckoning of periods in sections 101 and 106

[1] **111A.**—(1) Subsection (2) applies where an application is made under section 103(1), 104(1) or 105(1).

(2) In calculating the period of two years mentioned in section 101(6A)(a) or 106(3)(f), no account shall be taken of the period mentioned in subsection (3).

(3) The period is the period beginning with the date on which the application is made and—

(a) in the case of an application under section 103(1) or 104(1), ending on the date on which—

(i) an order under section 103(3) or, as the case may be, 104(2) is made, or

(ii) the application is otherwise finally determined or abandoned,

(b) in the case of an application under section 105(1), ending on the date on which—

(i) the order under section 103(3) or, as the case may be, 104(2) is varied or recalled, or

(ii) the application is otherwise finally determined or abandoned.

Transfer of tenancy

Transfer of tenancy

112.—(1) The court may, on the application of a non-entitled partner, make an order transferring the tenancy of a family home to that partner and providing, subject to subsection (12), for the payment by the non-entitled partner to the entitled partner of such compensation as seems to it to be just and reasonable in all the circumstances of the case.

(2) In an action—

(a) for dissolution of a civil partnership, the Court of Session or the sheriff,

(b) for declarator of nullity of a civil partnership, the Court of Session,

may, on granting decree or within such period as the court may specify on granting decree, make an order granting an application under subsection (1).

(3) In determining whether to grant an application under subsection (1), the court is to have regard to all the circumstances of the case including the matters specified in paragraphs (a) to (e) of section 103(3) and the suitability of the applicant to become the tenant and the applicant's capacity to perform the obligations under the lease of the family home.

(4) The non-entitled partner is to serve a copy of an application under subsection (1) on the landlord and, before making an order under subsection (1), the court is to give the landlord an opportunity of being heard by it.

(5) On the making of an order granting an application under subsection (1), the tenancy vests in the non-entitled partner without intimation to the landlord, subject to all the liabilities under the lease (other than liability for any arrears of rent for the period before the making of the order).

(6) The arrears mentioned in subsection (5) are to remain the liability of the original entitled partner.

(7) The clerk of court is to notify the landlord of the making of an order granting an application under subsection (1).

(8) It is not competent for a non-entitled partner to apply for an order under subsection (1) where the family home—

(a) is let to the entitled partner by the entitled partner's employer as an incident of employment, and the lease is subject to a requirement that the entitled partner must reside there,

(b) is or is part of an agricultural holding,

(c) is on, or pertains to—

(i) a croft,

(ii) the subject of a cottar, or

(iii) the holding of a landholder or of a statutory small tenant,

(d) is let on a long lease, or

(e) is part of the tenancy land of a tenant-at-will.

(9) In subsection (8)—

"agricultural holding" has the same meaning as in section 1 of the Agricultural Holdings (Scotland) Act 1991 (c.55),

"cottar" has the same meaning as in section 12(5) of the Crofters (Scotland) Act 1993 (c.44),

"croft" has the same meaning as in that Act of 1993,

"holding", in relation to a landholder and a statutory small tenant, "landholder" and "statutory small tenant" have the same meanings respectively as in sections 2(1), 2(2) and 32(1) of the Small Landholders (Scotland) Act 1911 (c.49),

"long lease" has the same meaning as in section 28(1) of the Land Registration (Scotland) Act 1979 (c.33), and

"tenant-at-will" has the same meaning as in section 20(8) of that Act of 1979.

(10) Where both civil partners are joint or common tenants of a family home, the court may, on the application of one of the civil partners, make an order vesting the tenancy in that civil partner solely and providing, subject to subsection (12), for the payment by the applicant to the other partner of such compensation as seems just and reasonable in the circumstances of the case.

(11) Subsections (2) to (9) apply for the purposes of an order under subsection (10) as they apply for the purposes of an order under subsection (1) but subject to the following modifications—

    (a) in subsection (3), for "tenant" there is substituted "sole tenant";

    (b) in subsection (4), for "non-entitled" there is substituted "applicant";

    (c) in subsection (5), for "non-entitled" there is substituted "applicant",

    (d) in subsection (6), for "liability of the original entitled partner" there is substituted "joint and several liability of both partners";

    (e) in subsection (8)—

        (i) for "a non-entitled" there is substituted "an applicant",

        (ii) for paragraph (a) there is substituted—

            "(a) is let to both partners by their employer as an incident of employment, and the lease is subject to a requirement that both partners must reside there;", and

        (iii) paragraphs (c) and (e) are omitted.

(12) Where the family home is a Scottish secure tenancy within the meaning of the Housing (Scotland) Act 2001 (asp 10), no account is to be taken, in assessing the amount of any compensation to be awarded under subsection (1) or (10), of the loss, by virtue of the transfer of the tenancy of the home, of a right to purchase the home under Part 3 of the Housing (Scotland) Act 1987 (c.26).

CHAPTER 4

INTERDICTS

Civil partners: competency of interdict

113.—(1) It shall not be incompetent for the Court of Session or the sheriff to entertain an application by one civil partner in a civil partnership for a relevant interdict by reason only that the civil partners are living together in civil partnership.

[1] (2) In subsection (1), "relevant interdict" means an interdict, including an interim interdict, which—

    (a) restrains or prohibits any conduct of one civil partner towards the other civil partner or a child of the family, or

    (b) subject to subsection (3), prohibits a civil partner from entering or remaining in—

        (i) a family home,

        (ii) any other residence occupied by the applicant civil partner,

        (iii) any place of work of the applicant civil partner,

        (iv) any school attended by a child in the permanent or temporary care of the applicant civil partner

[2] (3) Subsection (4) applies if in relation to a family home the non-applicant civil partner—

    (a) is an entitled partner, or

    (b) has occupancy rights.

[2] (4) Except where subsection (5) applies, the court may not grant a relevant interdict prohibiting the non-applicant civil partner from entering or remaining in the family home.

[2] (5) This subsection applies if—

    (a) the interdict is ancillary to an exclusion order, or

    (b) by virtue of section 101(4), the court refuses leave to exercise occupancy rights.

[2] (6) In this section and in sections 114 to 116, "applicant civil partner" means the civil partner who has applied for the interdict; and "non-applicant civil partner" is to be construed accordingly.

NOTE
1. Amended by Family Law (Scotland) Act 2006 (asp 2), s.33, Sch.1 and Sch.3.
2. Inserted by Family Law (Scotland) Act 2006 (asp 2), s.33, Sch.1.

Attachment of powers of arrest to relevant interdicts

114. [*Repealed by Family Law (Scotland) Act 2006 (asp 2), Sch.3 subject to savings specified in SSI 2006/212, art.13*].

Police powers after arrest

115. [*Repealed by Family Law (Scotland) Act 2006 (asp 2), Sch.3 subject to savings specified in SSI 2006/212, art.13*].

Procedure after arrest

116.—(1) The provisions of this section apply only where—
(a) the non-applicant civil partner has not been liberated under section 115(1), and
(b) the procurator fiscal decides that no criminal proceedings are to be taken in respect of the facts and circumstances which gave rise to the arrest.

(2) The non-applicant civil partner who has been arrested under section 114(4) is wherever practicable to be brought before the sheriff sitting as a court of summary criminal jurisdiction for the district in which that civil partner was arrested not later than in the course of the first day after the arrest, such day not being a Saturday, a Sunday or a court holiday prescribed for that court under section 8 of the Criminal Procedure (Scotland) Act 1995 (c.46).

(3) Nothing in subsection (2) prevents the non-applicant civil partner being brought before the sheriff on a Saturday, a Sunday or such a court holiday when the sheriff is, in pursuance of that section of that Act, sitting for the disposal of criminal business.

(4) Subsections (1) to (3) of section 15 of that Act (intimation to a named person) apply to a non-applicant civil partner who has been arrested under section 114(4) as they apply to a person who has been arrested in respect of any offence.

(5) The procurator fiscal is at the earliest opportunity, and in any event prior to the non-applicant civil partner being brought before the sheriff under subsection (2), to take all reasonable steps to intimate—
(a) to the applicant civil partner, and
(b) to the solicitor who acted for that civil partner when the interdict was granted or to any other solicitor who the procurator fiscal has reason to believe acts for the time being for that civil partner,
that the criminal proceedings referred to in subsection (1) will not be taken.

(6) On the non-applicant civil partner being brought before the sheriff under subsection (2) (as read with subsection (3)), the following procedures apply—
(a) the procurator fiscal is to present to the court a petition containing—
(i) a statement of the particulars of the non-applicant civil partner,
(ii) a statement of the facts and circumstances which gave rise to the arrest, and
(iii) a request that the non-applicant civil partner be detained for a further period not exceeding 2 days,
(b) if it appears to the sheriff that—
(i) the statement referred to in paragraph (a)(ii) ostensibly discloses a breach of interdict by the non-applicant civil partner,

(ii) proceedings for breach of interdict will be taken, and

(iii) there is a substantial risk of violence by the non-applicant civil partner against the applicant civil partner or any child of the family,

he may order the non-applicant civil partner to be detained for a further period not exceeding 2 days, and

(c) in any case to which paragraph (b) does not apply, the non-applicant civil partner is, unless in custody in respect of any other matter, to be released from custody.

(7) In computing the period of 2 days referred to in paragraphs (a) and (b) of subsection (6), no account is to be taken of a Saturday or Sunday or of any holiday in the court in which the proceedings for breach of interdict will require to be raised.

CHAPTER 5

DISSOLUTION, SEPARATION AND NULLITY

Dissolution and separation

Dissolution

117.—(1) An action for the dissolution of a civil partnership may be brought in the Court of Session or in the sheriff court.

(2) In such an action the court may grant decree, if, but only if, it is established that—

(a) the civil partnership has broken down irretrievably, or

(b) an interim gender recognition certificate under the Gender Recognition Act 2004 (c.7) has, after the date of registration of the civil partnership, been issued to either of the civil partners.

[1] (3) The irretrievable breakdown of a civil partnership is taken to be established if—

(a) since the date of registration of the civil partnership the defender has at any time behaved (whether or not as a result of mental abnormality and whether such behaviour has been active or passive) in such a way that the pursuer cannot reasonably be expected to cohabit with the defender,

(c) there has been no cohabitation between the civil partners at any time during a continuous period of one year after the date of registration of the civil partnership and immediately preceding the bringing of the action and the defender consents to the granting of decree of dissolution of the civil partnership, or

(d) there has been no cohabitation between the civil partners at any time during a continuous period of two years after that date and immediately preceding the bringing of the action.

(4) Provision is to be made by act of sederunt—

(a) for the purpose of ensuring that, in an action to which paragraph (c) of subsection (3) relates, the defender has been given such information as enables that civil partner to understand—

(i) the consequences of consenting to the granting of decree, and

(ii) the steps which must be taken to indicate such consent, and

(b) as to the manner in which the defender in such an action is to indicate such consent, and any withdrawal of such consent,

and where the defender has indicated (and not withdrawn) such consent in the prescribed manner, that indication is sufficient evidence of such consent.

(5) Provision is to be made by act of sederunt for the purpose of ensuring that, where in an action for the dissolution of a civil partnership the defender is suffering from mental illness, the court appoints a curator ad litem to the defender.

^{2}(6) ...

^{2}(7) ...

(8) In an action for dissolution of a civil partnership the standard of proof required to establish the ground of action is on balance of probability.

NOTE
1. Amended by Family Law (Scotland) Act 2006 (asp 2), s.33, Sch.1 and Sch.3.
2. Repealed by Family Law (Scotland) Act 2006 (asp 2), Sch.3.

Encouragement of reconciliation

118.—(1) At any time before granting decree in an action by virtue of paragraph (a) of section 117(2) for dissolution of a civil partnership, if it appears to the court that there is a reasonable prospect of a reconciliation between the civil partners it must continue, or further continue, the action for such period as it thinks proper to enable attempts to be made to effect such a reconciliation.

(2) If during any such continuation the civil partners cohabit with one another, no account is to be taken of such cohabitation for the purposes of that action.

Effect of resumption of cohabitation

119.—^{1}(1) ...

^{1}(2) ...

^{2}(3) In considering whether any period mentioned in paragraph (c) or (d) of section 117(3) has been continuous, no account is to be taken of any period or periods not exceeding 6 months in all during which the civil partners cohabited with one another; but no such period or periods during which the civil partners cohabited with one another is to count as part of the period of non-cohabitation required by any of those paragraphs.

NOTE
1. Repealed by Family Law (Scotland) Act 2006 (asp 2), Sch.3.
2. Amended by Family Law (Scotland) Act 2006 (asp 2), Sch.3.

Separation

120.—(1) An action for the separation of the civil partners in a civil partnership may be brought in the Court of Session or in the sheriff court.

(2) In such an action the court may grant decree if satisfied that the circumstances set out in any of paragraphs (a) to (d) of section 117(3) are established.

Dissolution following on decree of separation

121.—(1) The court may grant decree in an action for the dissolution of a civil partnership even though decree of separation has previously been granted to the pursuer on the same, or substantially the same, facts as those averred in support of that action; and in any such action the court may treat an extract decree of separation lodged in process as sufficient proof of the facts under which that decree was granted.

(2) Nothing in this section entitles a court to grant decree of dissolution of a civil partnership without receiving evidence from the pursuer.

Registration of dissolution of civil partnership

122.—(1) The Registrar General is to maintain at the General Register Office a register of decrees of dissolution of civil partnership (a register which shall be known as the "Register of Dissolutions of Civil Partnership").

(2) The Registrar General is to cause to be made and kept at the General Register Office an alphabetical index of the entries in that register.

(3) The register is to be in such form as may be prescribed.

(4) On payment to him of such fee or fees as may be prescribed, the Registrar General must, at any time when the General Register Office is open for that purpose—

    (a) cause a search of the index to be made on behalf of any person or permit any person to search the index himself,

    (b) issue to any person an extract of any entry in the register which that person may require.

(5) An extract of any entry in the register is to be sufficient evidence of the decree of dissolution to which it relates.

(6) The Registrar General may—

    (a) delete,

    (b) amend, or

    (c) substitute another entry for,

any entry in the register.

Nullity

Nullity

[1] **123.**—(1) Where two people register in Scotland as civil partners of each other, the civil partnership is void if, and only if—

    (a) they were not eligible to do so,

    (b) though they were so eligible, either of them did not consent to its formation, or

    (c) at the time of registration one of them who was capable of consenting to the formation of the civil partnership purported to give consent but did so by reason only of duress or error.

(2) In this section "error" means—

    (a) error as to the nature of civil partnership, or

    (b) a mistaken belief held by a person ("A") that the other person with whom A purported to register a civil partnership was the person with whom A had agreed to register a civil partnership.

NOTE

1. Amended by Family Law (Scotland) Act 2006 (asp 2), s.33, Sch.1.

Validity of civil partnerships registered outside Scotland

124.—(1) Where two people register as civil partners of each other in England and Wales—

    (a) the civil partnership is void if it would be void in England and Wales under section 49, and

    (b) the civil partnership is voidable if it would be voidable there under section 50(1)(a), (b), (c) or (e).

(2) Where two people register as civil partners of each other in Northern Ireland, the civil partnership is—

    (a) void, if it would be void in Northern Ireland under section 173, and

    (b) voidable, if it would be voidable there under section 174(1)(a), (b), (c) or (e).

(3) Subsection (4) applies where two people register as civil partners of each other under an Order in Council under—

    (a) section 210 (registration at British consulates etc.), or

    (b) section 211 (registration by armed forces personnel),

("the relevant section").

(4) The civil partnership is—

(a) void, if—

    (i) the condition in subsection (2)(a) or (b) of the relevant section is not met, or

    (ii) a requirement prescribed for the purposes of this paragraph by an Order in Council under the relevant section is not complied with, and

(b) voidable, if—

    (i) the appropriate part of the United Kingdom is England and Wales and the circumstances fall within section 50(1)(a), (b), (c) or (e), or

    (ii) the appropriate part of the United Kingdom is Northern Ireland and the circumstances fall within section 174(1)(a), (b), (c) or (e).

(5) The appropriate part of the United Kingdom is the part by reference to which the condition in subsection (2)(b) of the relevant section is met.

(6) Subsections (7) and (8) apply where two people have registered an apparent or alleged overseas relationship.

(7) The civil partnership is void if—

(a) the relationship is not an overseas relationship, or

(b) (even though the relationship is an overseas relationship), the parties are not treated under Chapter 2 of Part 5 as having formed a civil partnership.

(8) The civil partnership is voidable if—

(a) the overseas relationship is voidable under the relevant law,

(b) where either of the parties was domiciled in England and Wales at the time when the overseas relationship was registered, the circumstances fall within section 50(1)(a), (b), (c) or (e), or

(c) where either of the parties was domiciled in Northern Ireland at the time when the overseas relationship was registered, the circumstances fall within section 174(1)(a), (b), (c) or (e).

(9) Section 51 or (as the case may be) section 175 applies for the purposes of—

(a) subsections (1)(b), (2)(b) and (4)(b),

(b) subsection (8)(a), in so far as applicable in accordance with the relevant law, and

(c) subsection (8)(b) and (c).

(10) In subsections (8)(a) and (9)(b) "the relevant law" means the law of the country or territory where the overseas relationship was registered (including its rules of private international law).

(11) For the purposes of subsections (8) and (9)(b) and (c), references in sections 50 and 51 or (as the case may be) sections 174 and 175 to the formation of the civil partnership are to be read as references to the registration of the overseas relationship.

Special destinations: revocation on dissolution or annulment

Special destination: revocation on dissolution or annulment

[1] **124A.**—(1) Subsections (2) and (3) apply where—

(a) heritable property is held in the name of—

    (i) a person ("A") and A's civil partner ("B") and the survivor of them,

    (ii) A, B and another person and the survivor or survivors of them,

    (iii) A with a special destination on A's death, in favour of B,

(b) A and B's civil partnership is terminated by dissolution or annulment, and

(c) after the dissolution or annulment A dies.

(2) In relation to the succession to A's heritable property (or part of it) under the destination, B shall be deemed to have failed to survive A.

(3) If a person has in good faith and for value (whether by purchase or otherwise) acquired title to the heritable property, the title so acquired shall not be challengeable on the ground that, by virtue of subsection (2), the property falls to the estate of A.

(4) Subsection (2) shall not apply if the destination specifies that B is to take under the destination despite the termination of A and B's civil partnership by dissolution or annulment.

NOTE
1. Inserted by Family Law (Scotland) Act 2006 (asp 2), s.33, Sch.1.

Financial provision after overseas proceedings

Financial provision after overseas dissolution or annulment

125. Schedule 11 relates to applications for financial provision in Scotland after a civil partnership has been dissolved or annulled in a country or territory outside the British Islands.

CHAPTER 6

MISCELLANEOUS AND INTERPRETATION

Miscellaneous

Regulations

126.—(1) In this Chapter and in Chapters 2 and 5, "prescribed" means prescribed by regulations made by the Registrar General.

(2) Regulations so made may make provision (including provision as to fees) supplementing, in respect of the provision of services by or on behalf of the Registrar General or by local registration authorities (as defined by section 5(3) of the 1965 Act), the provisions of Chapter 2 of this Part.

(3) Any power to make regulations under subsection (1) or (2) is exercisable by statutory instrument; and no such regulations are to be made except with the approval of the Scottish Ministers.

(4) A statutory instrument containing regulations under subsection (1) or (2), or regulations under section 106(3)(a)(i), is subject to annulment in pursuance of a resolution of the Scottish Parliament.

Attachment

127. Where an attachment has been executed of furniture and plenishings of which the debtor's civil partner has the possession or use by virtue of an order under section 103(3) or (4), the sheriff, on the application of that civil partner made within 40 days after the execution of the attachment, may—
(a) declare the attachment null, or
(b) make such order as he thinks appropriate to protect such possession or use by that civil partner,
if satisfied that the purpose of the attachment was wholly or mainly to prevent such possession or use.

Promise or agreement to enter into civil partnership

128. No promise or agreement to enter into civil partnership creates any rights or obligations under the law of Scotland; and no action for breach of such a promise or agreement may be brought in any court in Scotland, whatever the law applicable to the promise or agreement.

Lord Advocate as party to action for nullity or dissolution of civil partnership

129. [*Repealed by Family Law (Scotland) Act 2006 (asp 2), Sch.3*].

Civil partner of accused a competent witness

130.—(1) The civil partner of an accused may be called as a witness—
(a) by the accused, or
(b) without the consent of the accused, by a co-accused or by the prosecutor.

(2) But the civil partner is not a compellable witness for the co-accused or for the prosecutor and is not compelled to disclose any communication made, while the civil partnership subsists, between the civil partners.

(3) The failure of a civil partner of an accused to give evidence is not to be commented on by the defence or the prosecutor.

Succession: legal rights arising by virtue of civil partnership

131.—(1) Where a person dies survived by a civil partner then, unless the circumstance is as mentioned in subsection (2), the civil partner has right to half of the moveable net estate belonging to the deceased at the time of death.

(2) That circumstance is that the person is also survived by issue, in which case the civil partner has right to a third of that moveable net estate and those issue have right to another third of it.

(3) In this section—
"issue" means issue however remote, and
"net estate" has the meaning given by section 36(1) (interpretation) of the Succession (Scotland) Act 1964 (c.41).

(4) Every testamentary disposition executed after the commencement of this section by which provision is made in favour of the civil partner of the testator and which does not contain a declaration to the effect that the provision so made is in full and final satisfaction of the right to any share in the testator's estate to which the civil partner is entitled by virtue of subsection (1) or (2), has effect (unless the disposition contains an express provision to the contrary) as if it contained such a declaration.

(5) In section 36(1) of the Succession (Scotland) Act 1964 (c.41), in the definition of "legal rights", for "and legitim" substitute "legitim and rights under section 131 of the Civil Partnership Act 2004".

Assurance policies

132. Section 2 of the Married Women's Policies of Assurance (Scotland) Act 1880 (c.26) (which provides that a policy of assurance may be effected in trust for a person's spouse, children or spouse and children) applies in relation to a policy of assurance—
(a) effected by a civil partner (in this section referred to as "A") on A's own life, and
(b) expressed upon the face of it to be for the benefit of A's civil partner, or of A's children, or of A's civil partner and children,
as it applies in relation to a policy of assurance effected as, and expressed upon the face of it to be for such benefit as, is mentioned in that section.

Council Tax: liability of civil partners

133. After section 77 of the Local Government Finance Act 1992 (c.14), insert—
"**Liability of civil partners**
77A.—(1) Where—
(a) a person who is liable to pay council tax in respect of any

chargeable dwelling and any day is in civil partnership with another person or living with another person in a relationship which has the characteristics of the relationship between civil partners; and

    (b) that other person is also a resident of the dwelling on that day but would not, apart from this section, be so liable,

those persons shall be jointly and severally liable to pay the council tax payable in respect of that dwelling and that day.

(2) Subsection (1) above shall not apply as respects any day on which the other person there mentioned falls to be disregarded for the purposes of discount—

    (a) by virtue of paragraph 2 of Schedule 1 to this Act (the severely mentally impaired); or

    (b) being a student, by virtue of paragraph 4 of that Schedule."

General provisions as to fees

134.—(1) Subject to such exceptions as may be prescribed, a district registrar may refuse to comply with any application voluntarily made to him under this Part until the appropriate fee, if any, provided for by or under this Part is paid to him; and any such fee, if not prepaid, is recoverable by the registrar to whom it is payable.

(2) Circumstances, of hardship or otherwise, may be prescribed in which fees provided for by or under this Part may be remitted by the Registrar General.

Interpretation

Interpretation of this Part

[1] **135.**—(1) In this Part, unless the context otherwise requires—

"the 1965 Act" means the Registration of Births, Deaths and Marriages (Scotland) Act 1965 (c.49);

"authorised registrar" has the meaning given by section 87;

"caravan" means a caravan which is mobile or affixed to land;

"child of the family" has the meaning given by section 101(7);

"civil partnership book" has the meaning given by section 89;

"civil partnership register" has the meaning given by section 95(2);

"civil partnership schedule" has the meaning given by section 94;

"the court" means the Court of Session or the sheriff;

"district" means a registration district as defined by section 5(1) of the 1965 Act;

"district registrar" has the meaning given by section 7(12) of the 1965 Act;

"entitled partner" and "non-entitled partner", subject to sections 106(2) and 111(2), have the meanings respectively assigned to them by section 101(1);

"exclusion order" has the meaning given by section 104(1);

"family" has the meaning given by section 101(7);

"family home" means, subject to subsection (2) any house, caravan, houseboat or other structure which has been provided or has been made available by one or both of the civil partners as, or has become, a family residence and includes any garden or other ground or building usually occupied with, or otherwise required for the amenity or convenience of, the house, caravan, houseboat or other structure but does not include a residence provided or made available by a person for one civil partner to reside in, whether with any child of the family or not, separately from the other civil partner;

"furniture and plenishings" means any article situated in a family home of civil partners which—

(a) is owned or hired by either civil partner or is being acquired by either civil partner under a hire-purchase agreement or conditional sale agreement, and

(b) is reasonably necessary to enable the home to be used as a family residence,

but does not include any vehicle, caravan or houseboat or such other structure as is mentioned in the definition of "family home";

"notice of proposed civil partnership" has the meaning given by section 88(1);

"occupancy rights" means the rights conferred by section 101(1);

"Registrar General" means the Registrar General of Births, Deaths and Marriages for Scotland;

"registration office" means a registration office provided under section 8(1) of the 1965 Act;

"tenant" includes—

(a) a sub-tenant,

(b) a statutory tenant as defined in section 3 of the Rent (Scotland) Act 1984 (c.58), and

(c) a statutory assured tenant as defined in section 16(1) of the Housing (Scotland) Act 1988 (c.43),

and "tenancy" is to be construed accordingly.

(2) If—

(a) the tenancy of a family home is transferred from one civil partner to the other by agreement or under any enactment, and

(b) following the transfer, the civil partner to whom the tenancy was transferred occupies the home but the other civil partner does not,

the home shall, on such transfer, cease to be a family home.

NOTE

1. Amended by Family Law (Scotland) Act 2006 (asp 2), s.33, Sch.1 and Sch.3.

The expression "relative" in the 1965 Act

136. In section 56(1) of the 1965 Act (interpretation), in the definition of "relative", at the end insert ", a civil partner and anyone related to the civil partner of the person as regards whom the expression is being construed".

Jurisdiction of Scottish courts

Jurisdiction of Scottish courts

225.—(1) The Court of Session has jurisdiction to entertain an action for the dissolution of a civil partnership or for separation of civil partners if (and only if)—

(a) the court has jurisdiction under section 219 regulations,

(b) no court has, or is recognised as having, jurisdiction under section 219 regulations and either civil partner is domiciled in Scotland on the date when the proceedings are begun, or

(c) the following conditions are met—

(i) the two people concerned registered as civil partners of each other in Scotland,

(ii) no court has, or is recognised as having, jurisdiction under section 219 regulations, and

(iii) it appears to the court to be in the interests of justice to assume jurisdiction in the case.

(2) The sheriff has jurisdiction to entertain an action for the dissolution of a civil partnership or for separation of civil partners if (and only if) the

requirements of paragraph (a) or (b) of subsection (1) are met and either civil partner—
- (a) was resident in the sheriffdom for a period of 40 days ending with the date when the action is begun, or
- (b) had been resident in the sheriffdom for a period of not less than 40 days ending not more than 40 days before that date and has no known residence in Scotland at that date.

(3) The Court of Session has jurisdiction to entertain an action for declarator of nullity of a civil partnership if (and only if)—
- (a) the Court has jurisdiction under section 219 regulations,
- (b) no court has, or is recognised as having, jurisdiction under section 219 regulations and either of the ostensible civil partners—
    - (i) is domiciled in Scotland on the date when the proceedings are begun, or
    - (ii) died before that date and either was at death domiciled in Scotland or had been habitually resident in Scotland throughout the period of 1 year ending with the date of death, or
- (c) the following conditions are met—
    - (i) the two people concerned registered as civil partners of each other in Scotland,
    - (ii) no court has, or is recognised as having, jurisdiction under section 219 regulations, and
    - (iii) it appears to the court to be in the interests of justice to assume jurisdiction in the case.

(4) At any time when proceedings are pending in respect of which a court has jurisdiction by virtue of any of subsections (1) to (3) (or this subsection) it also has jurisdiction to entertain other proceedings, in respect of the same civil partnership (or ostensible civil partnership), for dissolution, separation or (but only where the court is the Court of Session) declarator of nullity, even though that jurisdiction would not be exercisable under any of subsections (1) to (3).

Sisting of proceedings

226.—(1) Rules of court may make provision in relation to civil partnerships corresponding to the provision made in relation to marriages by Schedule 3 to the Domicile and Matrimonial Proceedings Act 1973 (c.45) (sisting of Scottish consistorial actions).

(2) The rules may in particular make provision—
- (a) for the provision of information by the pursuer and by any other person who has entered appearance in an action where proceedings relating to the same civil partnership (or ostensible civil partnership) are continuing in another jurisdiction, and
- (b) for an action to be sisted where there are concurrent proceedings elsewhere in respect of the same civil partnership (or ostensible civil partnership).

Scottish ancillary and collateral orders

227.—(1) This section applies where after the commencement of this Act an application is competently made to the Court of Session or the sheriff for the making, or the variation or recall, of an order which is ancillary or collateral to an action for—
- (a) the dissolution of a civil partnership,
- (b) the separation of civil partners, or
- (c) declarator of nullity of a civil partnership.

(2) And the section applies whether the application is made in the same proceedings or in other proceedings and whether it is made before or after the pronouncement of a final decree in the action.

(3) If the court has or, as the case may be, had jurisdiction to entertain the action, it has jurisdiction to entertain the application unless—

(a) jurisdiction to entertain the action was under section 219 regulations, and

(b) to make, vary or recall the order to which the application relates would contravene the regulations.

(4) Where the Court of Session has jurisdiction by virtue of this section to entertain an application for the variation or recall, as respects any person, of an order made by it and the order is one to which section 8 (variation and recall by the sheriff of certain orders made by the Court of Session) of the Law Reform (Miscellaneous Provisions) (Scotland) Act 1966 (c.19) applies, then for the purposes of any application under that section for the variation or recall of the order in so far as it relates to the person, the sheriff (as defined in that section) has jurisdiction to exercise the power conferred on him by that section.

(5) The reference in subsection (1) to an order which is ancillary or collateral is to an order relating to children, aliment, financial provision or expenses.

PROTECTION FROM ABUSE (SCOTLAND) ACT 2001

(2001 asp 14)

The Bill for this Act of the Scottish Parliament was passed by the Parliament on 4th October 2001 and received Royal Assent on 6th November 2001

An Act of the Scottish Parliament to enable a power of arrest to be attached to interdicts granted to protect individuals from abuse; to regulate the consequences of such attachment; and for connected purposes.

Attachment of power of arrest to interdict

1.—(1) A person who is applying for, or who has obtained, an interdict for the purpose of protection against abuse may apply to the court for a power of arrest to be attached to the interdict under this Act.

[1] (1A) In the case of an interdict which is—

(a) a matrimonial interdict (as defined by section 14(2) of the Matrimonial Homes (Family Protection) (Scotland) Act 1981 (c.59)) which is ancillary to—

(i) an exclusion order within the meaning of section 4(1) of that Act; or

(ii) an interim order under section 4(6) of that Act; or

(b) a relevant interdict (as defined by section 113(2) of the Civil Partnership Act 2004 (c.33)) which is ancillary to—

(i) an exclusion order within the meaning of section 104(1) of that Act; or

(ii) an interim order under section 104(6) of that Act,

the court must, on an application under subsection (1), attach a power of arrest to the interdict.

[2] (2) In the case of any other interdict the court must, on such application, attach a power of arrest to the interdict if satisfied that—

(a) the interdicted person has been given an opportunity to be heard by, or represented before, the court; and

(c) attaching the power of arrest is necessary to protect the applicant from a risk of abuse in breach of the interdict.

(3) The court, on attaching a power of arrest, must specify a date of expiry for the power, being a date not later than three years after the date when the power is attached.

NOTE
1. Inserted by Family Law (Scotland) Act 2006 (asp 2), s.32.
2. Amended by Family Law (Scotland) Act 2006 (asp 2), s.32 and Sch.3.

Duration, extension and recall

2.—(1) A power of arrest comes into effect only when it has been served on the interdicted person along with such documents as may be prescribed.

(2) A power of arrest ceases to have effect—

(a) on the date of expiry specified by the court;

(b) when it is recalled by the court; or

(c) when the interdict to which the power is attached is varied or recalled,

whichever is the earliest.

(3) The duration of a power of arrest must, on the application of the person who obtained it, be extended by the court, if satisfied that—

(a) the interdicted person has been given an opportunity to be heard by, or represented before, the court; and

(b) the extension is necessary to protect the applicant from a risk of abuse in breach of the interdict.

(4) The court, on extending the duration of a power of arrest, must specify a new date of expiry for the power, being a date not later than three years after the date when the extension is granted.

(5) Where the duration of a power of arrest has been extended—

(a) the extension comes into effect only when it has been served on the interdicted person along with such documents as may be prescribed; and

(b) subsection (2) applies as if the date referred to in paragraph (a) of that subsection were the new date of expiry specified by the court in granting the extension.

(6) Subsections (3), (4) and (5) apply to further extensions as they apply to an initial extension.

(7) A power of arrest must be recalled by the court if—

(a) the person who obtained it applies for recall; or

(b) the interdicted person applies for recall and the court is satisfied that—

　　(i) the person who obtained the power has been given an opportunity to be heard by, or represented before, the court; and

　　(ii) the power is no longer necessary to protect that person from a risk of abuse in breach of the interdict.

Notification to police

3.—(1) As soon as possible after—

(a) a power of arrest has been served;

(b) an extension of the duration of a power of arrest has been served;

(c) a recall of a power of arrest has been granted; or

(d) the relevant interdict has been varied or recalled,

the person who has obtained such power, extension, variation or recall, or such other person as may be prescribed, must deliver such documents as may be prescribed to the chief constable of any police area in which the relevant interdict has effect or (in the case of paragraph (d)) had effect before it was varied or recalled.

(2) In this section "relevant interdict" means the interdict to which the power of arrest is or was attached.

Powers and duties of police

4.—(1) Where a power of arrest attached to an interdict has effect a constable may arrest the interdicted person without warrant if the constable—

(a) has reasonable cause for suspecting that person of being in breach of the interdict; and

(b) considers that there would, if that person were not arrested, be a risk of abuse or further abuse by that person in breach of the interdict.

(2) A person who is arrested under subsection (1) must be informed immediately of the reason for the arrest and must thereafter be taken to a police station as quickly as is reasonably practicable and detained until—

(a) accused on petition or charged on complaint with an offence in respect of the facts and circumstances giving rise to the arrest; or

(b) brought before a court under section 5.

(3) A person who is detained under subsection (2) is entitled—

(a) to be informed immediately of the rights given by paragraphs (b) to (e);

(b) to have, on request, intimation of the detention and of the place of detention sent, without delay, to a solicitor and to one other person reasonably named by the detained person;

(c) to have, on request, intimation given to a solicitor that the solicitor's professional assistance is required;

(d) to have, on request, the solicitor informed, as soon as the information is available, of the court to which the detained person is to be taken and the date when that is to happen; and

(e) to have, on request, a private interview with the solicitor before any appearance in court under this Act.

(4) Where a person detained under subsection (2) appears to the officer in charge of the police station to be under 16 years of age the officer must where practicable, without delay and in addition to complying with subsection (3), send intimation of the detention and of the place of detention to any person known to have parental responsibilities and rights in relation to the detained person or to have care of that person; and any person to whom such intimation is given must be permitted reasonable access to the detained person.

(5) The following matters are to be recorded by the police in connection with the detention of a person under subsection (2)—

(a) the time at which the person was arrested;

(b) the police station to which the person was taken;

(c) the time when the person arrived at that police station;

(d) the address of any other place to which the person is, during the detention, thereafter taken;

(e) the time when the person was informed of the rights given by subsection (3);

(f) the time and nature of any request made by the person under subsection (3); and

(g) the time and nature of any action taken by a police officer under subsection (3) or (4).

(6) When a person has been arrested under this section the facts and circumstances giving rise to the arrest must be reported to the procurator fiscal as soon as is practicable.

Court appearance

5.—(1) If the procurator fiscal decides that no criminal proceedings are to be taken in respect of the facts and circumstances which gave rise to the arrest, the detained person must wherever practicable be brought before the sheriff sitting as a court of summary criminal jurisdiction for the district in which the person was arrested not later than in the course of the first day after the arrest, such day not being a Saturday, a Sunday or a court holiday for that court.

(2) Nothing in subsection (1) prevents the detained person from being brought before the sheriff on a Saturday, a Sunday or a court holiday if the sheriff is sitting on such a day for the disposal of criminal business.

(3) When the detained person is brought before the sheriff under this section the procurator fiscal must present to the court a petition—

    (a) giving particulars of the detained person;

    (b) stating the facts and circumstances which gave rise to the arrest;

    (c) giving any information known to the procurator fiscal about the circumstances which gave rise to the interdict and the attachment of the power of arrest;

    (d) giving any other information known to the procurator fiscal and relevant to an assessment of the risk of abuse or further abuse in breach of the interdict; and

    (e) requesting the court to consider whether, on the information presented, a further period of detention is justified.

(4) If it appears to the sheriff, after affording the detained person the opportunity to make representations, that—

    (a) the information presented to the court discloses a prima facie breach of the interdict by that person; and

    (b) there would, if further detention were not ordered, be a substantial risk of abuse or further abuse by that person in breach of the interdict,

the sheriff may order that person to be detained for a further period not exceeding 2 days.

(5) If the sheriff does not order further detention the detained person must, unless in custody in respect of any other matter, be released from custody.

Amendment of the Matrimonial Homes (Family Protection) (Scotland) Act 1981

6. [*Repealed by Family Law (Scotland) Act 2006 (asp 2), Sched. 3.*]

Interpretation

7. In this Act, unless the context otherwise requires—

    "abuse" includes violence, harassment, threatening conduct, and any other conduct giving rise, or likely to give rise, to physical or mental injury, fear, alarm or distress;

    "conduct" includes—

        (a) speech; and

        (b) presence in a specified place or area;

    "court" means the Court of Session or a sheriff;

    "documents" includes documents in electronic form;

    "interdict" includes interim interdict;

    "interdicted person" means—

        (a) in section 1, the person against whom the power of arrest is sought (being the person or one of the persons prohibited by the interdict mentioned in subsection (1) of that section); and

        (b) in sections 2 and 4, the person against whom the power of arrest has been granted;

    "parental responsibilities and rights" has the same meaning as in the Children (Scotland) Act 1995 (c.36);

    "person" means natural person;

    "power of arrest" means a power of arrest under this Act; and

    "prescribed" means prescribed by rules of court.

Short title and commencement

8.—(1) This Act may be cited as the Protection from Abuse (Scotland) Act 2001.

(2) This Act comes into force at the end of the period of three months beginning with the date of Royal Assent.

CHILDREN (SCOTLAND) ACT 1995

(1995, c.36)

.   .   .

An Act to reform the law of Scotland relating to children, to the adoption of children and to young persons who as children have been looked after by a local authority; to make new provision as respects the relationship between parent and child and guardian and child in the law of Scotland; to make provision as respects residential establishments for children and certain other residential establishments; and for connected purposes.

[July 19, 1995]

PART I

PARENTS, CHILDREN AND GUARDIANS

Parental responsibilities and parental rights

Parental responsibilities

1.—(1) Subject to section 3(1)(b) and (3) of this Act, a parent has in relation to his child the responsibility—
(a) to safeguard and promote the child's health, development and welfare;
(b) to provide, in a manner appropriate to the stage of development of the child—
(i) direction;
(ii) guidance,
to the child;
(c) if the child is not living with the parent, to maintain personal relations and direct contact with the child on a regular basis; and
(d) to act as the child's legal representative,
but only in so far as compliance with this section is practicable and in the interests of the child.
(2) "Child" means for the purposes of—
(a) paragraphs (a), (b)(i), (c) and (d) of subsection (1) above, a person under the age of sixteen years;
(b) paragraph (b)(ii) of that subsection, a person under the age of eighteen years.
(3) The responsibilities mentioned in paragraphs (a) to (d) of subsection (1) above are in this Act referred to as "parental responsibilities"; and the child, or any person acting on his behalf, shall have title to sue, or to defend, in any proceedings as respects those responsibilities.
(4) The parental responsibilities supersede any analogous duties imposed on a parent at common law; but this section is without prejudice to any other duty so imposed on him or to any duty imposed on him by, under or by virtue of any other provision of this Act or of any other enactment.

Parental rights

2.—(1) Subject to section 3(1)(b) and (3) of this Act, a parent, in order to enable him to fulfil his parental responsibilities in relation to his child, has the right—
(a) to have the child living with him or otherwise to regulate the child's residence;
(b) to control, direct or guide, in a manner appropriate to the stage of development of the child, the child's upbringing;
(c) if the child is not living with him, to maintain personal relations and direct contact with the child on a regular basis; and
(d) to act as the child's legal representative.
(2) Subject to subsection (3) below, where two or more persons have a parental right as respects a child, each of them may exercise that right without the consent of the other or, as the case may be, of any of the others, unless any decree or deed conferring the right, or regulating its exercise, otherwise provides.
(3) Without prejudice to any court order, no person shall be entitled to remove a child habitually resident in Scotland from, or to retain any such child outwith, the United Kingdom without the consent of a person described in subsection (6) below.
(4) The rights mentioned in paragraphs (a) to (d) of subsection (1) above are in this Act referred to as "parental rights"; and a parent, or any

person acting on his behalf, shall have title to sue, or to defend, in any proceedings as respects those rights.

(5) The parental rights supersede any analogous rights enjoyed by a parent at common law; but this section is without prejudice to any other right so enjoyed by him or to any right enjoyed by him by, under or by virtue of any other provision of this Act or of any other enactment.

(6) The description of a person referred to in subsection (3) above is a person (whether or not a parent of the child) who for the time being has and is exercising in relation to him a right mentioned in paragraph (a) or (c) of subsection (1) above; except that, where both the child's parents are persons
so described, the consent required for his removal or retention shall be that of them both.

(7) In this section, "child" means a person under the age of sixteen years.

Provisions relating both to parental responsibilities and to parental rights

3.—(1) Notwithstanding section 1(1) of the Law Reform (Parent and Child) (Scotland) Act 1986 (provision for disregarding whether a person's parents are not, or have not been, married to one another in establishing the legal relationship between him and any other person)—

    (a) a child's mother has parental responsibilities and parental rights in relation to him whether or not she is or has been married to his father; and

[1] (b) without prejudice to any arrangements which may be made under subsection (5) below and subject to any agreement which may be made under section 4 of this Act, his father has such responsibilities and rights in relation to him only if

      (i) married to the mother at the time of the child's conception or subsequently, or

      (ii) where not married to the mother at that time or subsequently, the father is registered as the child's father under any of the enactments mentioned in subsection (1A).

[2] (1A) Those enactments are—

    (a) section 18(1)(a), (b)(i) and (c) and (2)(b) of the Registration of Births, Deaths and Marriages (Scotland) Act 1965 (c.49);

    (b) sections 10(1)(a) to (e) and 10A(1)(a) to (e) of the Births and Deaths Registration Act 1953 (c.20); and

    (c) article 14(3)(a) to (e) of the Births and Deaths Registration (Northern Ireland) Order 1976 (S.I. 1976/1041).

(2) For the purposes of subsection (1)(b) above, the father shall be regarded as having been married to the mother at any time when he was a party to a purported marriage with her which was—

    (a) voidable; or

    (b) void but believed by them (whether by error of fact or of law) in good faith at that time to be valid.

(3) Subsection (1) above is without prejudice to any order made under section 11 of this Act or section 3(1) of the said Act of 1986 (provision analogous to the said section 11 but repealed by this Act) or to any other order, disposal or resolution affecting parental responsibilities or parental rights; and nothing in subsection (1) above or in this Part of this Act shall affect any other—

    (a) enactment (including any other provision of this Act or of that Act); or

    (b) rule of law,

by, under or by virtue of which a person may have imposed on him (or be relieved of) parental responsibilities or may be granted (or be deprived of) parental rights.

(4) The fact that a person has parental responsibilities or parental

rights in relation to a child shall not entitle that person to act in any way which would be incompatible with any court order relating to the child or the child's property, or with any supervision requirement made under section 70 of this Act.

(5) Without prejudice to section 4(1) of this Act, a person who has parental responsibilities or parental rights in relation to a child shall not abdicate those responsibilities or rights to anyone else but may arrange for some or all of them to be fulfilled or exercised on his behalf; and without prejudice to that generality any such arrangement may be made with a person who already has parental responsibilities or parental rights in relation to the child concerned.

(6) The making of an arrangement under subsection (5) above shall not affect any liability arising from a failure to fulfil parental responsibilities; and where any arrangements so made are such that the child is a foster child for the purposes of the Foster Children (Scotland) Act 1984, those arrangements are subject to the provisions of that Act.

NOTE
1. Amended by Family Law (Scotland) Act 2006 (asp 2), s.23.
2. Inserted by Family Law (Scotland) Act 2006 (asp 2), s.23.

Acquisition of parental rights and responsibilities by natural father

4.—(1) Where a child's mother has not been deprived of some or all of the parental responsibilities and parental rights in relation to him and, by virtue of subsection (1)(b) of section 3 of this Act, his father has no parental responsibilities or parental rights in relation to him, the father and mother, whatever age they may be, may by agreement provide that, as from the appropriate date, the father shall have the parental responsibilities and parental rights which (in the absence of any order under section 11 of this Act affecting those responsibilities and rights) he would have if married to the mother.

(2) No agreement under subsection (1) above shall have effect unless—
(a) in a form prescribed by the Secretary of State; and
(b) registered in the Books of Council and Session while the mother still has the parental responsibilities and parental rights which she had when the agreement was made.

(3) The date on which such registration as is mentioned in subsection (2)(b) above takes place shall be the "appropriate date" for the purposes of subsection (1) above.

(4) An agreement which has effect by virtue of subsection (2) above shall, subject only to section 11(11) of this Act, be irrevocable.

Care or control of child by person without parental responsibilities or parental rights

5.—(1) Subject to subsection (2) below, it shall be the responsibility of a person who has attained the age of sixteen years and who has care or control of a child under that age, but in relation to him either has no parental responsibilities or parental rights or does not have the parental responsibility mentioned in section 1(1)(a) of this Act, to do what is reasonable in all the circumstances to safeguard the child's health, development and welfare; and in fulfilling his responsibility under this section the person may in particular, even though he does not have the parental right mentioned in section 2(1)(d) of this Act, give consent to any surgical, medical or dental treatment or procedure where—
(a) the child is not able to give such consent on his own behalf; and
(b) it is not within the knowledge of the person that a parent of the child would refuse to give the consent in question.
(2) Nothing in this section shall apply to a person in so far as he has

care or control of a child in a school ("school" having the meaning given by section 135(1) of the Education (Scotland) Act 1980).

Views of children

6.—(1) A person shall, in reaching any major decision which involves—
(a) his fulfilling a parental responsibility or the responsibility mentioned in section 5(1) of this Act; or
(b) his exercising a parental right or giving consent by virtue of that section,

have regard so far as practicable to the views (if he wishes to express them) of the child concerned, taking account of the child's age and maturity, and to those of any other person who has parental responsibilities or parental rights in relation to the child (and wishes to express those views); and without prejudice to the generality of this subsection a child twelve years of age or more shall be presumed to be of sufficient age and maturity to form a view.

(2) A transaction entered into in good faith by a third party and a person acting as legal representative of a child shall not be challengeable on the ground only that the child, or a person with parental responsibilities or parental rights in relation to the child, was not consulted or that due regard was not given to his views before the transaction was entered into.

Guardianship

Appointment of guardians

7.—(1) A child's parent may appoint a person to be guardian of the child in the event of the parent's death; but—
(a) such appointment shall be of no effect unless—
(i) in writing and signed by the parent; and
(ii) the parent, at the time of death, was entitled to act as legal representative of the child (or would have been so entitled if he had survived until after the birth of the child); and
(b) any parental responsibilities or parental rights (or the right to appoint a further guardian under this section) which a surviving parent has in relation to the child shall subsist with those which, by, under or by virtue of this Part of this Act, the appointee so has.

(2) A guardian of a child may appoint a person to take his place as guardian in the event of the guardian's death; but such appointment shall be of no effect unless in writing and signed by the person making it.

(3) An appointment as guardian shall not take effect until accepted, either expressly or impliedly by acts which are not consistent with any other intention.

(4) If two or more persons are appointed as guardians, any one or more of them shall, unless the appointment expressly provides otherwise, be entitled to accept office even if both or all of them do not accept office.

(5) Subject to any order under section 11 or 86 of this Act, a person appointed as a child's guardian under this section shall have, in respect of the child, the responsibilities imposed, and the rights conferred, on a parent by sections 1 and 2 of this Act respectively; and sections 1 and 2 of this Act shall apply in relation to a guardian as they apply in relation to a parent.

(6) Without prejudice to the generality of subsection (1) of section 6 of this Act, a decision as to the appointment of a guardian under subsection (1) or (2) above shall be regarded for the purposes of that section (or of that section as applied by subsection (5) above) as a major decision which involves exercising a parental right.

Revocation and other termination of appointment

8.—(1) An appointment made under section 7(1) or (2) of this Act revokes an earlier such appointment (including one made in an unrevoked will or codicil) made by the same person in respect of the same child, unless it is clear (whether as a result of an express provision in the later appointment or by any necessary implication) that the purpose of the later appointment is to appoint an additional guardian.

(2) Subject to subsections (3) and (4) below, the revocation of an appointment made under section 7(1) or (2) of this Act (including one made in an unrevoked will or codicil) shall not take effect unless the revocation is in writing and is signed by the person making the revocation.

(3) An appointment under section 7(1) or (2) of this Act (other than one made in a will or codicil) is revoked if, with the intention of revoking the appointment, the person who made it—

(a) destroys the document by which it was made; or

(b) has some other person destroy that document in his presence.

(4) For the avoidance of doubt, an appointment made under section 7(1) or (2) of this Act in a will or codicil is revoked if the will or codicil is revoked.

(5) Once an appointment of a guardian has taken effect under section 7 of this Act, then, unless the terms of the appointment provide for earlier termination, it shall terminate only by virtue of—

(a) the child concerned attaining the age of eighteen years;

(b) the death of the child or the guardian; or

(c) the termination of the appointment by a court order under section 11 of this Act.

Administration of child's property

Safeguarding of child's property

9.—(1) Subject to section 13 of this Act, this section applies where—

(a) property is owned by or due to a child;

(b) the property is held by a person other than a parent or guardian of the child; and

(c) but for this section, the property would be required to be transferred to a parent having parental responsibilities in relation to the child or to a guardian for administration by that parent or guardian on behalf of the child.

(2) Subject to subsection (4) below, where this section applies and the person holding the property is an executor or trustee, then—

(a) if the value of the property exceeds £20,000, he shall; or

(b) if that value is not less than £5,000 and does not exceed £20,000, he may, apply to the Accountant of Court for a direction as to the administration of the property.

(3) Subject to subsection (4) below, where this section applies and the person holding the property is a person other than an executor or trustee, then, if the value of the property is not less than £5,000, that person may apply to the Accountant of Court for a direction as to the administration of the property.

(4) Where the parent or guardian mentioned in subsection (1)(c) above has been appointed a trustee under a trust deed to administer the property concerned, subsections (2) and (3) above shall not apply, and the person holding the property shall transfer it to the parent or guardian.

(5) On receipt of an application under subsection (2) or (3) above, the Accountant of Court may do one, or (in so far as the context admits) more than one, of the following—

(a) apply to the court for the appointment of a judicial factor (whether or not the parent or guardian mentioned in subsection (1)(c) above) to administer all or part of the property concerned and in the event of the court making such an appointment shall direct that the property, or as the case may be part, concerned be transferred to the factor;

(b) direct that all or part of the property concerned be transferred to himself;

(c) direct that all or, in a case where the parent or guardian so mentioned has not been appointed by virtue of paragraph (a) above, part of the property concerned be transferred to the parent or guardian, to be administered on behalf of the child.

(6) A direction under subsection (5)(c) above may include such conditions as the Accountant of Court considers appropriate, including in particular a condition—

(a) that in relation to the property concerned no capital expenditure shall be incurred without his approval; or

(b) that there shall be exhibited annually to him the securities and bank books which represent the capital of the estate.

(7) A person who has applied under subsection (2) or (3) above for a direction shall not thereafter transfer the property concerned except in accordance with a direction under subsection (5) above.

(8) The Secretary of State may from time to time prescribe a variation in any sum referred to in subsections (2) and (3) above.

(9) In this section "child" means a person under the age of sixteen years who is habitually resident in Scotland.

Obligations and rights of person administering child's property

10.—(1) A person acting as a child's legal representative in relation to the administration of the child's property—

(a) shall be required to act as a reasonable and prudent person would act on his own behalf; and

(b) subject to any order made under section 11 of this Act, shall be entitled to do anything which the child, if of full age and capacity, could do in relation to that property;

and subject to subsection (2) below, on ceasing to act as legal representative, shall be liable to account to the child for his intromissions with the child's property.

(2) No liability shall be incurred by virtue of subsection (1) above in respect of funds which have been used in the proper discharge of the person's responsibility to safeguard and promote the child's health, development and welfare.

Court orders

Court orders relating to parental responsibilities etc.

11.—(1) In the relevant circumstances in proceedings in the Court of Session or sheriff court, whether those proceedings are or are not independent of any other action, an order may be made under this subsection in relation to—

(a) parental responsibilities;

(b) parental rights;

(c) guardianship; or

(d) subject to section 14(1) and (2) of this Act, the administration of a child's property.

(1A) [*Repealed by European Communities (Matrimonial Jurisdiction and Judgements) (Scotland) Regulations SSI 2005/42, reg.9.*]

(2) The court may make such order under subsection (1) above as it thinks fit; and without prejudice to the generality of that subsection may in particular so make any of the following orders—

(a) an order depriving a person of some or all of his parental responsibilities or parental rights in relation to a child;

(b) an order—
  (i) imposing upon a person (provided he is at least sixteen years of age or is a parent of the child) such responsibilities; and
  (ii) giving that person such rights;

(c) an order regulating the arrangements as to—
  (i) with whom; or
  (ii) if with different persons alternately or periodically, with whom during what periods,
  a child under the age of sixteen years is to live (any such order being known as a "residence order");

(d) an order regulating the arrangements for maintaining personal relations and direct contact between a child under that age and a person with whom the child is not, or will not be, living (any such order being known as a "contact order");

(e) an order regulating any specific question which has arisen, or may arise, in connection with any of the matters mentioned in paragraphs (a) to (d) of subsection (1) of this section (any such order being known as a "specific issue order");

(f) an interdict prohibiting the taking of any step of a kind specified in the interdict in the fulfilment of parental responsibilities or the exercise of parental rights relating to a child or in the administration of a child's property;

(g) an order appointing a judicial factor to manage a child's property or remitting the matter to the Accountant of Court to report on suitable arrangements for the future management of the property; or

(h) an order appointing or removing a person as guardian of the child.

(3) The relevant circumstances mentioned in subsection (1) above are—

(a) that application for an order under that subsection is made by a person who—
  (i) not having, and never having had, parental responsibilities or parental rights in relation to the child, claims an interest;
  (ii) has parental responsibilities or parental rights in relation to the child;
  (iii) has had, but for a reason other than is mentioned in subsection (4) below no longer has, parental responsibilities or parental rights in relation to the child; or

(b) that although no such application has been made, the court (even if it declines to make any other order) considers it should make such an order.

(4) The reasons referred to in subsection (3)(a)(iii) above are that the parental responsibilities or parental rights have been–

(a) extinguished on the making of an adoption order;

(b) transferred to an adoption agency on the making of an order declaring the child free for adoption;

(c) extinguished by virtue of subsection (9) of section 30 of the Human Fertilisation and Embryology Act 1990 (provision for enactments about adoption to have effect with modifications) on the making of a parental order under subsection (1) of that section; or

(d) transferred to a local authority by a parental responsibilities order.

(5) In subsection (3)(a) above "person" includes (without prejudice to the generality of that subsection) the child concerned; but it does not include a local authority.

(6) In subsection (4) above—
  "adoption agency" and "adoption order" have the same meanings as they are given, in section 18 of the Adoption (Scotland) Act 1978, by section 65(1) of that Act; and

"parental responsibilities order" has the meaning given by section 86(1) of this Act.

(7) Subject to subsection (8) below, in considering whether or not to make an order under subsection (1) above and what order to make, the court—

(a) shall regard the welfare of the child concerned as its paramount consideration and shall not make any such order unless it considers that it would be better for the child that the order be made than that none should be made at all; and

(b) taking account of the child's age and maturity, shall so far as practicable—

(i) give him an opportunity to indicate whether he wishes to express his views;

(ii) if he does so wish, give him an opportunity to express them; and

(iii) have regard to such views as he may express.

[1] (7A) In carrying out the duties imposed by subsection (7)(a) above, the court shall have regard in particular to the matters mentioned in subsection (7B) below.

[1] (7B) Those matters are—

(a) the need to protect the child from—

(i) any abuse; or

(ii) the risk of any abuse,

which affects, or might affect, the child;

(b) the effect such abuse, or the risk of such abuse, might have on the child;

(c) the ability of a person—

(i) who has carried out abuse which affects or might affect the child; or

(ii) who might carry out such abuse,

to care for, or otherwise meet the needs of, the child; and

(d) the effect any abuse, or the risk of any abuse, might have on the carrying out of responsibilities in connection with the welfare of the child by a person who has (or, by virtue of an order under subsection (1), would have) those responsibilities.

[1] (7C) In subsection (7B) above—

"abuse" includes—

(a) violence, harassment, threatening conduct and any other conduct giving rise, or likely to give rise, to physical or mental injury, fear, alarm or distress;

(b) abuse of a person other than the child; and

(c) domestic abuse;

"conduct" includes—

(a) speech; and

(b) presence in a specified place or area.

[1] (7D) Where—

(a) the court is considering making an order under subsection (1) above; and

(b) in pursuance of the order two or more relevant persons would have to co-operate with one another as respects matters affecting the child,

the court shall consider whether it would be appropriate to make the order.

[1] (7E) In subsection (7D) above, "relevant person", in relation to a child, means—

(a) a person having parental responsibilities or parental rights in respect of the child; or

(b) where a parent of the child does not have parental responsibilities or parental rights in respect of the child, a parent of the child.

(8) The court shall, notwithstanding subsection (7) above, endeavour to ensure that any order which it makes, or any determination by it not to make an order, does not adversely affect the position of a person who has, in good faith and for value, acquired any property of the child concerned, or any right or interest in such property.

(9) Nothing in paragraph (b) of subsection (7) above requires a child to be legally represented, if he does not wish to be, in proceedings in the course of which the court implements that paragraph.

(10) Without prejudice to the generality of paragraph (b) of subsection (7) above, a child twelve years of age or more shall be presumed to be of sufficient age and maturity to form a view for the purposes both of that paragraph and of subsection (9) above.

(11) An order under subsection (1) above shall have the effect of depriving a person of a parental responsibility or parental right only in so far as the order expressly so provides and only to the extent necessary to give effect to the order; but in making any such order as is mentioned in paragraph (a) or (b) of subsection (2) above the court may revoke any agreement which, in relation to the child concerned, has effect by virtue of section 4(2) of this Act.

(12) Where the court makes a residence order which requires that a child live with a person who, immediately before the order is made does not have in relation to the child all the parental responsibilities mentioned in paragraphs (a), (b) and (d) of section 1(1), and the parental rights mentioned in paragraphs (b) and (d) of section 2(1), of this Act (those which he does not so have being in this subsection referred to as the "relevant responsibilities and rights") that person shall, subject to the provisions of the order or of any other order made under subsection (1) above, have the relevant responsibilities and rights while the residence order remains in force.

(13) Any reference in this section to an order includes a reference to an interim order or to an order varying or discharging an order.

NOTE
1.   Inserted by Family Law (Scotland) Act 2006 (asp 2), s.24.

Restrictions on decrees for divorce, separation or annulment affecting children

12.—(1) In any action for divorce, judicial separation or declarator of nullity of marriage, the court shall, where this section applies, consider (in the light of such information as is before the court as to the arrangements which have been, or are proposed to be, made for the upbringing of each child by virtue of which it applies) whether to exercise with respect to him the powers conferred by section 11 or 54 of this Act.

(2) Where, in any case to which this section applies, the court is of the opinion that—

   (a) the circumstances of the case require, or are likely to require, it to exercise any power under section 11 or 54 of this Act with respect to the child concerned;

   (b) it is not in a position to exercise that power without giving further consideration to the case; and

   (c) there are exceptional circumstances which make it desirable in the interests of that child that it should not grant decree in the action until it is in a position to exercise such a power,

it shall postpone its decision on the granting of decree in the action until it is in such a position.

(3) This section applies where a child of the family has not reached the age of sixteen years at the date when the question first arises as to whether the court should give such consideration as is mentioned in subsection (1) above.

[1] (4) In this section "child of the family", in relation to

(a) the parties to a marriage, means—
    (i) a child of both of them; or
    (ii) any other child, not being a child who is placed with them as foster parents by a local authority or voluntary organisation, who has been treated by both of them as a child of their family.
  or
(b) the partners in a civil partnership, means a child who has been treated by both partners as a child of the family which their partnership constitutes.

NOTE
  1. As amended by Family Law (Scotland) Act 2006 (asp 2), Sch.2.

Awards of damages to children

13.—(1) Where in any court proceedings a sum of money becomes payable to, or for the benefit of, a child under the age of sixteen years, the court may make such order relating to the payment and management of the sum for the benefit of the child as it thinks fit.

(2) Without prejudice to the generality of subsection (1) above, the court may in an order under this section—
(a) appoint a judicial factor to invest, apply or otherwise deal with the money for the benefit of the child concerned;
(b) order the money to be paid—
    (i) to the sheriff clerk or the Accountant of Court; or
    (ii) to a parent or guardian of that child,
to be invested, applied or otherwise dealt with, under directions of the court, for the benefit of that child; or
(c) order the money to be paid directly to that child.

(3) Where payment is made to a person in accordance with an order under this section, a receipt given by him shall be a sufficient discharge of the obligation to make the payment.

Jurisdiction and choice of law

Jurisdiction and choice of law in relation to certain matters

14.—(1) The Court of Session shall have jurisdiction to entertain an application for an order relating to the administration of a child's property if the child is habitually resident in, or the property is situated in, Scotland.

(2) A sheriff shall have jurisdiction to entertain such an application if the child is habitually resident in, or the property is situated in, the sheriffdom.

(3) Subject to subsection (4) below, any question arising under this Part of this Act—
(a) concerning—
    (i) parental responsibilities or parental rights; or
    (ii) the responsibilities or rights of a guardian,
in relation to a child shall, in so far as it is not also a question such as is mentioned in paragraph (b) below, be determined by the law of the place of the child's habitual residence at the time when the question arises;
(b) concerning the immediate protection of a child shall be determined by the law of the place where the child is when the question arises; and
(c) as to whether a person is validly appointed or constituted guardian of a child shall be determined by the law of the place of the child's habitual residence on the date when the appointment was made (the date of death of the testator being taken to be the date of

appointment where an appointment was made by will), or the event constituting the guardianship occurred.

(4) Nothing in any provision of law in accordance with which, under subsection (3) above, a question which arises in relation to an application for, or the making of, an order under subsection (1) of section 11 of this Act falls to be determined, shall affect the application of subsection (7) of that section.

[1](5) The provisions of sections 9, 11, 13 and this section are subject to sections 2 and 3 of Chapter II of Council Regulation (EC) No. 2201/2003 of the 27th November 2003 concerning jurisdiction and the recognition and enforcement of judgments in matrimonial matters and matters of parental responsibility.

NOTE
1. Inserted by the European Communities (Matrimonial Jurisdiction and Judgments) (Scotland) Regulations 2005 (SSI 2005/42), reg. 5(2).

Interpretation

Interpretation of Part I

15.—(1) In this Part of this Act—
"child" means, where the expression is not otherwise defined, a person under the age of eighteen years;
"contact order" has the meaning given by section 11(2)(d) of this Act;
"parent", in relation to any person, means, subject to Part IV of the Adoption (Scotland) Act 1978 and sections 27 to 30 of the Human Fertilisation and Embryology Act 1990 and any regulations made under subsection (9) of the said section 30, someone, of whatever age, who is that person's genetic father or mother;
"parental responsibilities" has the meaning given by section 1(3) of this Act;
"parental rights" has the meaning given by section 2(4) of this Act;
"residence order" has the meaning given by section 11(2)(c) of this Act;
"specific issue order" has the meaning given by section 11(2)(e) of this Act; and
"transaction" has the meaning given by section 9 of the Age of Legal Capacity (Scotland) Act 1991 (except that, for the purposes of subsection (5)(b) below, paragraph (d) of the definition in question shall be disregarded).

(2) No provision in this Part of this Act shall affect any legal proceedings commenced, or any application made to a court, before that provision comes into effect; except that where, before section 11 of this Act comes into force, there has been final decree in a cause in which, as respects a child, an order for custody or access, or an order which is analogous to any such order as is mentioned in subsection (2) of that section, has been made, any application on or after the date on which the section does come into force for variation or recall of the order shall proceed as if the order had been made under that section.

(3) In subsection (2) above, the reference to final decree is to a decree or interlocutor which, taken by itself or along with previous interlocutors, disposes of the whole subject matter of the cause.

(4) Any reference in this Part of this Act to a person—
(a) having parental rights or responsibilities;
(b) acting as a legal representative; or
(c) being appointed a guardian,
is to a natural person only.

(5) Any reference in this Part of this Act to a person acting as the legal

representative of a child is a reference to that person, in the interests of the child—

(a) administering any property belonging to the child; and

(b) acting in, or giving consent to, any transaction where the child is incapable of so acting or consenting on his own behalf.

(6) Where a child has legal capacity to sue, or to defend, in any civil proceedings, he may nevertheless consent to be represented in those proceedings by any person who, had the child lacked that capacity, would have had the responsibility to act as his legal representative.

LAW REFORM (PARENT AND CHILD) (SCOTLAND) ACT 1986

(1986, c.9)

ARRANGEMENT OF SECTIONS

An Act to make fresh provision in the law of Scotland with respect to the consequences of birth out of wedlock, the rights and duties of parents, the determination of parentage and the taking of blood samples in relation to the determination of parentage; to amend the law as to guardianship; and for connected purposes.

[March 26, 1986]

Abolition of status of illegitimacy

1.—[1] (1) No person whose status is governed by Scots law shall be illegitimate; and accordingly the fact that a person's parents are not or have not been married to each other shall be left out of account in—

(a) determining the person's legal status; or

(b) establishing the legal relationship between the person and any other person.

[2] (2) Any reference (however expressed) in any enactment or deed to any relative shall, unless the contrary intention appears in the enactment or deed, be construed in accordance with subsection (1) above.

(3) *[Repealed by Family Law (Scotland) Act 2006, Sch.3]*.

[3] (4) Nothing in this section shall apply to the construction or effect of—

(a) any enactment passed or made before the commencement of section 21 of the Family Law (Scotland) Act 2006 (asp 2);

(b) any deed executed before such commencement;

[4] (5) In subsection (4), "enactment" includes an Act of the Scottish Parliament.

[4](6) It shall no longer be competent to bring an action for declarator of legitimacy, legitimation or illegitimacy.

NOTE
1. Substituted by Family Law (Scotland) Act 2006 (asp 2), s.21.
2. Amended by Family Law (Scotland) Act 2006 (asp 2), Sch.3.
3. Amended by Family Law (Scotland) Act 2006 (asp 2), s.21 and Sch.3.
4. Inserted by Family Law (Scotland) Act 2006 (asp 2), s.21.

2.–4. [*Repealed by the Children (Scotland) Act 1995 (c.36), s.105(4) and Sched. 5.*]

Presumptions

5.—(1) A man shall be presumed to be the father of a child—
(a) if he was married to the mother of the child at any time in the period beginning with the conception and ending with the birth of the child;
(b) where paragraph (a) above does not apply, if both he and the mother of the child have acknowledged that he is the father and he has been registered as such in any register kept under section 13 (register of births and still-births) or section 44 (register of corrections etc.) of the Registration of Births, Deaths and Marriages (Scotland) Act 1965 or in any corresponding register kept under statutory authority in any part of the United Kingdom other than Scotland.

(2) Subsection (1)(a) above shall apply in the case of a void, voidable or irregular marriage as it applies in the case of a valid and regular marriage.

(3) Without prejudice to the effect under any rule of law which a decree of declarator in an action to which section 7 of this Act applies may have in relation to the parties, a decree of declarator in such an action shall give rise to a presumption to the same effect as the decree; and any such presumption shall displace any contrary presumption howsoever arising.

(4) Any presumption under this section may be rebutted by proof on a balance of probabilities.

Determination of parentage by blood sample

[1]**6.**—(1) This section applies where, for the purpose of obtaining evidence relating to the determination of parentage in civil proceedings, a sample of blood or other body fluid or of body tissue is sought by a party to the proceedings or by a curator ad litem.

[2](2) Where such a sample is sought from a child under the age of 16 years, consent to the taking of the sample may be given by any person having parental responsibilities (within the meaning of section 1(3) of the Children (Scotland) Act 1995) in relation to him or having care and control of him.

(3) Where such a sample is sought from any person who is incapable of giving consent, the court may consent to the taking of the sample where—
(a) there is no person who is entitled to give such consent, or
(b) there is such a person, but it is not reasonably practicable to obtain his consent in the circumstances, or he is unwilling to accept the responsibility of giving or withholding consent.

(4) The court shall not consent under subsection (3) above to the taking of such a sample from any person unless the court is satisfied that the taking of the sample would not be detrimental to the person's health.

NOTE
1. As amended by the Law Reform (Miscellaneous Provisions) (Scotland) Act 1990 (c.40), s.70(3).

2. As amended by the Age of Legal Capacity (Scotland) Act 1991 (c.50), Sch.1, para.42 and the Children (Scotland) Act 1995 (c.36), s.105(4) and Sch.4, para.38(3).

Actions for declarator

7.—(1) An action for declarator of parentage or non-parentage may be brought in the Court of Session or the sheriff court.

(2) Such an action may be brought in the Court of Session if and only if the child was born in Scotland or the alleged or presumed parent or the child—

(a) is domiciled in Scotland on the date when the action is brought;
(b) was habitually resident in Scotland for not less than one year immediately preceding that date; or
(c) died before that date and either—
   (i) was at the date of death domiciled in Scotland; or
   (ii) had been habitually resident in Scotland for not less than one year immediately preceding the date of death.

(3) Such an action may be brought in the sheriff court if and only if—

(a) the child was born in the sheriffdom, or
(b) an action could have been brought in the Court of Session under subsection (2) above and the alleged or presumed parent or the child was habitually resident in the sheriffdom on the date when the action is brought or on the date of his death.

(4) [*Repealed by the Civil Evidence (Scotland) Act 1988 (c.32), Sch.*]

[1] (5) Nothing in any rule of law or enactment shall prevent the court making in any proceedings an incidental finding as to parentage or non-parentage for the purposes of those proceedings.

(6) In this section "the alleged or presumed parent" includes a person who claims or is alleged to be or not to be the parent.

NOTE
1. Amended by Family Law (Scotland) Act 2006 (asp 2), Sch.2, subject to savings specified in SSI 2006/212, art.10.

Interpretation

[1,2,3] **8.** In this Act, unless the context otherwise requires, the following expressions shall have the following meanings respectively assigned to them—

[4] "action for declarator" includes an application for declarator contained in other proceedings but does not include an appeal under section 20(1)(a) or (b) (Appeals) of the Child Support Act 1991 made to the court by virtue of an order made under section 45 (jurisdiction of the courts in certain proceedings) of that Act;

"the court" means the Court of Session or the sheriff;

"deed" means any disposition, contract, instrument or writing whether inter vivos or mortis causa;

"non-parentage" means that a person is not or was not the parent, or is not or was not the child, of another person;

"parent" includes natural parent;

"parentage" means that a person is or was the parent, or is or was the child, of another person;

NOTE
1. Amended by Age of Legal Capacity (Scotland) Act 1991 (c.50), Sch.1, para.43 and Sch.2.
2. "Child" and "parental rights" repealed by the Children (Scotland) Act 1995 (c.36), s.105(5) and Sch.5.
3. Prospectively amended by the Child Support Appeals (Jurisdiction of Courts) (Scotland) Order 2003 (SSI 2003/96), art.7.

4. As amended by the Child Support Appeals (Jurisdiction of Courts) (Scotland) Order 2003 (SSI 2006/96), s.7.

Savings and supplementary provisions

9.—[1](1) Nothing in this Act shall—

(b) subject to subsection (1A) below, except to the extent that Schedules 1 and 2 to this Act otherwise provide, affect the law relating to adoption of children;

(c) apply to any title coat of arms, honour or dignity transmissible on the death of the holder thereof or affect the succession thereto or the devolution thereof (including, in particular, the competence of bringing an action of declarator of legitimacy, legitimation or illegitimacy in connection with such succession or devolution);

(ca) affect the functions of the Lord Lyon King of Arms so far as relating to the granting of arms;

(d) affect the right of legitim out of, or the right of succession to, the estate of any person who died before the commencement of this Act.

[2](1A) Subsections (1) and (2) of section 1 of this Act shall apply in relation to adopted children.

(2) The court may at any time vary or recall any order made under section 3 of this Act or consent given by it under section 6 of this Act.

NOTE

1. Amended by Family Law (Scotland) Act 2006 (asp 2), s.21.
2. Inserted by Family Law (Scotland) Act 2006 (asp 2), Sch.2.

Transitional provisions, amendments and repeals

10.—(1) The enactments specified in Schedule 1 to this Act shall have effect subject to the amendments set out in that Schedule.

(2) The enactments specified in Schedule 2 to this Act are hereby repealed to the extent set out in the third column of that Schedule.

Citation, commencement and extent

11.—(1) This Act may be cited as the Law Reform (Parent and Child) (Scotland) Act 1986.

(2) This Act shall come into operation on such day as the Secretary of State may appoint by order made by statutory instrument.

(3) An order under subsection (2) above may contain such transitional provisions and savings as appear to the Secretary of State necessary or expedient in connection with the coming into operation of this Act.

(4) This Act shall extend to Scotland only.

.   .   .

FAMILY LAW (SCOTLAND) ACT 1985

(1985, c.37)

ARRANGEMENT OF SECTIONS

Aliment

An Act to make fresh provision in the law of Scotland regarding aliment; regarding financial and other consequences of decrees of divorce and of declarator of nullity of marriage; regarding property rights and legal capacity of married persons; and for connected purposes.

[July 16, 1985]

Aliment

Obligation of aliment

1.—(1) From the commencement of this Act, an obligation of aliment shall be owed by, and only by—
   (a) a husband to his wife;
   (b) a wife to her husband;
¹(bb) a partner in a civil partnership to the other partner,
   (c) a father or mother to his or her child;
   (d) a person to a child (other than a child who has been boarded out with him by a local or other public authority or a voluntary

organisation) who has been accepted by him as a child of his family.

(2) For the purposes of this Act, an obligation of aliment is an obligation to provide such support as is reasonable in the circumstances, having regard to the matters to which a court is required or entitled to have regard under section 4 of this Act in determining the amount of aliment to award in an action for aliment.

(3) Any obligation of aliment arising under a decree or by operation of law and subsisting immediately before the commencement of this Act shall, except insofar as consistent with this section, cease to have effect as from the commencement of this Act.

(4) Nothing in this section shall affect any arrears due under a decree at the date of termination or cessation of an obligation of aliment, nor any rule of law by which a person who is owed an obligation of aliment may claim aliment from the executor of a deceased person or from any person enriched by the succession to the estate of a deceased person.

(5) In subsection (1) above—
   "child" means a person—
   (a) under the age of 18 years; or
   (b) over that age and under the age of 25 years who is reasonably and appropriately undergoing instruction at an educational establishment, or training for employment or for a trade, profession or vocation;
   "husband" and "wife" include the parties to a valid polygamous marriage.

NOTE
   1. As inserted by the Civil Partnership Act 2004 c.33, Sch.28.

Actions for aliment

2.—(1) A claim for aliment only (whether or not expenses are also sought) may be made, against any person owing an obligation of aliment, in the Court of Session or the sheriff court.

(2) Unless the court considers it inappropriate in any particular case, a claim for aliment may also be made, against any person owing an obligation of aliment, in proceedings—
   (a) for divorce, separation, declarator of marriage or declarator of nullity of marriage;
   [3](aa) for dissolution of a civil partnership, separation of civil partners or declarator of nullity of a civil partnership,
   (b) relating to orders for financial provision;
   [1](c) concerning parental responsibilities or parental rights (within the meaning of sections 1(3) and 2(4) respectively of the Children (Scotland) Act 1995) or guardianship in relation to children;
   (d) concerning parentage or legitimacy;
   (e) of any other kind, where the court considers it appropriate to include a claim for aliment.

(3) In this Act "action for aliment" means a claim for aliment in proceedings referred to in subsection (1) or (2) above.

[2](4) An action for aliment may be brought—
   (a) by a person (including a child) to whom the obligation of aliment is owed;
   (b) by the curator bonis of an incapax;
   (c) on behalf of a child under the age of 18 years, by—
      (i) the parent or guardian of the child;
      [1](iii) a person with whom the child lives or who is seeking a residence order (within the meaning of section 11(2)(c) of the Children (Scotland) Act 1995) in respect of the child.

(5) A woman (whether married or not) may bring an action for aliment

on behalf of her unborn child as if the child had been born, but no such action shall be heard or disposed of prior to the birth of the child.

(6) It shall be competent to bring an action for aliment, notwithstanding that the person for or on behalf of whom aliment is being claimed is living in the same household as the defender.

(7) It shall be a defence to an action for aliment brought by virtue of subsection (6) above that the defender is fulfilling the obligation of aliment, and intends to continue doing so.

(8) It shall be a defence to an action for aliment by or on behalf of a person other than a child under the age of 16 years that the defender is making an offer, which it is reasonable to expect the person concerned to accept, to receive that person into his household and to fulfil the obligation of aliment.

[4] (9) For the purposes of subsection (8) above, in considering whether it is reasonable to expect a person to accept an offer, the court shall have regard among other things to any conduct, decree or other circumstances which appear to the court to be relevant: but the fact that a husband and wife or the partners in a civil partnership have agreed to live apart shall not of itself be regarded as making it unreasonable to expect a person to accept such an offer.

(10) A person bringing an action for aliment under subsection (4)(c) above may give a good receipt for aliment paid under the decree in the action.

NOTE
1. Substituted by the Children (Scotland) Act 1995 (c.36), Sch.4, para.36.
2. As amended by the Age of Legal Capacity (Scotland) Act 1991 (c.50), Sch.1, para.40 and Sch.2.
3. As inserted by the Civil Partnership Act 2004 c.33, Sch.28.
4. As amended by the Civil Partnership Act 2004 c.33, Sch.28.

Powers of court in action for aliment

3.—(1) The court may, if it thinks fit, grant decree in an action for aliment, and in granting such decree shall have power—
   (a) to order the making of periodical payments, whether for a definite or an indefinite period or until the happening of a specified event;
   (b) to order the making of alimentary payments of an occasional or special nature, including payments in respect of inlying, funeral or educational expenses;
   (c) to backdate an award of aliment under this Act—
      (i) to the date of the bringing of the action or to such later date as the court thinks fit; or
      (ii) on special cause shown, to a date prior to the bringing of the action;
   (d) to award less than the amount claimed even if the claim is undisputed.

(2) Nothing in subsection (1) above shall empower the court to substitute a lump sum for a periodical payment.

Amount of aliment

4.—(1) In determining the amount of aliment to award in an action for aliment, the court shall, subject to subsection (3) below, have regard—
   (a) to the needs and resources of the parties;
   (b) to the earning capacities of the parties;
   (c) generally to all the circumstances of the case.

(2) Where two or more parties owe an obligation of aliment to another person, there shall be no order of liability, but the court, in deciding how much, if any, aliment to award against any of those persons, shall have

regard, among the other circumstances of the case, to the obligation of aliment owed by any other person.

(3) In having regard under subsection (1)(c) above generally to all the circumstances of the case, the court—

   (a) may, if it thinks fit, take account of any support, financial or otherwise, given by the defender to any person whom he maintains as a dependant in his household, whether or not the defender owes an obligation of aliment to that person; and

   (b) shall not take account of any conduct of a party unless it would be manifestly inequitable to leave it out of account.

[1] (4) Where a court makes an award of aliment in an action brought by or on behalf of a child under the age of 16 years, it may include in that award such provision as it considers to be in all the circumstances reasonable in respect of the expenses incurred wholly or partly by the person having care of the child for the purpose of caring for the child.

NOTE

   1.   Added by the Child Support Act 1991 (c.48), Sch.5, para.5.

Variation or recall of decree of aliment

5.—(1) A decree granted in an action for aliment brought before or after the commencement of this Act may, on an application by or on behalf of either party to the action, be varied or recalled by an order of the court if since the date of the decree there has been a material change of circumstances.

[1] (1A) Without prejudice to the generality of subsection (1) above, the making of a maintenance calculation with respect to a child for whom the decree of aliment was granted is a material change of circumstances for the purposes of that subsection.

(2) The provisions of this Act shall apply to applications and orders under subsection (1) above as they apply to actions for aliment and decrees in such actions, subject to any necessary modifications.

(3) On an application under subsection (1) above, the court may, pending determination of the application, make such interim order as it thinks fit.

(4) Where the court backdates an order under subsection (1) above, the court may order any sums paid under the decree to be repaid.

NOTE

   1.   Inserted by SI 1993/660. As amended by the Child Support and Pensions Act 2000 (c.19), s.26 and Sch.3, para.5(2).

Interim aliment

[1] **6.**—(1) A claim for interim aliment shall be competent—

   (a) in an action for aliment, by the person who claims aliment against the other person;

   (b) in an action for divorce, separation, declarator of marriage or declarator of nullity of marriage, by either party against the other party,

   [2] (c) in an action for dissolution of a civil partnership, separation of civil partners or declarator of nullity of a civil partnership, by either partner against the other partner,

on behalf of the claimant and any person on whose behalf he is entitled to act under section 2(4) of this Act.

(2) Where a claim under subsection (1) above has been made, then, whether or not the claim is disputed, the court may award by way of interim aliment the sum claimed or any lesser sum or may refuse to make such an award.

(3) An award under subsection (2) above shall consist of an award of periodical payments payable only until the date of the disposal of the action in which the award was made or such earlier date as the court may specify.

(4) An award under subsection (2) above may be varied or recalled by an order of the court; and the provisions of this section shall apply to an award so varied and the claim therefor as they applied to the original award and the claim therefor.

NOTE
  1. As amended by the Civil Partnership Act 2004 c.33, Sch.28.
  2. As inserted by the Civil Partnership Act 2004 c.33, Sch.28.

Agreements on aliment

7.—(1) Any provision in an agreement which purports to exclude future liability for aliment or to restrict any right to bring an action for aliment shall have no effect unless the provision was fair and reasonable in all the circumstances of the agreement at the time it was entered into.

(2) Where a person who owes an obligation of aliment to another person has entered into an agreement to pay aliment to or for the benefit of the other person, on a material change of circumstances application may be made to the court by or on behalf of either person for variation of the amount payable under the agreement or for termination of the agreement.

[1] (2ZA) On an application under subsection (2) above, the court may—
  (a) pending determination of the application, make such interim order as it thinks fit;
  (b) make an order backdating a variation of the amount payable under the agreement to—
     (i) the date of the application or such later date as the court thinks fit; or
     (ii) on special cause shown, a date prior to the date of the application.

[1] (2ZB) Where the court makes an order under subsection (2ZA)(b) above, it may order any sums paid under the agreement to be repaid on such terms (including terms relating to repayment by instalments) as the court thinks fit.

[1] (2ZC) Nothing in subsection (2ZA) shall empower the court to substitute a lump sum for a periodical payment.

[2] (2A) Without prejudice to the generality of subsection (2) above, the making of a maintenance calculation with respect to a child to whom or for whose benefit aliment is payable under such an agreement is a material change of circumstances for the purposes of that subsection.

(3) Subsections (8) and (9) of section 2 of this Act (which afford a defence to an action for aliment in certain circumstances) shall apply to an action to enforce such an agreement as is referred to in subsection (2) above as they apply to an action for aliment.

[3] (4) In this section "the court" means the court which would have jurisdiction and competence to entertain an action for aliment between the parties to the agreement to which the application under that subsection relates.

(5) In this section "agreement" means an agreement entered into before or after the commencement of this Act and includes a unilateral voluntary obligation.

NOTE
  1. Inserted by Family Law (Scotland) Act 2006 (asp 2), s.20.
  2. Inserted by SI 1993/660. As amended by the Child Support and Pensions Act 2000 (c.19), s.26 and Sch.3, para.5(3).
  3. Amended by Family Law (Scotland) Act 2006 (asp 2), s.20.

Orders for financial provision

[1]**8.**—(1) In an action for divorce, either party to the marriage and in an action for dissolution of a civil partnership, either partner may apply to the court for one or more of the following orders—

[2](a) an order for the payment of a capital sum to him by the other party to the action;

[3](aa) an order for the transfer of property to him by the other party to the action;

(b) an order for the making of a periodical allowance to him by the other party to the action;

[4](baa) a pension sharing order;

[5](ba) an order under section 12(A)(2) or (3) of this Act;

(c) an incidental order within the meaning of section 14(2) of this Act.

(2) Subject to sections 12 to 15 of this Act, where an application has been made under subsection (1) above, the court shall make such order, if any, as is—

(a) justified by the principles set out in section 9 of this Act; and

(b) reasonable having regard to the resources of the parties.

(3) An order under subsection (2) above is in this Act referred to as an "order for financial provision".

[4](4) The court shall not, in the same proceedings, make both a pension sharing order and an order under section 12A(2) or (3) of this Act in relation to the same pension arrangement.

[6](4A) The court shall not make a pension sharing order, or an order under section 12A(2) or (3) of this Act, in relation to matrimonial property, or partnership property, consisting of compensation such as is mentioned in section 10(5A).

(5) Where, as regards a pension arrangement, the parties to a marriage or the partners in a civil partnership have in effect a qualifying agreement which contains a term relating to pension sharing, the court shall not—

(a) make an order under section 12A(2) or (3) of this Act; or

(b) make a pension sharing order,

relating to the arrangement unless it also sets aside the agreement or term under section 16(1)(b) of this Act.

(6) The court shall not make a pension sharing order in relation to the rights of a person under a pension arrangement if there is in force an order under section 12A(2) or (3) of this Act which relates to benefits or future benefits to which he is entitled under the pension arrangement.

(7) In subsection (5) above—

(a) "term relating to pension sharing" shall be construed in accordance with section 16(2A) of this Act; and

(b) "qualifying agreement" has the same meaning as in section 28(3) of the Welfare Reform and Pensions Act 1999.

NOTE
1. As amended by the Civil Partnership Act 2004 c.33, Sch.28.
2. As amended by the Law Reform (Miscellaneous Provisions) (Scotland) Act 1990 (c.40), Sch.8, para.34 and Sch.9.
3. Inserted by the Law Reform (Miscellaneous Provisions) (Scotland) Act 1990 (c.40), Sch.8, para.34.
4. Inserted by the Welfare Reform and Pensions Act 1999 (c.30), s.20(1) and Sch.12, para.6.
5. Inserted by the Pensions Act 1995 (c.26), s.167(1). Section 167(4) of the Pensions Act 1995 provides that "nothing in the provisions mentioned in section 166(5) [of the 1995 Act] applies to a court exercising its powers under section 8(orders for financial provision on divorce, etc.) or 12A (orders for payment of capital sum: pensions lump sums) of the 1985 Act in respect of any benefits under a pension scheme which fall within subsection (5)(b) of section 10 of that Act ("pension scheme" having the meaning given in subsection (10) of that section)."
6. Inserted by the Family Law (Scotland) Act 2006 (asp 2), s.17.

Pension sharing orders: apportionment of charges

[1] **[8A.** If a pension sharing order relates to rights under a pension arrangement, the court may include in the order provision about the apportionment between the parties of any charge under section 41 of the Welfare Reform and Pensions Act 1999 (charges in respect of pension sharing costs) or under corresponding Northern Ireland legislation.]

NOTE
1. Inserted by the Welfare Reform and Pensions Act 1999 (c.30), Sch.12, para.7.

Principles to be applied

[1] **9.**—(1) The principles which the court shall apply in deciding what order for financial provision, if any, to make are that—
  (a) the net value of the matrimonial property should be shared fairly between the parties to the marriage or as the case may be the net value of the partnership property should be so shared between the partners in the civil partnership;
  (b) fair account should be taken of any economic advantage derived by either party from contributions by the other, and of any economic disadvantage suffered by either person in the interests of the other person or of the family;
  (c) any economic burden of caring, should be shared fairly between the persons—
      (i) after divorce, for a child of the marriage under the age of 16 years;
      (ii) after dissolution of the civil partnership, for a child under that age who has been accepted by both partners as a child of the family.
  (d) a person who has been dependent to a substantial degree on the financial support of the other person should be awarded such financial provision as is reasonable to enable him to adjust, over a period of not more than three years from
      (i) the date of the decree of divorce, to the loss of that support on divorce;
      (ii) the date of the decree of dissolution of the civil partnership, to the loss of that support on dissolution,
  (e) a person who at the time of the divorce or of the dissolution of the civil partnership, seems likely to suffer serious financial hardship as a result of the divorce or dissolution should be awarded such financial provision as is reasonable to relieve him of hardship over a reasonable period.
(2) In subsection (1)(b) above and section 11(2) of this Act—
  "economic advantage" means advantage gained whether before or during the marriage or civil partnership and includes gains in capital, in income and in earning capacity, and "economic disadvantage" shall be construed accordingly;
  "contributions" means contributions made whether before or during the marriage or civil partnership; and includes indirect and non-financial contributions and, in particular, any such contribution made by looking after the family home or caring for the family.

NOTE
1. As amended by the Civil Partnership Act 2004 c.33, Sch.28.

Sharing of value of matrimonial property

[1] **10.**—(1) In applying the principle set out in section 9(1)(a) of this Act,

the net value of the matrimonial property or partnership property shall be taken to be shared fairly between the persons when it is shared equally or in such other proportions as are justified by special circumstances.

[2] (2) Subject to subsection (3A) below the net value of the property shall be the value of the property at the relevant date after deduction of any debts incurred by one or both of the parties to the marriage or as the case may be of the partners—

(a) before the marriage so far as they relate to the matrimonial property or before the registration of the partnership so far as they relate to the partnership property, and

(b) during the marriage or partnership,

which are outstanding at that date.

(3) In this section "the relevant date" means whichever is the earlier of—

(a) subject to subsection (7) below, the date on which the persons ceased to cohabit;

(b) the date of service of the summons in the action for divorce or for dissolution of the civil partnership.

[3] (3A) In its application to property transferred by virtue of an order under section 8(1)(aa) of this Act this section shall have effect as if—

(a) in subsection (2) above, for "relevant date" there were substituted "appropriate valuation date";

(b) after that subsection there were inserted—

"(2A) Subject to subsection (2B), in this section the "appropriate valuation date" means—

(a) where the parties to the marriage or, as the case may be, the partners agree on a date, that date;

(b) where there is no such agreement, the date of the making of the order under section 8(1)(aa).

(2B) If the court considers that, because of the exceptional circumstances of the case, subsection (2A)(b) should not apply, the appropriate valuation date shall be such other date (being a date as near as may be to the date referred to in subsection (2A)(b)) as the court may determine; and

(c) subsection (3) did not apply.

[4] (4) Subject to subsections (5) and (5A) below, in this section and in section 11 of this Act "the matrimonial property" means all the property belonging to the parties or either of them at the relevant date which was acquired by them or him (otherwise than by way of gift or succession from a third party)—

(a) before the marriage for use by them as a family home or as furniture or plenishings for such home; or

(b) during the marriage but before the relevant date.

[4] (4A) Subject to subsections (5) and (5A) below, in this section and in section 11 of this Act "the partnership property" means all the property belonging to the partners or either of them at the relevant date which was acquired by them or by one of them (otherwise than by way of gift or succession from a third party)—

(a) before the registration of the partnership for use by them as a family home or as furniture or plenishings for such a home, or

(b) during the partnership but before the relevant date.

[4,5] (5) The proportion of any rights or interests of either person—

(a) under a life policy or similar arrangement; and

(b) in any benefits under a pension arrangement which either person has or may have (including such benefits payable in respect of the death of either person), and

which is referable to the period to which subsection (4)(b) or (4A)(b) above refers shall be taken to form part of the matrimonial property or partnership property.

[6] (5A) Where either person is entitled to compensation payable under Chapter 3 of Part 2 of the Pensions Act 2004 (c.35) or any provision in force in Northern Ireland corresponding to that Chapter, the proportion of the compensation which is referable to the period to which subsection (4)(b) or (4A)(b) above refers shall be taken to form part of the matrimonial property or partnership property.

(6) In subsection (1) above "special circumstances", without prejudice to the generality of the words, may include—

(a) the terms of any agreement between the persons on the ownership or division of any of the matrimonial property or partnership property;

(b) the source of the funds or assets used to acquire any of the matrimonial property or partnership property where those funds or assets were not derived from the income or efforts of the persons during the marriage;

(c) any destruction, dissipation or alienation of property by either person;

(d) the nature of the matrimonial property, the use made of it (including use for business purposes or as a family home) and the extent to which it is reasonable to expect it to be realised or divided or used as security;

(e) the actual or prospective liability for any expenses of valuation or transfer of property in connection with the divorce or the dissolution of the civil partnership.

(7) For the purposes of subsection (3) above no account shall be taken of any cessation of cohabitation where the persons thereafter resumed cohabitation, except where the persons ceased to cohabit for a continuous period of 90 days or more before resuming cohabitation for a period or periods of less than 90 days in all.

[7] (8) The Secretary of State may by regulations make provision about calculation and verification in relation to the valuation for the purposes of this Act of benefits under a pension arrangement or relevant state scheme rights.

[7] (8A) Regulations under subsection (8) above may include—

(a) provision for calculation or verification in accordance with guidance from time to time prepared by a prescribed person; and

(b) provision by reference to regulations under section 30 or 49(4) of the Welfare Reform and Pensions Act 1999.

[6] (8B) The Scottish Ministers may by regulations make provision for or in connection with the verification, or apportionment, of compensation such as is mentioned in subsection (5A).

[8] (9) Regulations under subsection (8) or (8B) above may make different provision for different purposes and shall be made by statutory instrument which shall be subject to annulment in pursuance of a resolution of either House of Parliament.

(10) [*Repealed by the Welfare Reform and Pensions Act 1999 (c.30), Sch.12, para.8(6).*]

(11) [*Repealed by the Welfare Reform and Pensions Act 1999 (c.30), Sch.12, para.8(6).*]

NOTE

1. Amended by the Civil Partnership Act 2004 c.33, Sch.28.
2. Amended by the Family Law (Scotland) Act 2006 (asp 2), s.16.
3. Inserted by the Family Law (Scotland) Act 2006 (asp 2), s.16.
4. Amended by the Family Law (Scotland) Act 2006 (asp 2), s.17.
5. Amended by the Pensions Act 1995 (c.26), s.167(2)(a) and by the Family Law Act 1996 (c.27), s.17(a). As amended by the Welfare Reform and Pensions Act 1999 (c.30), Sch.12, para.8(2).
6. Inserted by the Family Law (Scotland) Act 2006 (asp 2), s.17.

7. Inserted by the Pensions Act 1995 (c.26), s.167(2)(b). Substituted by the Welfare Reform and Pensions Act 1999 (c.30), Sch.12, para.8(3).
8. Inserted by the Family Law Act 1996 (c.27), s.17(b). As amended by the Welfare Reform and Pensions Act 1999 (c.30), Sch.12, para.8(5) and (6). As amended by the Family Law (Scotland) Act 2006 (asp 2), s.17.

Factors to be taken into account

[1] **11.**—(1) In applying the principles set out in section 9 of this Act, the following provisions of this section shall have effect.

(2) For the purposes of section 9(1)(b) of this Act, the court shall have regard to the extent to which—

(a) the economic advantages or disadvantages sustained by either person have been balanced by the economic advantages or disadvantages sustained by the other person, and

(b) any resulting imbalance has been or will be corrected by a sharing of the value of the matrimonial property or the partnership property or otherwise.

(3) For the purposes of section 9(1)(c) of this Act, the court shall have regard to—

(a) any decree or arrangement for aliment for the child;

(b) any expenditure or loss of earning capacity caused by the need to care for the child;

(c) the need to provide suitable accommodation for the child;

(d) the age and health of the child;

(e) the educational, financial and other circumstances of the child;

(f) the availability and cost of suitable child-care facilities or services;

(g) the needs and resources of the persons; and

(h) all the other circumstances of the case.

(4) For the purposes of section 9(1)(d) of this Act, the court shall have regard to—

(a) the age, health and earning capacity of the person who is claiming the financial provision;

(b) the duration and extent of the dependence of that person prior to divorce or to the dissolution of the civil partnership;

(c) any intention of that person to undertake a course of education or training;

(d) the needs and resources of the persons; and

(e) all the other circumstances of the case.

(5) For the purposes of section 9(1)(e) of this Act, the court shall have regard to—

(a) the age, health and earning capacity of the person who is claiming the financial provision;

(b) the duration of the marriage or of the civil partnership;

(c) the standard of living of the persons during the marriage or civil partnership;

(d) the needs and resources of the persons; and

(e) all the other circumstances of the case.

(6) In having regard under subsections (3) to (5) above to all the other circumstances of the case, the court may, if it thinks fit, take account of any support, financial or otherwise, given by the person who is to make the financial provision to any person whom he maintains as a dependant in his household whether or not he owes an obligation of aliment to that person.

(7) In applying the principles set out in section 9 of this Act, the court shall not take account of the conduct of either party to the marriage or as the case may be of either partner unless—

(a) the conduct has adversely affected the financial resources which are relevant to the decision of the court on a claim for financial provision; or

(b) in relation to section 9(1)(d) or (e), it would be manifestly inequitable to leave the conduct out of account.

NOTE
1. As amended by the Civil Partnership Act 2004 c.33, Sch.28.

Orders for payment of capital sum or transfer of property

[1] **12.**—(1) An order under section 8(2) of this Act for payment of a capital sum or transfer of property may be made—
(a) on granting decree of divorce or of dissolution of a civil partnership; or
(b) within such period as the court on granting the decree may specify.
(2) The court, on making an order referred to in subsection (1) above, may stipulate that it shall come into effect at a specified future date.
(3) The court, on making an order under section 8(2) of this Act for payment of a capital sum, may order that the capital sum shall be payable by instalments.
(4) Where an order referred to in subsection (1) above has been made, the court may, on an application by—
(a) either party to the marriage
(b) either partner,
on a material change of circumstances, vary the date or method of payment of the capital sum or the date of transfer of property.

NOTE
1. As amended by the Civil Partnership Act 2004 c.33, Sch.28.

Orders for payment of capital sum: pensions lump sums

[1,2] **12A.**—(1) This section applies where the court makes an order under section 8(2) of this Act for payment of a capital sum (a "capital sum order") by a party to the marriage or a partner in a civil partnership ("the liable person") in circumstances where—
(a) the matrimonial property or the partnership property within the meaning of section 10 of this Act includes any rights or interests in benefits under a pension arrangement which the liable person has or may have (whether such benefits are payable to him or in respect of his death); and
(b) those benefits include a lump sum payable to him or in respect of his death.
(2) Where the benefits referred to in subsection (1) above include a lump sum payable to the liable person, the court, on making the capital sum order, may make an order requiring the person responsible for the pension arrangement in question to pay the whole or part of that sum, when it becomes due, to the other party to the marriage or as the case may be to the other partner ("the other person").
(3) Where the benefits referred to in subsection (1) above include a lump sum payable in respect of the death of the liable person, the court, on making the capital sum order, may make an order—
(a) if the person responsible for the pension arrangement in question has power to determine the person to whom the sum, or any part of it, is to be paid, requiring them to pay the whole or part of that sum, when it becomes due, to the other person;
(b) if the liable person has power to nominate the person to whom the sum, or any part of it, is to be paid, requiring the liable person to nominate the other person in respect of the whole or part of that sum;
(c) in any other case, requiring the person responsible for the pension

115

arrangement in question to pay the whole or part of that sum, when it becomes due, to the other person instead of to the person to whom, apart from the order, it would be paid.

(4) Any payment by the person responsible for the pension arrangement under an order under subsection (2) or (3) above—

(a) shall discharge so much of the [liability of the person responsible for the pension arrangement] to or in respect of the liable person as corresponds to the amount of the payment; and

(b) shall be treated for all purposes as a payment made by the liable person in or towards the discharge of his liability under the capital sum order.

(5) Where the liability of the liable person under the capital sum order has been discharged in whole or in part, other than by a payment by the [person responsible for the pension arrangement] under an order under subsection (2) or (3) above, the court may, on an application by any person having an interest, recall any order under either of those subsections or vary the amount specified in such an order, as appears to the court appropriate in the circumstances.

(6) Where—

(a) an order under subsection (2) or (3) above imposes any requirement on the person responsible for a pension arrangement ("the first arrangement") and the liable person acquires transfer credits under another arrangement ("the new arrangement") which are derived (directly or indirectly) from a transfer from the first arrangement of all his accrued rights under that arrangement; and

(b) the trustees or managers of the new [arrangement] [has] been given notice in accordance with regulations under subsection (8) below,

the order shall have effect as if it had been made instead in respect of the person responsible for the new arrangement; and in this subsection "transfer credits" has the same meaning as in the Pension Schemes Act 1993.

(7) Without prejudice to subsection (6) above, the court may, on an application by any person having an interest, vary an order under subsection (2) or (3) above by substituting for the person responsible for the pension arrangement specified in the order the person responsible for any other pension arrangement under which any lump sum referred to in subsection (1) above is payable to the liable person or in respect of his death.

[3] (7A) Where—

(a) the court makes an order under subsection (3); and

(b) after the making of the order the Board gives the trustees or managers of the scheme a notice under section 160 of the Pensions Act 2004 (c.35) ("the 2004 Act"), or the Northern Ireland provision, in relation to the scheme,

the order shall, on the giving of such notice, be recalled.

[3] (7B) Subsection (7C) applies where—

(a) the court makes an order under subsection (2) imposing requirements on the trustees or managers of an occupational pension scheme; and

(b) after the making of the order the Board gives the trustees or managers of the scheme a notice under section 160 of the 2004 Act, or the Northern Ireland provision, in relation to the scheme.

[3] (7C) The order shall have effect from the time when the notice is given—

(a) as if—

(i) references to the trustees or managers of the scheme were references to the Board; and

(ii) references to any lump sum to which the person with benefits under a pension arrangement is or might become entitled under the scheme were references to the amount of any compensation payable under that Chapter of the 2004 Act, or the Northern Ireland provision, to which that person is or might become entitled in respect of the lump sum; and

(b) subject to such other modifications as may be prescribed by regulations by the Scottish Ministers.

(8) The Secretary of State may by regulations—

(a) require notices to be given in respect of changes of circumstances relevant to orders under subsection (2) or (3) above;

(b) [*Repealed by the Welfare Reform and Pensions Act 1999 (c.30), Sch.13, Pt II.*]

[4] (9) Regulations under subsections (7C)(b) and (8) above shall be made by statutory instrument which shall be subject to annulment in pursuance of a resolution of either House of Parliament.

(10) The definition of "benefits under a pension scheme" in section 27 of this Act does not apply to this section.

[3] (11) In subsections (7A) to (7C) "the Northern Ireland provision", in relation to a provision of the 2004 Act, means any provision in force in Northern Ireland corresponding to the provision of that Act.

NOTE

1. Inserted by the Pensions Act 1995 (c.26), s.167(3). Section 167(4) of the Pensions Act 1995 provides that "nothing in the provisions mentioned in section 166(5) [of the 1995 Act] applies to a court exercising its powers under section 8 (orders for financial provision on divorce, etc.) or 12A (orders for payment of capital sum: pensions lump sums) of the 1985 Act in respect of any benefits under a pension scheme which fall within subsection (5)(b) of section 10 of that Act ("pension scheme" having the meaning given in subsection (10) of that section)." As amended by the Welfare Reform and Pensions Act 1999 (c.30), Sch.12, para.9A.

2. Amended by the Civil Partnership Act 2004 c.33, Sch.28 and the Family Law (Scotland) Act 2006 (asp 2), Sch.2.

3. Inserted by Family Law (Scotland) Act 2006 (asp 2), s.17.

4. Amended by Family Law (Scotland) Act 2006 (asp 2), s.17.

Orders for periodical allowance

[1,3] **13.**—(1) An order under section 8(2) of this Act for a periodical allowance may be made—

(a) on granting decree of divorce or of dissolution;

(b) within such period as the court on granting the decree may specify; or

(c) after such decree where—

    (i) no such order has been made previously;

    (ii) application for the order has been made after the date of decree; and

    (iii) since the date of decree there has been a change of circumstances.

(2) The court shall not make an order for a periodical allowance under section 8(2) of this Act unless—

(a) the order is justified by a principle set out in paragraph (c), (d) or (e) of section 9(1) of this Act; and

[1] (b) it is satisfied that an order for payment of a capital sum or for transfer of property [, or a pension sharing order,] under that section would be inappropriate or insufficient to satisfy the requirements of the said section 8(2).

(3) An order under section 8(2) of this Act for a periodical allowance may be for a definite or an indefinite period or until the happening of a specified event.

(4) Where an order for a periodical allowance has been made under section 8(2) of this Act, and since the date of the order there has been a material change of circumstances, the court shall, on an application by or on behalf of either party to the marriage or his executor, or as the case may be either partner or his executor, have power by subsequent order—

(a) to vary or recall the order for a periodical allowance;

(b) to backdate such variation or recall to the date of the application therefor or, on cause shown, to an earlier date;

(c) to convert the order into an order for payment of a capital sum or for a transfer of property.

[2] (4A) Without prejudice to the generality of subsection (4) above, the making of a maintenance calculation with respect to a child who has his home with a person to whom the periodical allowance is made (being a child to whom the person making the allowance has an obligation of aliment) is a material change of circumstances for the purposes of that subsection.

(5) The provisions of this Act shall apply to applications and orders under subsection (4) above as they apply to applications for periodical allowance and orders on such applications.

(6) Where the court backdates an order under subsection (4)(b) above, the court may order any sums paid by way of periodical allowance to be repaid.

(7) An order for a periodical allowance made under section 8(2) of this Act—

(a) shall, if subsisting at the death of the person making the payment, continue to operate against the person's estate, but without prejudice to the making of an order under subsection (4) above;

(b) shall cease to have effect on the person receiving payment—

(i) marrying,

(ii) entering into a civil partnership, or

(iii) dying,

except in relation to any arrears due under it.

NOTE

1. As amended by the Welfare Reform and Pensions Act 1999 (c.30), Sch.12, para.10.

2. Inserted by SI 1993/660. As amended by the Child Support and Pensions Act 2000 (c.19), s.26 and Sch.3, para.5(4).

3. As amended by the Civil Partnership Act 2004 c.33, Sch.28.

Incidental orders

[1,3] **14.**—(1) Subject to subsection (3) below, an incidental order may be made under section 8(2) of this Act before, on or after the granting or refusal of decree of divorce or of dissolution of a civil partnership.

(2) In this Act, "an incidental order" means one or more of the following orders—

(a) an order for the sale of property;

(b) an order for the valuation of property;

(c) an order determining any dispute between the parties to the marriage or as the case may be the partners, as to their respective property rights by means of a declarator thereof or otherwise;

(d) an order regulating the occupation of—

(i) the matrimonial home or

(ii) the family home of the partnership,

or the use of furniture and plenishings therein or excluding either person from such occupation;

(e) an order regulating liability, as between the persons, for outgoings in respect of—

(i) the matrimonial home, or

        (ii) the family home of the partnership,
or furniture or plenishings therein;

(f) an order that security shall be given for any financial provision;

(g) an order that payments shall be made or property transferred to any curator bonis or trustee or other person for the benefit of the person by whom or on whose behalf application has been made under section 8(1) of this Act for an incidental order;

(h) an order setting aside or varying any term in an antenuptial or postnuptial marriage settlement or in any corresponding settlement in respect of the civil partnership;

(j) an order as to the date from which any interest on any amount awarded shall run;

² (ja) in relation to a deed relating to moveable property, an order dispensing with the execution of the deed by the grantor and directing the sheriff clerk to execute the deed;

(k) any ancillary order which is expedient to give effect to the principles set out in section 9 of this Act or to any order made under section 8(2) of this Act.

(3) An incidental order referred to in subsection (2)(d) or (e) above may be made only on or after the granting of the decree.

(4) An incidental order may be varied or recalled by subsequent order on cause shown.

(5) So long as an incidental order granting a party to a marriage the right to occupy a matrimonial home or the right to use furniture and plenishings therein remains in force then—

(a) section 2(1), (2), (5)(a) and (9) of the Matrimonial Homes (Family Protection) (Scotland) Act 1981 (which confer certain general powers of management on a spouse in relation to a matrimonial home), and

³ (b) subject to section 15(3) of this Act, section 12 of the said Act of 1981 and section 41 of the Bankruptcy (Scotland) Act 1985 (which protect the occupancy rights of a spouse against arrangements intended to defeat them),

shall, except to the extent that the order otherwise provides, apply in relation to the order—

(i) as if that party were a non-entitled spouse and the other party were an entitled spouse within the meaning of section 1(1) or 6(2) of the said Act of 1981 as the case may require;

(ii) as if the right to occupy a matrimonial home under that order were "occupancy rights" within the meaning of the said Act of 1981; and

(iii) with any other necessary modifications; and

subject to section 15(3) of this Act, section 11 of the said Act of 1981 (protection of spouse in relation to furniture and plenishings) shall apply in relation to the order as if that party were a spouse within the meaning of the said section 11 and the order were an order under section 3(3) or (4) of the said Act of 1981.

(5A) So long as an incidental order granting a partner in a civil partnership the right to occupy a family home or the right to use furnishings and plenishings therein remains in force then—

(a) section 102(1), (2), (5)(a) and (9) of the Civil Partnership Act 2004, and

(b) subject to section 15(3) of this Act, section 111 of that Act,

shall, except to the extent that the order otherwise provides, apply in relation to the order in accordance with subsection (5B).

(5B) Those provisions apply—

(a) as if that partner were a non-entitled partner and the other partner were an entitled partner within the meaning of section 101 or 106(2) of that Act as the case may require,

(b) as if the right to occupy a family home under that order were a right specified in paragraph (a) or (b) of section 101(1) of that Act, and

(c) with any other necessary modification.

(6) In subsection (2)(h) above, "settlement" includes a settlement by way of a policy of assurance to which section 2 of the Married Women's Policies of Assurance (Scotland) Act 1880 relates.

(7) Notwithstanding subsection (1) above, the Court of Session may by Act of Sederunt make rules restricting the categories of incidental order which may be made under section 8(2) of this Act before the granting of decree of divorce or of dissolution of a civil partnership.

NOTE
1. As amended by the Civil Partnership Act 2004 c.33, Sch.28.
2. Inserted by Family Law (Scotland) Act 2006 (asp 2), s.20.
3. As amended by the Bankruptcy (Scotland) Act 1985 (c.66), Sch.7, para.23.

Rights of third parties

15.—(1) The court shall not make an order under section 8(2) of this Act for the transfer of property if the consent of a third party which is necessary under any obligation, enactment or rule of law has not been obtained.

(2) The court shall not make an order under section 8(2) of this Act for the transfer of property subject to security without the consent of the creditor unless he has been given an opportunity of being heard by the court.

(3) Neither an incidental order, nor any rights conferred by such an order, shall prejudice any rights of any third party insofar as those rights existed immediately before the making of the order.

Agreements on financial provision

[1] **16.**—(1) Where the parties to a marriage or the partners in a civil partnership have entered into an agreement as to financial provision to be made on divorce or on dissolution of the civil partnership, the court may make an order setting aside or varying—

(a) any term of the agreement relating to a periodical allowance where the agreement expressly provides for the subsequent setting aside or variation by the court of that term; or

(b) the agreement or any term of it where the agreement was not fair and reasonable at the time it was entered into.

(2) The court may make an order—

(a) under subsection (1)(a) above at any time after granting decree of divorce or of dissolution of civil partnership; and

[3] (b) under subsection (1)(b) above, if the agreement does not contain a term relating to pension sharing, on granting decree of divorce or dissolution of the civil partnership or within such time as the court may specify on granting decree of divorce or of dissolution of civil partnership; or

[2] (c) under subsection (1)(b) above, if the agreement contains a term relating to pension sharing—

(i) where the order sets aside the agreement or sets aside or varies the term relating to pension sharing, on granting decree of divorce or of dissolution of civil partnership; and

(ii) where the order sets aside or varies any other term of the agreement, on granting decree of divorce or dissolution of the civil partnership or within such time thereafter as the court may specify on granting decree of divorce or of dissolution of civil partnership.

[3](2A) In subsection (2) above, a term relating to pension sharing is a term corresponding to provision which may be made in a pension sharing order and satisfying the requirements set out in section 28(1)(f) or 48(1)(f) of the Welfare Reform and Pensions Act 1999.

[4](2B) Subsection (2C) applies where—

(a) the parties to a marriage or the partners in a civil partnership have entered into an agreement as to financial provision to be made on divorce or on dissolution of the civil partnership; and

(b) the agreement includes provision in respect of a person's rights or interests or benefits under an occupational pension scheme.

[4](2C) The Board of the Pension Protection Fund's subsequently assuming responsibility for the occupational pension scheme in accordance with Chapter 3 of Part 2 of the Pension Act 2004 (c.35) or any provision in force in Northern Ireland corresponding to that Chapter shall not affect—

(a) the power of the court under subsection (1)(b) to make an order setting aside or varying the agreement or any term of it;

(b) on an appeal, the powers of the appeal court in relation to the order.

(3) Without prejudice to subsections (1) and (2) above, where the parties to a marriage or the partners in a civil partnership have entered into an agreement as to financial provision to be made on divorce or on dissolution of the civil partnership and—

(a) the estate of the person by whom any periodical allowance is payable under the agreement has, since the date when the agreement was entered into, been sequestrated, the award of sequestration has not been recalled and the person has not been discharged;

(b) an analogous remedy within the meaning of section 10(5) of the Bankruptcy (Scotland) Act 1985 has, since that date, come into force and remains in force in respect of that person's estate;

(c) that person's estate is being administered by a trustee acting under a voluntary trust deed granted since that date by the person for the benefit of his creditors generally or is subject to an analogous arrangement; or

[5](d) by virtue of the making of a maintenance calculation, child support maintenance has become payable by either party to the agreement with respect to a child to whom or for whose benefit periodical allowance is paid under that agreement,

the court may, on or at any time after granting decree of divorce or of dissolution of the civil partnership, make an order setting aside or varying any term of the agreement relating to the periodical allowance.

(4) Any term of an agreement purporting to exclude the right to apply for an order under subsection (1)(b) or (3) above shall be void.

(5) In this section, "agreement" means an agreement entered into before or after the commencement of this Act.

NOTE

1. As amended by the Civil Partnership Act 2004 c.33, Sch.28 and the Family Law (Scotland) Act 2006 (asp 2), Sch.2.

2. As amended by the Welfare Reform and Pensions Act 1999 (c.30), Sch.12, para.11(3) and by Family Law (Scotland) Act 2006 (asp 2), Sch.2.

3. Inserted by the Welfare Reform and Pensions Act 1999 (c.30), Sch.12, para.11(2) and amended by Family Law (Scotland) Act 2006 (asp 2), Sch.2.

4. Inserted by Family Law (Scotland) Act 2006 (asp 2), s.17.

5. As amended by the Child Support and Pensions Act 2000 (c.19), s.26 and Sch.3, para.5(5).

Financial provision on declarator of nullity of marriage

[1] **17.**—(1) Subject to the following provisions of this section, the provisions of this Act shall apply to actions for declarator of nullity of marriage or of a civil partnership as they apply to actions for divorce or for dissolution of a civil partnership; and in this Act, unless the context otherwise requires, "action for divorce" includes an action for declarator of nullity of marriage and "action for dissolution of a civil partnership" includes an action for declarator of nullity of a civil partnership and, in relation to such an action, "decree", "divorce" and "dissolution of a civil partnership" and "divorce" shall be construed accordingly.

(2) In an action for declarator of nullity of marriage or civil partnership, it shall be competent for either party to claim interim aliment under section 6(1) of this Act notwithstanding that he denies the existence of the marriage or civil partnership.

(3) Any rule of law by virtue of which either party to an action for declarator of nullity of marriage may require restitution of property upon the granting of such declarator shall cease to have effect.

NOTE
1. As amended by the Civil Partnership Act 2004 c.33, Sch.28.

Supplemental

Orders relating to avoidance transactions

[1] **18.**—(1) Where a claim has been made (whether before or after the commencement of this Act), being—

(a) an action for aliment,
(b) a claim for an order for financial provision, or
(c) an application for variation or recall of a decree in such an action or of an order for financial provision,

the person making the claim may, not later than one year from the date of the disposal of the claim, apply to the court for an order—

(i) setting aside or varying any transfer of, or transaction involving, property effected by the other person not more than five years before the date of the making of the claim; or
(ii) interdicting the other person from effecting any such transfer or transaction.

(2) Subject to subsection (3) below, on an application under subsection (1) above for an order the court may, if it is satisfied that the transfer or transaction had the effect of, or is likely to have the effect of, defeating in whole or in part any claim referred to in subsection (1) above, make the order applied for or such other order as it thinks fit.

(3) An order under subsection (2) above shall not prejudice any rights of a third party in or to the property where that third party—

(a) has in good faith acquired the property or any of it or any rights in relation to it for value; or
(b) derives title to such property or rights from any person who has done so.

(4) Where the court makes an order under subsection (2) above, it may include in the order such terms and conditions as it thinks fit and may make any ancillary order which it considers expedient to ensure that the order is effective.

NOTE
1. As amended by the Civil Partnership Act 2004 c.33, Sch.28.

Inhibition and arrestment

19.—(1) Where a claim has been made, being—

(a) an action for aliment, or

(b) a claim for an order for financial provision,

the court shall have power, on cause shown, to grant warrant for inhibition or warrant for arrestment on the dependence of the action in which the claim is made and, if it thinks fit, to limit the inhibition to any particular property or to limit the arrestment to any particular property or to funds not exceeding a specified value.

(2) In subsection (1) above, "the court" means the Court of Session in relation to a warrant for inhibition and the Court of Session or the sheriff, as the case may require, in relation to a warrant for arrestment on the dependence.

(3) This section is without prejudice to section 1 of the Law Reform (Miscellaneous Provisions) (Scotland) Act 1966 (wages, pensions, etc., to be exempt from arrestment on the dependence of an action).

Provision of details of resources

20. In an action—

(a) for aliment;

(b) which includes a claim for an order for financial provision; or

(c) which includes a claim for interim aliment,

the court may order either party to provide details of his resources or those relating to a child or incapax on whose behalf he is acting.

Award of aliment or custody where divorce or separation refused

[1,2] **21.** A court which refuses a decree of divorce, separation or dissolution of a civil partnership shall not, by virtue of such refusal, be prevented from making an order for aliment.

NOTE

1. As amended by the Children (Scotland) Act 1995 (c.36), s.105(5) and Sch.5.

2. As amended by the Civil Partnership Act 2004 c.33, Sch.28.

Expenses of action

[1] **22.** The expenses incurred by a person in pursuing or defending—

(a) an action for aliment brought—

    (i) by either party to a marriage, or

    (ii) by either party in a civil partnership,

on his own behalf against the other party or partner

(b) an action for divorce, separation (whether of the parties marriage or the civil partners in a civil partnership), declarator of marriage or declarator of nullity of marriage;

(bb) an action for dissolution of a civil partnership, declarator that a civil partnership exists or declarator of nullity of a civil partnership,

(c) an application made after the commencement of this Act for variation or recall of a decree of aliment or an order for financial provision in an action brought before or after the commencement of this Act,

shall not be regarded as necessaries for which the other party to the marriage or the other partner in the civil partnership is liable.

NOTE

1. As amended by the Civil Partnership Act 2004 c.33, Sch.28.

Actions for aliment of small amounts

23. *[Substitutes new s.3 of the Sheriff Courts (Civil Jurisdiction and Procedure) (Scotland) Act 1963.]*

Matrimonial property, etc.

Marriage not to affect property rights or legal capacity

[1] **24.**—(1) Subject to the provisions of any enactment (including this Act), marriage shall not of itself affect—

(a) the respective rights of the parties to the marriage, or as the case may be the partners in the civil partnership in relation to their property;

(b) the legal capacity of those parties or partners.

(2) Nothing in subsection (1) above affects the law of succession.

NOTE

    1. As amended by the Civil Partnership Act 2004 c.33, Sch.28.

Presumption of equal shares in household goods

[1] **25.**—(1) If any question arises (whether during or after a marriage or civil partnership) as to the respective rights of ownership of the parties to a marriage in any household goods obtained in prospect of or during the marriage or civil partnership other than by gift or succession from a third party, it shall be presumed, unless the contrary is proved, that each has a right to an equal share in the goods in question.

(2) For the purposes of subsection (1) above, the contrary shall not be treated as proved by reason only that while—

(a) the parties were married

(b) the partners were in civil partnership,

and living together the goods in question were purchased from a third party by either party alone or by both in unequal shares.

(3) In this section "household goods" means any goods (including decorative or ornamental goods) kept or used at any time during the marriage or civil partnership in any family home for the joint domestic purposes of the parties to the marriage or the partners, other than—

(a) money or securities;

(b) any motor car, caravan or other road vehicle;

(c) any domestic animal.

NOTE

    1. As amended by the Civil Partnership Act 2004 c.33, Sch.28.

Presumption of equal shares in money and property derived from house-keeping allowance

[1] **26.** If any question arises (whether during or after a marriage or civil partnership) as to the right of a party to a marriage or as the case may be of a partner in a civil partnership to money derived from any allowance made by either party or partner for their joint household expenses or for similar purposes, or to any property acquired out of such money, the money or property shall, in the absence of any agreement between them to the contrary, be treated as belonging to each party or partner in equal shares.

NOTE

    1. As amended by the Civil Partnership Act 2004 c.33, Sch.28.

Interpretation

27.—(1) In this Act, unless the context otherwise requires—

"action" means an action brought after the commencement of this Act;

"action for aliment" has the meaning assigned to it by section 2(3) of this Act;

"aliment" does not include aliment *pendente lite* or interim aliment under section 6 of this Act;

[1] "benefits under a pension arrangement" includes any benefits by way of pension, including relevant state scheme rights, whether under a pension arrangement or not;

"caravan" means a caravan which is mobile or affixed to the land;

[2] "child" includes a child whether or not his parents have ever been married to one another, and any reference to the child of a marriage (whether or not subsisting) includes a child (other than a child who has been boarded out with the parties, or one of them, by a local or other public authority or a voluntary organisation) who has been accepted by the parties as a child of the family;

[3] "child support maintenance" has the meaning assigned to it by section 3(6) of the Child Support Act 1991;

[4] "civil partnership", in relation to an action for declarator of nullity of a civil partnership, means purported civil partnership,

"the court" means the Court of Session or the sheriff, as the case may require;

"decree" in an action for aliment includes an order of the court awarding aliment;

[5] "family" includes a one-parent family and in relation to a civil partnership means the members of the civil partnership together with any child accepted by them both as a child of the family;

"incidental order" has the meaning assigned to it by section 14(2) of this Act;

[3] "maintenance calculation" has the meaning assigned to it by section 54 of the Child Support Act 1991;

"marriage", in relation to an action for declarator of nullity of marriage, means purported marriage;

[6] "matrimonial home" has the meaning assigned to it by section 22 of the Matrimonial Homes (Family Protection) (Scotland) Act 1981 as amended by section 13(10) of the Law Reform (Miscellaneous Provisions) (Scotland) Act 1985;

"needs" means present and foreseeable needs;

"obligation of aliment" shall be construed in accordance with section 1(2) of this Act;

"order for financial provision" means an order under section 8(2) of this Act and, in sections 18(1) and 22(c) of this Act, also includes an order under section 5(2) of the Divorce (Scotland) Act 1976;

[4] "partner", in relation to a civil partnership, includes a person who was a partner in a civil partnership which has been terminated and an ostensible partner in a civil partnership which has been annulled,

"party to a marriage" and "party to the marriage" include a party to a marriage which has been terminated or annulled;

[1] "pension arrangement" means—

(a) any occupational pension scheme within the meaning of the Pension Schemes Act 1993;

(b) a personal pension scheme within the meaning of that Act;

(c) a retirement annuity contract;

(d) an annuity or insurance policy purchased or transferred for the purpose of giving effect to rights under an occupational pension scheme or a personal pension scheme;

(e) an annuity purchased or entered into for the purpose of discharging liability in respect of a pension credit under section 29(1)(b) of the Welfare Reform and Pensions Act 1999 or under corresponding Northern Ireland legislation;

[1] "pension sharing order" is an order which—

(a) provides that one party's—

    (i) shareable rights under a specified pension arrangement,

    or

    (ii) shareable state scheme rights,

    be subject to pension sharing for the benefit of the other party, and

(b) specifies the percentage value, or the amount, to be transferred;

[1] ["person responsible for a pension arrangement" means—

(a) in the case of an occupational pension scheme or a personal pension scheme, the trustees or managers of the scheme;

(b) in the case of a retirement annuity contract or an annuity falling within paragraph (d) or (e) of the definition of "pension arrangement" above, the provider of the annuity;

(c) in the case of an insurance policy falling within paragraph (d) of the definition of that expression, the insurer;]

"property" in sections 8, 12, 13 and 15 of this Act does not include a tenancy transferable under section 13 of the Matrimonial Homes (Family Protection) (Scotland) Act 1981;

[1] "relevant state scheme rights" means—

(a) entitlement, or prospective entitlement, to a Category A retirement pension by virtue of section 44(3)(b) of the Social Security Contributions and Benefits Act 1992 or under corresponding Northern Ireland legislation; and

(b) entitlement, or prospective entitlement, to a pension under section 55A of the Social Security Contributions and Benefits Act 1992 (shared additional pension) or under corresponding Northern Ireland legislation;

"resources" means present and foreseeable resources;

[1] "retirement annuity contract" means a contract or scheme approved under Chapter III of Part XIV of the Income and Corporation Taxes Act 1988;

[1] "trustees or managers" in relation to an occupational pension scheme or a personal pension scheme means—

(a) in the case of a scheme established under a trust, the trustees of the scheme; and

(b) in any other case, the managers of the scheme;

"voluntary organisation" means a body, other than a local or other public authority, the activities of which are not carried on for profit.

[1] [(1A) In subsection (1), in the definition of "pension sharing order"—

(a) the reference to shareable rights under a pension arrangement is to rights in relation to which pension sharing is available under Chapter I of Part IV of the Welfare Reform and Pensions Act 1999, or under corresponding Northern Ireland legislation, and

(b) the reference to shareable state scheme rights is to rights in relation to which pension sharing is available under Chapter II of Part IV of the Welfare Reform and Pensions Act 1999, or under corresponding Northern Ireland legislation.]

(2) For the purposes of this Act, the parties to a marriage shall be held to cohabit with one another only when they are in fact living together as man and wife.

NOTE
1. Inserted amended by the Welfare Reform and Pensions Act 1999 (c.30), s.20(3) and (4) and Sch.12, para.12.
2. As amended by the Law Reform (Parent and Child) (Scotland) Act 1986 (c.9), Sch.1, para.21.
3. Inserted by SI 1993/660. As amended by the Child Support and Pensions Act 2000 (c.19), s.26 and Sch.3, para.5(6).
4. Inserted by the Civil Partnership Act 2004 c.33, Sch.28 and amended by the Family Law (Scotland) Act 2006, Sch.2.
5. As amended by the Civil Partnership Act 2004 c.33, Sch.28.
6. As amended by the Law Reform (Miscellaneous Provisions) (Scotland) Act 1985 (c.73), Sch.2, para.31.

Amendments, repeals and savings

28.—(1) The enactments specified in Schedule 1 to this Act shall have effect subject to the amendments set out therein.

(2) The enactments specified in columns 1 and 2 of Schedule 2 to this Act are repealed to the extent specified in column 3 of that Schedule.

(3) Nothing in subsection (2) above shall affect the operation of section 5 (orders for financial provision) of the Divorce (Scotland) Act 1976 in relation to an action for divorce brought before the commencement of this Act; but in the continued operation of that section the powers of the court—

(a) to make an order for payment of periodical allowance under subsection (2) thereof; and

(b) to vary such an order under subsection (4) thereof,

shall include power to make such an order for a definite or an indefinite period or until the happening of a specified event.

Citation, commencement and extent

29.—(1) This Act may be cited as the Family Law (Scotland) Act 1985.

[1] (2) This Act shall come into operation on such day as the Secretary of State may appoint by order made by statutory instrument, and different days may be appointed for different purposes.

(3) An order under subsection (2) above may contain such transitional provisions and savings as appear to the Secretary of State necessary or expedient in connection with the provisions brought into force (whether wholly or partly) by the order.

(4) So much of section 28 of, and Schedule 1 to, this Act as affects the operation of the Maintenance Orders Act 1950 and the Maintenance Orders (Reciprocal Enforcement) Act 1972 shall extend to England and Wales and to Northern Ireland as well as to Scotland, but save as aforesaid this Act shall extend to Scotland only.

.   .   .

MATRIMONIAL HOMES (FAMILY PROTECTION) (SCOTLAND) ACT 1981

(1981, c.59)

An Act to make new provision for Scotland as to the rights of occupancy of spouses in a matrimonial home and of cohabiting couples in the house where they cohabit; to provide for the transfer of the tenancy of a matrimonial home between the spouses in certain circumstances during marriage and on granting decree of divorce or nullity of marriage, and for the transfer of the tenancy of a house occupied by a cohabiting couple between the partners in certain circumstances; to strengthen the law relating to matrimonial interdicts; and for connected purposes.

[October 30, 1981]

Protection of occupancy rights of one spouse against the other

Right of spouse without title to occupy matrimonial home

[1] **1.**—(1) Where, apart from the provisions of this Act, one spouse is entitled, or permitted by a third party, to occupy a matrimonial home (an "entitled spouse") and the other spouse is not so entitled or permitted (a "non-entitled spouse"), the non-entitled spouse shall, subject to the provisions of this Act, have the following rights—

    (a) if in occupation, a right to continue to occupy the matrimonial home;

    (b) if not in occupation, a right to enter into and occupy the matrimonial home.

(1A) The rights conferred by subsection (1) above to continue to occupy or, as the case may be, to enter and occupy the matrimonial home include, without prejudice to their generality, the right to do so together with any child of the family.

(2) In subsection (1) above, an "entitled spouse" includes a spouse who is entitled, or permitted by a third party, to occupy a matrimonial home along with an individual who is not the other spouse only if that individual has waived his or her right of occupation in favour of the spouse so entitled or permitted.

(3) If the entitled spouse refuses to allow the non-entitled spouse to exercise the right conferred by subsection (1)(b) above, the non-entitled spouse may exercise that right only with the leave of the court under section 3(3) or (4) of this Act.

(4) In this Act, the rights mentioned in paragraphs (a) and (b) of subsection (1) above are referred to as occupancy rights.

(5) A non-entitled spouse may renounce in writing his or her occupancy rights only—

    (a) in a particular matrimonial home; or

    (b) in a particular property which it is intended by the spouses will become a matrimonial home.

(6) A renunciation under subsection (5) above shall have effect only if at the time of making the renunciation, the non-entitled spouse has sworn or affirmed before a notary public that it was made freely and without coercion of any kind. In this subsection, "notary public" includes any person duly authorised by the law of the country (other than Scotland) in which the swearing or affirmation takes place to administer oaths or receive affirmations in that other country.

[2] (7) Subject to subsection (5), if—

    (a) there has been no cohabitation between an entitled spouse and a non-entitled spouse during a continuous period of two years; and

    (b) during that period the non-entitled spouse has not occupied the matrimonial home,

the non-entitled spouse shall, on the expiry of that period, cease to have occupancy rights in the matrimonial home.

[2] (8) A non-entitled spouse who has ceased to have occupancy rights by virtue of subsection (7) may not apply to the court for an order under section 3(1).

NOTE

   1. Amended by the Law Reform (Miscellaneous Provisions) (Scotland) Act 1985 (c.73), s.13.

2. Inserted by Family Law (Scotland) Act 2006 (asp 2), s.5 subject to transitional provisions specified in SSI 2006/212, art.3.

Subsidiary and consequential rights

[1] **2.**—(1) For the purpose of securing the occupancy rights of a non-entitled spouse, that spouse shall, in relation to a matrimonial home, be entitled without the consent of the entitled spouse—

(a) to make any payment due by the entitled spouse in respect of rent, rates, secured loan instalments, interest or other outgoings (not being outgoings on repairs or improvements);

(b) to perform any other obligation incumbent on the entitled spouse (not being an obligation in respect of non-essential repairs or improvements);

(c) to enforce performance of an obligation by a third party which that third party has undertaken to the entitled spouse to the extent that the entitled spouse may enforce such performance;

(d) to carry out such essential repairs as the entitled spouse may carry out;

(e) to carry out such non-essential repairs or improvements as may be authorised by an order of the court, being such repairs or improvements as the entitled spouse may carry out and which the court considers to be appropriate for the reasonable enjoyment of the occupancy rights;

(f) to take such other steps, for the purpose of protecting the occupancy rights of the non-entitled spouse, as the entitled spouse may take to protect the occupancy rights of the entitled spouse.

(2) Any payment made under subsection (1)(a) above or any obligation performed under subsection (1)(b) above shall have effect in relation to the rights of a third party as if the payment were made or the obligation were performed by the entitled spouse; and the performance of an obligation which has been enforced under subsection (1)(c) above shall have effect as if it had been enforced by the entitled spouse.

(3) Where there is an entitled and a non-entitled spouse, the court, on the application of either of them, may, having regard in particular to the respective financial circumstances of the spouses, make an order apportioning expenditure incurred or to be incurred by either spouse—

(a) without the consent of the other spouse, on any of the items mentioned in paragraphs (a) and (d) of subsection (1) above;

(b) with the consent of the other spouse, on anything relating to a matrimonial home.

(4) Where both spouses are entitled, or permitted by a third party, to occupy a matrimonial home—

(a) either spouse shall be entitled, without the consent of the other spouse, to carry out such non-essential repairs or improvements as may be authorised by an order of the court, being such repairs or improvements as the court considers to be appropriate for the reasonable enjoyment of the occupancy rights;

(b) the court, on the application of either spouse, may, having regard in particular to the respective financial circumstances of the spouses, make an order apportioning expenditure incurred or to be incurred by either spouse, with or without the consent of the other spouse, on anything relating to the matrimonial home.

(5) Where one spouse owns or hires, or is acquiring under a hire-purchase or conditional sale agreement, furniture and plenishings in a matrimonial home—

(a) the other spouse may, without the consent of the first mentioned spouse—

(i) make any payment due by the first mentioned spouse which is necessary, or take any other step which the first mentioned spouse is entitled to take, to secure the possession or use of any such furniture and plenishings (and any such payment shall have effect in relation to the rights of a third party as if it were made by the first mentioned spouse); or

(ii) carry out such essential repairs to the furniture and plenishings as the first mentioned spouse is entitled to carry out;

(b) the court, on the application of either spouse, may, having regard in particular to the respective financial circumstances of the spouses, make an order apportioning expenditure incurred or to be incurred by either spouse—

(i) without the consent of the other spouse, in making payments under a hire, hire-purchase or conditional sale agreement, or in paying interest charges in respect of the furniture and plenishings, or in carrying out essential repairs to the furniture and plenishings; or

(ii) with the consent of the other spouse, on anything relating to the furniture and plenishings.

(6) An order under subsection (3), (4)(b) or (5)(b) above may require one spouse to make a payment to the other spouse in implementation of the apportionment.

(7) Any application under subsection (3), (4)(b) or 5 (b) above shall be made within five years of the date on which any payment in respect of such incurred expenditure was made.

(8) Where—

(a) the entitled spouse is a tenant of a matrimonial home; and

(b) possession thereof is necessary in order to continue the tenancy; and

(c) the entitled spouse abandons such possession,

the tenancy shall be continued by such possession by the non-entitled spouse.

(9) In this section "improvements" includes alterations and enlargement.

Regulation by court of rights of occupancy of matrimonial home

[1] **3.**—(1) Subject to subsection 1(7) of this Act where there is an entitled and a non-entitled spouse, or where both spouses are entitled, or permitted by a third party, to occupy a matrimonial home, either spouse may apply to the court for an order—

(a) declaring the occupancy rights of the applicant spouse;

(b) enforcing the occupancy rights of the applicant spouse;

(c) restricting the occupancy rights of the non-applicant spouse;

(d) regulating the exercise by either spouse of his or her occupancy rights;

(e) protecting the occupancy rights of the applicant spouse in relation to the other spouse.

(2) Where one spouse owns or hires, or is acquiring under a hire-purchase or conditional sale agreement, furniture and plenishings in a matrimonial home, the other spouse, if he or she has occupancy rights in that home, may apply to the court for an order granting to the applicant the possession or use in the matrimonial home of any such furniture and plenishings; but, subject to section 2 of this Act, an order under this subsection shall not prejudice the rights of any third party in relation to the non-performance of any obligation under such hire-purchase or conditional sale agreement.

(3) The court shall grant an application under subsection (1)(a) above if it appears to the court that the application relates to a matrimonial home; and, on an application under any of paragraphs (b) to (e) of subsection (1) or under subsection (2) above, the court may make such order relating

to the application as appears to it to be just and reasonable having regard to all the circumstances of the case including—

    (a) the conduct of the spouses in relation to each other and otherwise;

    (b) the respective needs and financial resources of the spouses;

    (c) the needs of any child of the family;

    (d) the extent (if any) to which—

        (i) the matrimonial home; and

        (ii) in relation only to an order under subsection (2) above, any item of furniture and plenishings referred to in that subsection,

    is used in connection with a trade, business or profession of either spouse; and

    (e) whether the entitled spouse offers or has offered to make available to the non-entitled spouse any suitable alternative accommodation.

(4) Pending the making of an order under subsection (3) above, the court, on the application of either spouse, may make such interim order as it may consider necessary or expedient in relation to—

    (a) the residence of either spouse in the home to which the application relates;

    (b) the personal effects of either spouse or of any child of the family; or

    (c) the furniture and plenishings:

Provided that an interim order may be made only if the non-applicant spouse has been afforded an opportunity of being heard by or represented before the court.

(5) The court shall not make an order under subsection (3) or (4) above if it appears that the effect of the order would be to exclude the non-applicant spouse from the matrimonial home.

(6) If the court makes an order under subsection (3) or (4) above which requires the delivery to one spouse of anything which has been left in or removed from the matrimonial home, it may also grant a warrant authorising a messenger-at-arms or sheriff officer to enter the matrimonial home or other premises occupied by the other spouse and to search for and take possession of the thing required to be delivered, if need be by opening shut and lockfast places, and to deliver the thing in accordance with the said order:

Provided that a warrant granted under this subsection shall be executed only after expiry of the period of a charge, being such period as the court shall specify in the order for delivery.

(7) Where it appears to the court—

    (a) on the application of a non-entitled spouse, that that spouse has suffered a loss of occupancy rights or that the quality of the non-entitled spouse's occupation of a matrimonial home has been impaired; or

    (b) on the application of a spouse who has been given the possession or use of furniture and plenishings by virtue of an order under subsection (3) above, that the applicant has suffered a loss of such possession or use or that the quality of the applicant's possession or use of the furniture and plenishings has been impaired,

in consequence of any act or default on the part of the other spouse which was intended to result in such loss or impairment, it may order that other spouse to pay to the applicant such compensation as the court in the circumstances considers just and reasonable in respect of that loss or impairment.

(8) A spouse may renounce in writing the right to apply under subsection (2) above for the possession or use of any item of furniture and plenishings.

NOTE

1. Amended by Family Law (Scotland) Act 2006 (asp 2), Sch.2.

Exclusion orders

4.—[1] (1) Where there is an entitled and a non-entitled spouse, or where both spouses are entitled, or permitted by a third party, to occupy a matrimonial home, either spouse, whether or not that spouse is in occupation at the time of the application, may apply to the court for an order (in this Act referred to as "an exclusion order") suspending the occupancy rights of the other spouse ("the non-applicant spouse") in a matrimonial home.

(2) Subject to subsection (3) below, the court shall make an exclusion order if it appears to the court that the making of the order is necessary for the protection of the applicant or any child of the family from any conduct or threatened or reasonably apprehended conduct of the non-applicant spouse which is or would be injurious to the physical or mental health of the applicant or child.

(3) The court shall not make an exclusion order if it appears to the court that the making of the order would be unjustified or unreasonable—

    (a) having regard to all the circumstances of the case including the matters specified in paragraphs (a) to (e) of section 3(3) of this Act; and

    (b) where the matrimonial home—

        (i) is or is part of an agricultural holding within the meaning of section 1 of the Agricultural Holdings (Scotland) Act 1949; or

        (ii) is let, or is a home in respect of which possession is given, to the non-applicant spouse or to both spouses by an employer as an incident of employment,

    subject to a requirement that the non-applicant spouse or, as the case may be, both spouses must reside in the matrimonial home, having regard to that requirement and the likely consequences of the exclusion of the non-applicant spouse from the matrimonial home.

(4) In making an exclusion order the court shall, on the application of the applicant spouse,—

    (a) grant a warrant for the summary ejection of the non-applicant spouse from the matrimonial home;

    (b) grant an interdict prohibiting the non-applicant spouse from entering the matrimonial home without the express permission of the applicant;

    (c) grant an interdict prohibiting the removal by the non-applicant spouse, except with the written consent of the applicant or by a further order of the court, of any furniture and plenishings in the matrimonial home;

unless, in relation to paragraph (a) or (c) above, the non-applicant spouse satisfies the court that it is unnecessary for it to grant such a remedy.

(5) In making an exclusion order the court may—

    (a) grant an interdict prohibiting the non-applicant spouse from entering or remaining in a specified area in the vicinity of the matrimonial home;

    (b) where the warrant for the summary ejection of the non-applicant spouse has been granted in his or her absence, give directions as to the preservation of the non-applicant spouse's goods and effects which remain in the matrimonial home;

    (c) on the application of either spouse, make the exclusion order or the warrant or interdict mentioned in paragraph (a), (b) or (c) of subsection (4) above or paragraph (a) of this subsection subject to such terms and conditions as the court may prescribe;

    (d) on application as aforesaid, make such other order as it may consider necessary for the proper enforcement of an order made under subsection (4) above or paragraph (a), (b) or (c) of this subsection.

(6) Pending the making of an exclusion order, the court may, on the application of the applicant spouse, make an interim order suspending the occupancy rights of the non-applicant spouse in the matrimonial home to which the application for the exclusion order relates; and subsections (4) and (5) above shall apply to such interim order as they apply to an exclusion order:

Provided that an interim order may be made only if the non-applicant spouse has been afforded an opportunity of being heard by or represented before the court.

(7) Without prejudice to subsections (1) and (6) above, where both spouses are entitled, or permitted by a third party, to occupy a matrimonial home, it shall be incompetent for one spouse to bring an action of ejection from the matrimonial home against the other spouse.

NOTE
1. As amended by the Law Reform (Miscellaneous Provisions) (Scotland) Act 1985 (c.73), s.13(5).

Duration of orders under sections 3 and 4

5.—(1) The court may, on the application of either spouse, vary or recall any order made by it under section 3 or 4 of this Act, but, subject to subsection (2) below, any such order shall, unless previously so varied or recalled, cease to have effect—

(a) on the termination of the marriage; or
(b) subject to section 6(1) of this Act, where there is an entitled and a non-entitled spouse, on the entitled spouse ceasing to be an entitled spouse in respect of the matrimonial home to which the order relates; or
(c) where both spouses are entitled, or permitted by a third party, to occupy the matrimonial home, on both spouses ceasing to be so entitled or permitted.

(2) Without prejudice to the generality of subsection (1) above, an order under section 3(3) or (4) of this Act which grants the possession or use of furniture and plenishings shall cease to have effect if the furniture and plenishings cease to be permitted by a third party to be retained in the matrimonial home.

Occupancy rights in relation to dealings with third parties

Continued exercise of occupancy rights after dealing

6.—(1) Subject to subsection (3) below—

(a) the continued exercise of the rights conferred on a non-entitled spouse by the provisions of this Act in respect of a matrimonial home shall not be prejudiced by reason only of any dealing of the entitled spouse relating to that home; and
(b) a third party shall not by reason only of such a dealing be entitled to occupy that matrimonial home or any part of it.

[1](1A) The occupancy rights of a non-entitled spouse in relation to a matrimonial home shall not be exercisable in relation to the home where, following a dealing of the entitled spouse relating to the home—

(a) a person acquires the home, or an interest in it, in good faith and for value from a person other than the person who is or, as the case may be, was the entitled spouse; or
(b) a person derives title to the home from a person who acquired title as mentioned in paragraph (a).

(2) In this section and section 7 of this Act—

"dealing" includes the grant of a heritable security and the creation of a trust but does not include a conveyance under section 80 of the Lands Clauses Consolidation (Scotland) Act 1845;

"entitled spouse" does not include a spouse who, apart from the provisions of this Act,—

(a) is permitted by a third party to occupy a matrimonial home; or

(b) is entitled to occupy a matrimonial home along with an individual who is not the other spouse, whether or not that individual has waived his or her right of occupation in favour of the spouse so entitled;

and "non-entitled spouse" shall be construed accordingly.

(3) This section shall not apply in any case where—

(a) the non-entitled spouse in writing either—

    (i) consents or has consented to the dealing, and any consent shall be in such form as the Secretary of State may, by regulations made by statutory instrument, prescribe; or

    (ii) renounces or has renounced his or her occupancy rights in relation to the matrimonial home or property to which the dealing relates;

(b) the court has made an order under section 7 of this Act dispensing with the consent of the non-entitled spouse to the dealing;

(c) the dealing occurred, or implements, a binding obligation entered into by the entitled spouse before his or her marriage to the non-entitled spouse;

(d) the dealing occurred, or implements, a binding obligation entered into before the commencement of this Act;

[2](e) the dealing comprises a transfer for value to a third party who has acted in good faith, if there is produced to the third party by the transferor—

    (i) a written declaration signed by the transferor, or a person acting on behalf of the transferor under a power of attorney or as a guardian (within the meaning of the Adults with Incapacity (Scotland) Act 2000 (asp 4)), that the subjects of the transfer are not, or were not at the time of the dealing, a matrimonial home in relation to which a spouse of the transferor has or had occupancy rights; or

    (ii) a renunciation of occupancy rights or consent to the dealing which bears to have been properly made or given by the non-entitled spouse or a person acting on behalf of the non-entitled spouse under a power of attorney or as a guardian (within the meaning of the Adults with Incapacity (Scotland) Act 2000 (asp 4)).

[3](f) the entitled spouse has permanently ceased to be entitled to occupy the matrimonial home, and at any time thereafter a continuous period of 2 years has elapsed during which the non-entitled spouse has not occupied the matrimonial home.

(4) *[Amends the Land Registration (Scotland) Act 1979, ss.6(4), 9(4) and 28.]*

NOTE

1. Inserted by Family Law (Scotland) Act 2006 (asp 2), s.6.

2. As amended by the Law Reform (Miscellaneous Provisions) (Scotland) Act 1985 (c.73), s.13(6), with effect from 30th November 1985, by the Law Reform (Miscellaneous Provisions) (Scotland) Act 1990 (c.40), Sch.8, para.31(1) and Sch.9 and by the Family Law (Scotland) Act 2006 (asp 2), s.6.

3. Amended by Family Law (Scotland) Act 2006 (asp 2), s.6 subject to transitional provisions (SSI 2006/212).

Dispensation by court with spouse's consent to dealing

7.—[1] (1) Subject to subsections (1A) and (1D) below, the court may, on the application of an entitled spouse or any other person having an interest, make an order dispensing with the consent of a non-entitled spouse to a dealing which has taken place or a proposed dealing, if—

    (a) such consent is unreasonably withheld;

    (b) such consent cannot be given by reason of physical or mental disability;

    (c) the non-entitled spouse cannot be found after reasonable steps have been taken to trace him or her; or

[2] (d) the non-entitled spouse is under legal disability by reason of nonage.

[3] (1A) Subsection (1B) applies if, in relation to a proposed sale—

    (a) negotiations with a third party have not begun; or

    (b) negotiations have begun but a price has not been agreed.

(1B) An order under subsection (1) dispensing with consent may be made only if—

    (a) the price agreed for the sale is no less than such amount as the court specifies in the order; and

    (b) the contract for the sale is concluded before the expiry of such period as may be so specified.

(1C) Subsection (1D) applies if the proposed dealing is the grant of a heritable security.

(1D) An order under subsection (1) dispensing with consent may be made only if—

    (a) the heritable security is granted for a loan of no more than such amount as the court specifies in the order; and

    (b) the security is executed before the expiry of such period as may be so specified.

(2) For the purposes of subsection (1)(a) above, a non-entitled spouse shall have unreasonably withheld consent to a dealing which has taken place or a proposed dealing, where it appears to the court—

    (a) that the non-entitled spouse has led the entitled spouse to believe that he or she would consent to the dealing and that the non-entitled spouse would not be prejudiced by any change in the circumstances of the case since such apparent consent was given; or

    (b) that the entitled spouse has, having taken all reasonable steps to do so, been unable to obtain an answer to a request for consent.

(3) The court, in considering whether to make an order under subsection (1) above, shall have regard to all the circumstances of the case including the matters specified in paragraphs (a) to (e) of section 3(3) of this Act.

[3] (3A) If the court refuses an application for an order under subsection (1), it may make an order requiring a non-entitled spouse who is or becomes the occupier of the matrimonial home—

    (a) to make such payments to the owner of the home in respect of that spouse's occupation of it as may be specified in the order;

    (b) to comply with such other conditions relating to that spouse's occupation of the matrimonial home as may be so specified.

(4) Where—

    (a) an application is made for an order under this section; and

    (b) an action is or has been raised by a non-entitled spouse to enforce occupancy rights,

the action shall be sisted until the conclusion of the proceedings on the application.

(5) *[Repealed by the Family Law (Scotland) Act 1985 (c.37), Sch.2.]*

NOTE
  1. Amended by Family Law (Scotland) Act 2006 (asp 2), s.7.

2. Amended by the Age of Legal Capacity (Scotland) Act 1991 (c.50), s.10 and Sch.1, para.37.
3. Inserted by Family Law (Scotland) Act 2006 (asp 2), s.7.

Interests of heritable creditors

[1] **8.**—(1) The rights of a third party with an interest in the matrimonial home as a creditor under a secured loan in relation to the non-performance of any obligation under the loan shall not be prejudiced by reason only of the occupancy rights of the non-entitled spouse; but where a non-entitled spouse has or obtains occupation of a matrimonial home and—

(a) the entitled spouse is not in occupation; and
(b) there is a third party with such an interest in the matrimonial home,

the court may, on the application of the third party, make an order requiring the non-entitled spouse to make any payment due by the entitled spouse in respect of the loan.

[2] (2) This section shall not apply to secured loans in respect of which the security was granted prior to the commencement of section 13 of the Law Reform (Miscellaneous Provisions) (Scotland) Act 1985 unless the third party in granting the secured loan acted in good faith and there was produced to the third party by the entitled spouse—

(a) an affidavit sworn or affirmed by the entitled spouse declaring that there is no non-entitled spouse; or
(b) a renunciation of occupancy rights or consent to the taking of the loan which bears to have been properly made or given by the non-entitled spouse.

[3] (2A) This section shall not apply to secured loans in respect of which the security was granted after the commencement of section 13 of the Law Reform (Miscellaneous Provisions) (Scotland) Act 1985 unless the third party in granting the secured loan acted in good faith and there was produced to the third party by the grantor—

[4] (a) a written declaration signed by the grantor declaring that the security subjects are not or were not at the time of the granting of the security a matrimonial home in relation to which a spouse of the grantor has or had occupancy rights; or
(b) a renunciation of occupancy rights or consent to the granting of the security which bears to have been properly made or given by the non-entitled spouse.

[3] (2B) For the purposes of subsections (2) and (2A) above, the time of granting a security, in the case of a heritable security, is the date of delivery of the deed creating the security.

NOTE

1. As amended by the Law Reform (Miscellaneous Provisions) (Scotland) Act 1990 (c.40), Sch.8, para.31(2) and Sch.9.
2. As amended by the Law Reform (Miscellaneous Provisions) (Scotland) Act 1985 (c.73), s.13(7).
3. Inserted by the Law Reform (Miscellaneous Provisions) (Scotland) Act 1985 (c.73), s.13(8).
4. As amended by the Family Law (Scotland) Act 2006 (Consequential Modifications) Order (SSI 2006/384), art.5.

Provisions where both spouses have title

9.—(1) Subject to subsection (2) below, where, apart from the provisions of this Act, both spouses are entitled to occupy a matrimonial home—

  (a) the rights in that home of one spouse shall not be prejudiced by reason only of any dealing of the other spouse; and

  (b) a third party shall not by reason only of such a dealing be entitled to occupy that matrimonial home or any part of it.

(2) The definition of "dealing" in section 6(2) of this Act and sections 6(3) and 7 of this Act shall apply for the purposes of subsection (1) above as they apply for the purposes of section 6(1) of this Act subject to the following modifications—

  (a) any reference to the entitled spouse and to the non-entitled spouse shall be construed as a reference to a spouse who has entered into, or as the case may be, proposes to enter into a dealing and to the other spouse respectively; and

  (b) in paragraph (b) of section 7(4) the reference to occupancy rights shall be construed as a reference to any rights in the matrimonial home.

Reckoning of non-cohabitation periods in sections 1 and 6

Effect of court action under section 3, 4 or 5 on reckoning of periods in sections 1 and 6

[1]**9A.**—(1) Subsection (2) applies where an application is made under section 3(1), 4(1) or 5(1) of this Act.

(2) In calculating the period of two years mentioned in section 1(7)(a) or 6(3)(f) of this Act, no account shall be taken of the period mentioned in subsection (3) below.

(3) The period is the period beginning with the date on which the application is made and—

  (a) in the case of an application under section 3(1) or 4(1) of this Act, ending on the date on which—

    (i) an order under section 3(3) or, as the case may be, 4(2) of this Act is made; or

    (ii) the application is otherwise finally determined or abandoned;

  (b) in the case of an application under section 5(1) of this Act, ending on the date on which—

    (i) the order under section 3(3) or, as the case may be, 4(2) is varied or recalled; or

    (ii) the application is otherwise finally determined or abandoned.

NOTE
  1. Inserted by Family Law (Scotland) Act 2006 (asp 2), s.8 subject to transitional provisions (SSI 2006/212).

Protection of rights of spouse against arrangements intended to defeat them

10. *[Repealed by the Bankruptcy (Scotland) Act 1985 (c.66), Sch.8.]*

Poinding

[1]**11.** Where an attachment has been executed of furniture and plenishings of which the debtor's spouse has the possession or use by virtue of an order under section 3(3) or (4) of this Act, the sheriff, on the application of that spouse within 40 days of the date of execution of the attachment, may—

  (a) declare that the attachment is null; or

  (b) make such order as he thinks appropriate to protect such possession or use by that spouse,

if he is satisfied that the purpose of the diligence was wholly or mainly to prevent such possession or use.

NOTE
1. Applied by the Family Law (Scotland) Act 1985 (c.37), s.14(5). As amended by the Debt Arrangement and Attachment (Scotland) Act 2002 (asp 17), Sch.3, para.13.

Adjudication

[1] **12.**—(1) Where a matrimonial home of which there is an entitled spouse and a non-entitled spouse is adjudged, the Court of Session, on the application of the non-entitled spouse within 40 days of the date of the decree of adjudication, may—
  (a) order the reduction of the decree; or
  (b) make such order as it thinks appropriate to protect the occupancy rights of the non-entitled spouse,
if it is satisfied that the purpose of the diligence was wholly or mainly to defeat the occupancy rights of the non-entitled spouse.

(2) In this section, "entitled spouse" and "non-entitled spouse" have the same meanings respectively as in section 6(2) of this Act.

NOTE
1. Applied by the Family Law (Scotland) Act 1985 (c.37), s.14(5).

Transfer of tenancy

Transfer of tenancy

13.—(1) The court may, on the application of a non-entitled spouse, make an order transferring the tenancy of a matrimonial home to that spouse and providing, subject to subsection (11) below, for the payment by the non-entitled spouse to the entitled spouse of such compensation as seems just and reasonable in all the circumstances of the case.

[1] (2) In an action—
  (a) for divorce, the Court of Session or a sheriff;
  (b) for nullity of marriage, the Court of Session,
may, on granting decree or within such period as the court may specify on granting decree, make an order granting an application under subsection (1) above.

(3) In determining whether to grant an application under subsection (1) above, the court shall have regard to all the circumstances of the case including the matters specified in paragraphs (a) to (e) of section 3(3) of this Act and the suitability of the applicant to become the tenant and the applicant's capacity to perform the obligations under the lease of the matrimonial home.

(4) The non-entitled spouse shall serve a copy of an application under subsection (1) above on the landlord and, before making an order under subsection (1) above, the court shall give the landlord an opportunity of being heard by it.

(5) On the making of an order granting an application under subsection (1) above, the tenancy shall vest in the non-entitled spouse without intimation to the landlord, subject to all the liabilities under the lease (other than any arrears of rent for the period before the making of the order, which shall remain the liability of the original entitled spouse).

(6) The clerk of court shall notify the landlord of the making of an order granting an application under subsection (1) above.

(7) It shall not be competent for a non-entitled spouse to apply for an order under subsection (1) above where the matrimonial home—
  (a) is let to the entitled spouse by his or her employer as an incident of employment, and the lease is subject to a requirement that the entitled spouse must reside therein;
  (b) is or is part of an agricultural holding;

  (c) is on or pertains to a croft or the subject of a cottar or the holding of a landholder or a statutory small tenant;

  (d) is let on a long lease;

  (e) is part of the tenancy land of a tenant-at-will.

[2] (8) In subsection (6) above—

"agricultural lease" means a lease constituting a 1991 Act tenancy within the meaning of the Agricultural Holdings (Scotland) Act 2003 (asp 11) or a lease constituting a limited duration tenancy or a short limited duration tenancy (within the meaning of that Act);

"cottar" has the same meaning as in section 28(4) of the Crofters (Scotland) Act 1955;

"croft" has the same meaning as in the Crofters (Scotland) Act 1955;

"holding", in relation to a landholder and a statutory small tenant, "landholder" and "statutory small tenant" have the same meanings respectively as in sections 2(1), 2(2) and 32(1) of the Small Landholders (Scotland) Act 1911;

"long lease" has the same meaning as in section 28(1) of the Land Registration (Scotland) Act 1979;

"tenant-at-will" has the same meaning as in section 20(8) of the Land Registration (Scotland) Act 1979.

(9) Where both spouses are joint or common tenants of a matrimonial home, the court may, on the application of one of the spouses, make an order vesting the tenancy in that spouse solely and providing, subject to subsection (11) below, for the payment by the applicant to the other spouse of such compensation as seems just and reasonable in the circumstances of the case.

(10) Subsections (2) to (8) above shall apply for the purposes of an order under subsection (9) above as they apply for the purposes of an order under subsection (1) above subject to the following modifications—

  (a) in subsection (3) for the word "tenant" there shall be substituted the words "sole tenant";

  (b) in subsection (4) for the words "non-entitled" there should be substituted the word "applicant";

  (c) in subsection (5) for the words "non-entitled" and "liability of the original entitled spouse" there shall be substituted respectively the words "applicant" and "joint and several liability of both spouses";

  (d) in subsection (7)—

    (i) for the words "a non-entitled" there shall be substituted the words "an applicant";

    (ii) for paragraph (a) there shall be substituted the following paragraph—

      "(a) is let to both spouses by their employer as an incident of employment, and the lease is subject to a requirement that both spouses must reside there;";

    (iii) paragraphs (c) and (e) shall be omitted.

[3] (11) Where the matrimonial home is a Scottish secure tenancy within the meaning of the Housing (Scotland) Act 2001 (asp 10), no account shall be taken, in assessing the amount of any compensation to be awarded under subsection (1) or (9) above, of the loss, by virtue of the transfer of the tenancy of the home, of a right to purchase the home under Part III of the Housing (Scotland) Act 1987 (c.26).

(12) *[Amends the Housing (Scotland) Act 1987, s.48(1) and Sch.3, Pt I.]*

NOTE

  1. As amended by the Family Law (Scotland) Act 1985 (c.37), Sch.1, para.11.

  2. As amended by the Agricultural Holdings (Scotland) Act 2003 (asp 11), Sch.1.

3. As amended by the Housing (Scotland) Act 1987 (c.26), Sch.23, para.26 and by the Housing (Scotland) Act 2001 (asp 10), Sch.10, para.7.
4. Prospectively amended by the Agricultural Holdings (Scotland) Act 2003 (asp 11), Sch.1, para.5.

Matrimonial interdicts

Interdict competent where spouses live together

14.—(1) It shall not be incompetent for the court to entertain an application by a spouse for a matrimonial interdict by reason only that the spouses are living together as man and wife.

(2) In this section of this Act—

"matrimonial interdict" means an interdict including an interim interdict which—

(a) restrains or prohibits any conduct of one spouse towards the other spouse or a child of the family, or

[1](b) subject to subsection (3), prohibits a spouse from entering or remaining in—

(i) a matrimonial home;

(ii) any other residence occupied by the applicant spouse;

(iii) any place of work of the applicant spouse;

(iv) any school attended by a child in the permanent or temporary care of the applicant spouse.

[2](3) Subsection (4) applies if in relation to a matrimonial home the non-applicant spouse—

(a) is an entitled spouse; or

(b) has occupancy rights.

[2](4) Except where subsection (5) applies, the court may not grant a matrimonial interdict prohibiting the non-applicant spouse from entering or remaining in the matrimonial home.

[2](5) This subsection applies if—

(a) the interdict is ancillary to an exclusion order; or

(b) by virtue of section 1(3), the court refuses leave to exercise occupancy rights.

[2](6) In this section and in sections 15 to 17, "applicant spouse" means the spouse who has applied for the interdict; and "non-applicant spouse" shall be construed accordingly.

NOTE

1. Substituted by Family Law (Scotland) Act 2006 (asp 2), s.10.
2. Inserted by Family Law (Scotland) Act 2006 (asp 2), s.10.

Attachment of powers of arrest to matrimonial interdicts

15. [*Repealed by Family Law (Scotland) Act 2006 (asp 2), Sch.3 subject to savings specified in SSI 2006/212, art.13.*]

Police powers after arrest

16. [*Repealed by Family Law (Scotland) Act 2006 (asp 2), Sch.3 subject to savings specified in SSI 2006/212, art.13.*]

Procedure after arrest

17. [*Repealed by Family Law (Scotland) Act 2006 (asp 2), Sch.3 subject to savings specified in SSI 2006/212, art.13.*]

Cohabiting couples

Occupancy rights of cohabiting couples

18.—[1](1) If a man and a woman are living with each other as if they were man and wife or two persons of the same sex are living together as if they were civil partners (in either case "a cohabiting couple") in a house which, apart from the provisions of this section—

(a) one of them (an "entitled partner") is entitled, or permitted by a third party, to occupy; and

(b) the other (a "non-entitled partner") is not so entitled or permitted to occupy,

the court may, on the application of the non-entitled partner, if it appears that the entitled partner and the non-entitled partner are a cohabiting couple in that house, grant occupancy rights therein to the applicant for such period, not exceeding six months, as the court may specify:

Provided that the court may extend the said period for a further period or periods, no such period exceeding 6 months.

(2) In determining whether for the purpose of subsection (1) above two persons are a cohabiting couple the court shall have regard to all the circumstances of the case including—

(a) the time for which it appears they have been living together; and

(b) whether there is any child—

(i) of whom they are the parents; or

(ii) who they have treated as a child of theirs.

(3) While an order granting an application under subsection (1) above or an extension of such an order is in force, or where both partners of a cohabiting couple are entitled, or permitted by a third party, to occupy the house where they are cohabiting, the following provisions of this Act shall subject to any necessary modifications—

(a) apply to the cohabiting couple as they apply to parties to a marriage; and

[2] (b) have effect in relation to any child residing with the cohabiting couple as they have effect in relation to a child of the family,

section 2;

section 3, except subsection (1)(a);

section 4;

in section 5(1), the words from the beginning to "Act" where it first occurs;

section 13;

and

section 22,

and any reference in these provisions to a matrimonial home shall be construed as a reference to a house.

(4) Any order under section 3 or 4 of this Act as applied to a cohabiting couple by subsection (3) above shall have effect—

(a) if one of them is a non-entitled partner, for such a period, not exceeding the period or periods which from time to time may be specified in any order under subsection (1) above for which occupancy rights have been granted under that subsection, as may be specified in the order;

(b) if they are both entitled, or permitted by a third party, to occupy the house, until a further order of the court.

(5) Nothing in this section shall prejudice the rights of any third party having an interest in the house referred to in subsection (1) above.

[3] (6) In this section—

"house" includes a caravan, houseboat or other structure in which the couple are cohabiting and any garden or other ground or building attached to, and usually occupied with, or otherwise required for the amenity or convenience of, the house, caravan, houseboat or other structure;

"occupancy rights" means the following rights of a non-entitled partner—

(a) if in occupation, a right to continue to occupy the house;

141

(b) if not in occupation, a right to enter into and occupy the house;

and, without prejudice to the generality of these rights, includes the right to continue to occupy or, as the case may be, to enter and occupy the house together with any child residing with the cohabiting couple;

"entitled partner" includes a partner who is entitled, or permitted by a third party, to occupy the house along with an individual who is not the other partner only if that individual has waived his or her right of occupation in favour of the partner so entitled or permitted.

NOTE

1. Amended by the Law Reform (Miscellaneous Provisions) (Scotland) Act 1985 (c.73), s.13(9) and the Family Law (Scotland) Act 2006 (asp 2), s.34.
2. Amended by Family Law (Scotland) Act 2006 (asp 2), s.31.
3. Amended by the Law Reform (Miscellaneous Provisions) (Scotland) Act 1985 (c.73), s.13(9).

Domestic interdicts

Meaning of "domestic interdict"

[1]**18A.**—(1) In section 18B, "domestic interdict" means—

(a) an interdict granted on the application of a person ("A") who is (or was) living with another person ("B") as if they were husband and wife against B for any of the purposes mentioned in subsection (2); or

(b) an interdict granted on the application of a person ("C") who is (or was) living with another person ("D") as if they were civil partners against D for any of the purposes mentioned in subsection (2).

(2) Those purposes are—

(a) restraining or prohibiting such conduct of the defender towards—
    (i) the pursuer; or
    (ii) any child in the permanent or temporary care of the pursuer, as the court may specify;

(b) prohibiting the defender from entering or remaining in—
    (i) a family home occupied by the pursuer and the defender;
    (ii) any other residence occupied by the pursuer;
    (iii) any place of work of the pursuer;
    (iv) any school attended by a child in the permanent or temporary care of the pursuer.

(3) In this section and in section 18B—

"family home" means, subject to subsection (4), any house, caravan, houseboat or other structure which has been provided or has been made available by the pursuer or the defender (or both of them) as (or has become) a family residence for them and includes any garden or other ground or building usually occupied with, or otherwise required for the amenity or convenience of, the house, caravan, houseboat or other structure; but does not include a residence provided or made available by any person for the pursuer or, as the case may be, the defender to reside in (whether or not with any child of the pursuer and the defender) separately from the defender or, as the case may be, the pursuer; and

"interdict" includes interim interdict.

(4) If the tenancy of a family home is transferred from a pursuer to a defender (or, as the case may be, from a defender to a pursuer) by agreement or under any enactment, the home shall, on such transfer, cease to be a family home.

(5) In subsection (3), "child of the pursuer and the defender" includes any child or grandchild of the pursuer or the defender, and any person

142

who has been brought up or treated by the pursuer or the defender as if the person were a child of the pursuer or, as the case may be, the defender, whatever the age of such a child, grandchild or person.

NOTE
    1. Inserted by Family Law (Scotland) Act 2006 (asp 2), s.31.

Domestic interdicts: further provision

[1] **18B.**—(1) Subsection (2) applies if the defender—
(a) is entitled to occupy a family home;
(b) is permitted by a third party to occupy it; or
(c) has, by virtue of section 18(1), occupancy rights in it.
(2) Except where subsection (3) applies, the court may not grant a domestic interdict prohibiting the defender from entering or remaining in the family home.
(3) This subsection applies if—
(a) the interdict is ancillary to an exclusion order; or
(b) an order under section 18(1) granting or extending occupancy rights is recalled.

NOTE
    1. Inserted by Family Law (Scotland) Act 2006 (asp 2), s.31.

Miscellaneous and General

Rights of occupancy in relation to division and sale

19. Where a spouse brings an action for the division and sale of a matrimonial home which the spouses own in common, the court, after having regard to all the circumstances of the case including—
(a) the matters specified in paragraphs (a) to (d) of section 3(3) of this Act; and
(b) whether the spouse bringing the action offers or has offered to make available to the other spouse any suitable alternative accommodation,
may refuse to grant decree in that action or may postpone the granting of decree for such period as it may consider reasonable in the circumstances or may grant decree subject to such conditions as it may prescribe.

Spouse's consent in relation to calling up of standard securities over matrimonial homes

20. [*Amends the Conveyancing and Feudal Reform (Scotland) Act 1970, s.19(10).*]

Procedural provision

21. [*Repealed by Family Law (Scotland) Act 2006 (asp 2), Sch.2.*]

Interpretation

[1] **22.**—(1) In this Act—
    "caravan" mean a caravan which is mobile or affixed to the land;
    [2]"child of the family" includes any child or grandchild of either spouse, and any person who has been brought up or treated by either spouse as if he or she were a child of that spouse, whatever the age of such a child, grandchild or person may be;
    "the court" means the Court of Session or the sheriff;
    "furniture and plenishings" means any article situated in a matrimonial home which—

(a) is owned or hired by either spouse or is being acquired by either spouse under a hire-purchase agreement or conditional sale agreement; and

(b) is reasonably necessary to enable the home to be used as a family residence,

but does not include any vehicle, caravan or houseboat, or such other structure as is mentioned in the definition of "matrimonial home";

"matrimonial home" means subject to subsection (2), any house, caravan, houseboat or other structure which has been provided or has been made available by one or both of the spouses as, or has become, a family residence and includes any garden or other ground or building usually occupied with, or otherwise required for the amenity or convenience of, the house, caravan, houseboat or other structure but does not include a residence provided or made available by a person for one spouse to reside in, whether with any child of the family or not, separately from the other spouse;

"occupancy rights" has, subject to section 18(6) of this Act, the meaning assigned by section 1(4) of this Act;

"the sheriff" includes the sheriff having jurisdiction in the district where the matrimonial home is situated;

"tenant" includes sub-tenant and a statutory tenant as defined in section 3 of the Rent (Scotland) Act 1984 and a statutory assured tenant as defined in section 16(1) of the Housing (Scotland) Act 1988 and "tenancy" shall be construed accordingly;

"entitled spouse" and "non-entitled spouse", subject to sections 6(2) and 12(2) of this Act, have the meanings respectively assigned to them by section 1 of this Act.

(2) If—

(a) the tenancy of a matrimonial home is transferred from one spouse to the other by agreement or under any enactment; and

(b) following the transfer, the spouse to whom the tenancy was transferred occupies the home but the other spouse does not,

the home shall, on such transfer, cease to be a matrimonial home.

NOTE

1. As amended by the Law Reform (Miscellaneous Provisions) (Scotland) Act 1985 (c.73), s.13(10), and the Housing (Scotland) Act 1988 (c.43), Sch.9, para.3 and the Family (Scotland) Act 2006 (asp 2), Sch.2.

2. As amended by the Children (Scotland) Act 1995 (c.36), s.105(4) and Sch.4, para.30.

Short title, commencement and extent

23.—(1) This Act may be cited as the Matrimonial Homes (Family Protection) (Scotland) Act 1981.

[1] (2) This Act (except this section) shall come into operation on such day as the Secretary of State may by order made by statutory instrument appoint, and different days may be so appointed for different provisions and for different purposes.

(3) This Act extends to Scotland only.

[1] MARRIAGE (SCOTLAND) ACT 1977

(1977, c.15)

An Act to make new provision for Scotland as respects the law relating to the constitution of marriage, and for connected purposes.

NOTE
1. As amended by the Marriage (Prohibited Degrees of Relationship) Act 1986 (c.16), Sch.2.

Minimum age for marriage

Minimum age for marriage

1.—(1) No person domiciled in Scotland may marry before he attains the age of 16.

(2) A marriage solemnised in Scotland between persons either of whom is under the age of 16 shall be void.

Marriage of related persons

2.—[1] (1) Subject to subsection (1A) below, a marriage between a man and any woman related to him in a degree specified in column 1 of Schedule 1 to this Act, or between a woman and any man related to her in a degree specified in column 2 of that Schedule shall be void if solemnised—

(a) in Scotland; or

(b) at a time when either party is domiciled in Scotland.

[2] (1A) Subsection (1) above does not apply to a marriage between a man and any woman related to him in a degree specified in column 1 of paragraph 2 of Schedule 1 to this Act, or between a woman and any man related to her in a degree specified in column 2 of that paragraph, if—

(a) both parties have attained the age of 21 at the time of the marriage; and

(b) the younger party has not at any time before attaining the age of 18 lived in the same household as the other party and been treated by the other party as a child of his family.

(1B) [*Repealed by Family Law (Scotland) Act 2006 (asp 2), s.1.*]

(2) For the purposes of this section a degree of relationship exists—

(a) in the case of a degree specified in paragraph 1 of Schedule 1 to this Act, whether it is of the full blood or the half blood;

(b) [*Repealed by the Law Reform (Parent and Child) (Scotland) Act 1986 (c.55), Sch.2.*]

(3) Where a person is related to another person in a degree not specified in Schedule 1 to this Act that degree of relationship shall not, in Scots law, bar a valid marriage between them; but this subsection is without prejudice to—

(a) the effect which a degree of relationship not so specified may have under the provisions of a system of law other than Scots law in a case where such provisions apply as the law of the place of celebration of a marriage or as the law of a person's domicile; or

(b) any rule of law that a marriage may not be contracted between persons either of whom is married to a third person.

[3] (4) References in this section and in Schedule 1 to this Act to relationships and degrees of relationship shall be construed in accordance with section 1(1) of the Law Reform (Parent and Child) (Scotland) Act 1986.

[2] (5) Where the parties to an intended marriage are related in a degree specified in paragraph 2 of Schedule 1 to this Act, either party may (whether or not an objection to the marriage has been submitted in accordance with section 5(1) of this Act) apply to the Court of Session for a declarator that the conditions specified in paragraphs (a) and (b) of subsection (1A) above are fulfilled in relation to the intended marriage.

[3] (6) Subsections (1A) and (1B) above and paragraphs 2 and 2A of Schedule 1 to this Act have effect subject to the following modifications in

the case of a party to a marriage whose gender has become the acquired gender under the Gender Recognition Act 2004 ("the relevant person").

(7) Any reference in those provisions to a former wife or former husband of the relevant person includes (respectively) any former husband or former wife of the relevant person.

(8) [*Repealed by the Family Law (Scotland) Act 2006 (Consequential Modifications) Order (SSI 2006/384), art.4(b).*]

NOTE
1. As amended by the Marriage (Prohibited Degrees of Relationship) Act 1986 (c.16), Sch.2, para.2 and by Family Law (Scotland) Act 2006 (asp 2), s.1.
2. Inserted by the Marriage (Prohibited Degrees of Relationship) Act 1986 (c.16), Sch.2, para.2.
3. Inserted by the Law Reform (Parent and Child) (Scotland) Act 1986 (c.9), Sch.1, para.17.
4. Inserted by the Gender Recognition Act 2004 (c.7), Sch.4, para.7.

. . .

Void marriages

Grounds on which marriage void

20A.—(1) Where subsection (2) or (3) applies in relation to a marriage solemnised in Scotland, the marriage shall be void.

(2) This subsection applies if at the time of the marriage ceremony a party to the marriage who was capable of consenting to the marriage purported to give consent but did so by reason only of duress or error.

(3) This subsection applies if at the time of the marriage ceremony a party to the marriage was incapable of—
   (a) understanding the nature of marriage; and
   (b) consenting to the marriage.

(4) If a party to a marriage purported to give consent to the marriage other than by reason only of duress or error, the marriage shall not be void by reason only of that party's having tacitly withheld consent to the marriage at the time when it was solemnised.

(5) In this section "error" means—
   (a) error as to the nature of the ceremony; or
   (b) a mistaken belief held by a person ("A") that the other party at the ceremony with whom A purported to enter into a marriage was the person whom A had agreed to marry.

DIVORCE (SCOTLAND) ACT 1976

(1976, c.39)

An Act to amend the law of Scotland relating to divorce and separation; to facilitate reconciliation of the parties in consistorial causes; to amend the law as to the power of the court to make orders relating to financial provision arising out of divorce and to settlements and other dealings by a party to the marriage, and as to the power of the court to award aliment to spouses in actions for aliment; to abolish the oath of calumny; and for purposes connected with the matters aforesaid.

[July 22, 1976]

Divorce

Grounds of Divorce

¹**1.**—(1) In an action for divorce the court may grant decree of divorce if, but only if, it is established in accordance with the following provisions of this Act that

(a) the marriage has broken down irretrievably,

or

(b) an interim gender recognition certificate under the Gender Recognition Act 2004 has, after the date of the marriage, been issued to either party to the marriage.

References in this Act (other than in section 5(1) and 13 of this Act) to an action for divorce are to be construed as references to such an action brought after the commencement of this Act.

NOTE

1. As amended by the Gender Recognition Act 2004 (c.7), Sch.2, para.6.

(2) The irretrievable breakdown of a marriage shall, subject to the following provisions of this Act, be taken to be established in an action for divorce if—

(a) since the date of the marriage the defender has committed adultery; or

(b) since the date of the marriage the defender has at any time behaved (whether or not as a result of mental abnormality and whether such behaviour has been active or passive) in such a way that the pursuer cannot reasonably be expected to cohabit with the defender; or

(c) [*Repealed by Family Law (Scotland) Act 2006 (asp 2), s.12.*]

¹(d) there has been no cohabitation between the parties at any time during a continuous period of one year after the date of the marriage and immediately preceding the bringing of the action and the defender consents to the granting of decree of divorce; or

(e) there has been no cohabitation between the parties at any time during a continuous period of two years after the date of the marriage and immediately preceding the bringing of the action.

(3) The irretrievable breakdown of a marriage shall not be taken to be established in an action for divorce by reason of subsection (2)(a) of this section if the adultery mentioned in the said subsection (2)(a) has been connived at in such a way as to raise the defence of *lenocinium* or has been condoned by the pursuer's cohabitation with the defender in the knowledge or belief that the defender has committed the adultery.

(4) Provision shall be made by act of sederunt—

(a) for the purpose of ensuring that, where in an action for divorce to which subsection (2)(d) of this section relates the defender consents to the granting of decree, he has been given such information as will enable him to understand—

(i) the consequences to him of his consenting as aforesaid; and

(ii) the steps which he must take to indicate his consent; and

(b) prescribing the manner in which the defender in such an action shall indicate his consent, and any withdrawal of such consent, to the granting of decree;

and where the defender has indicated (and not withdrawn) his consent in the prescribed manner, such indication shall be sufficient evidence of such consent.

(5) [*Repealed by Family Law (Scotland) Act 2006 (asp 2), s.12.*]

(6) In an action for divorce the standard of proof required to establish the ground of the action shall be on balance of probability.

NOTE

  1.   Amended by Family Law (Scotland) Act 2006 (asp 2), s.11.

Encouragement of reconciliation

2.—(1) At any time before granting decree under paragraph (a) of section 1(1), if it appears to the court that there is a reasonable prospect of a reconciliation between the parties, it shall continue, or further continue, the action for such period as it thinks proper to enable attempts to be made to effect such a reconciliation; and if during any such continuation the parties cohabit with one another, no account shall be taken of such cohabitation for the purposes of that action.

(2) Adultery shall not be held to have been condoned within the meaning of section 1(3) of this Act by reason only of the fact that after the commission of the adultery the pursuer has continued or resumed cohabitation with the defender, provided that the pursuer has not cohabited with the defender at any time after the end of the period of three months from the date on which such cohabitation as is referred to in the said section 1(3) was continued or resumed as aforesaid.

(3) [*Repealed by Family Law (Scotland) Act 2006 (asp 2), Sch.3.*]

[1](4) In considering whether any period mentioned in paragraph (d) or (e) of section 1(2) of this Act has been continuous no account shall be taken of any period or periods not exceeding six months in all during which the parties cohabited with one another; but no such period or periods during which the parties cohabited with one another shall count as part of the period of non-cohabitation required by any of those paragraphs.

NOTE

  1.   Amended by Family Law (Scotland) Act 2006 (asp 2), Sch.3.

Action for divorce following on decree of separation

3.—(1) The court may grant decree in an action for divorce notwithstanding that decree of separation has previously been granted to the pursuer on the same, or substantially the same, facts as those averred in support of the action for divorce; and in any such action (other than an action for divorce by reason of section 1(2)(a) of this Act) the court may treat an extract decree of separation lodged in process as sufficient proof of the facts upon which such decree was granted.

(2) Nothing in this section shall entitle the court to grant decree of divorce without receiving evidence from the pursuer.

Postponement of decree of divorce where religious impediment to remarry exists

[1]**3A.**—(1) Notwithstanding that irretrievable breakdown of a marriage has been established in an action for divorce, the court may—

  (a) on the application of a party ("the applicant"); and
  (b) if satisfied—
       (i) that subsection (2) applies; and
       (ii) that it is just and reasonable to do so,

postpone the grant of decree in the action until it is satisfied that the other party has complied with subsection (3).

(2) This subsection applies where—

  (a) the applicant is prevented from entering into a religious marriage by virtue of a requirement of the religion of that marriage; and
  (b) the other party can act so as to remove, or enable or contribute to the removal of, the impediment which prevents that marriage.

(3) A party complies with this subsection by acting in the way described in subsection (2)(b).

(4) The court may, whether or not on the application of a party and notwithstanding that subsection (2) applies, recall a postponement under subsection (1).

(5) The court may, before recalling a postponement under subsection (1), order the other party to produce a certificate from a relevant religious body confirming that the other party has acted in the way described in subsection 2(b).

(6) For the purposes of subsection (5), a religious body is "relevant" if the applicant considers the body competent to provide the confirmation referred to in that subsection.

(7) In this section—

"religious marriage" means a marriage solemnised by a marriage celebrant of a prescribed religious body, and "religion of that marriage" shall be construed accordingly;

"prescribed" means prescribed by regulations made by the Scottish Ministers.

(8) Any reference in this section to a marriage celebrant of a prescribed religious body is a reference to—

(a) a minister, clergyman, pastor or priest of such a body;

(b) a person who has, on the nomination of such a body, been registered under section 9 of the Marriage (Scotland) Act 1977 (c.15) as empowered to solemnise marriages; or

(c) any person who is recognised by such a body as entitled to solemnise marriages on its behalf.

(9) Regulations under subsection (7) shall be made by statutory instrument; and any such instrument shall be subject to annulment in pursuance of a resolution of the Scottish Parliament.

NOTE
1. Inserted by Family Law (Scotland) Act 2006 (asp 2), s.15.

Actions for separation

4.—(1) Sections 1, 2 and 11 of this Act shall apply to an action for separation or separation and aliment brought after the commencement of this Act and decree in such action as those sections apply to an action for divorce and decree therein subject to—

(a) the modification that any reference to irretrievable breakdown of a marriage shall be construed as a reference to grounds justifying decree of separation of the parties to a marriage; and

(b) all other necessary modifications.

(2) In an action for separation or separation and aliment brought after the commencement of this Act, decree of separation shall not be pronounced except in accordance with the provisions of this section.

Financial provision for spouses and children

Orders for financial provision

[1] **5.**—(1) In an action for divorce (whether brought before or after the commencement of this Act), either party to the marriage may, at any time prior to decree being granted, apply to the court for any one or more of the following orders—

(a) an order for the payment to him or for his benefit by the other party to the marriage of a periodical allowance;

(b) an order for the payment to him or for his benefit by the other party to the marriage of a capital sum;

(c) an order varying the terms of any settlement made in

contemplation of or during the marriage so far as taking effect on or after the termination of the marriage:

Provided that any reference in this subsection to payment by the other party to the marriage shall include a reference to payment out of any estate belonging to that party or held for his benefit.

(2) Where an application under the foregoing subsection has been made in an action, the court, on granting decree in that action, shall make with respect to the application such order, if any, as it thinks fit, having regard to the respective means of the parties to the marriage and to all the circumstances of the case, including any settlement or other arrangements made for financial provision for any child of the marriage.

(3) Where an application for an order for the payment of a periodical allowance under subsection (1)(a) of this section has been withdrawn or refused, or where no such application has been made, either party to the marriage may apply to the court for such an order after the date of the granting of decree of divorce if since that date there has been a change in the circumstances of either of the parties to the marriage; and the court shall make with respect to that application such order, if any, as it thinks fit, having regard to the factors mentioned in subsection (2) of this section.

[2](4) Any order made under this section relating to the payment of a periodical allowance may, on an application by or on behalf of either party to the marriage (or his executor) on a change of circumstances, be varied or recalled by a subsequent order.

(5) Any order made under this section relating to payment of a periodical allowance—

(a) shall, on the death of the person by whom the periodical allowance is payable, continue to operate against that person's estate, but without prejudice to the making of an order under the last foregoing subsection;

(b) shall cease to have effect on the remarriage or death of the person to whom or for whose benefit the periodical allowance is payable, except in relation to any arrears due under it on the date of such remarriage or death.

(6) Provision shall be made by act of sederunt to impose upon the pursuer in an action for divorce to which section 1(2)(d) or 1(2)(e) of this Act relates a duty to inform the defender of his right to apply for—

(a) financial provision under this Act,

(b) an order providing for the custody, maintenance and education of any child of the marriage under section 9 of the Conjugal Rights (Scotland) Amendment Act 1861,

in such form and manner as the act of sederunt may require, and, for the purposes of this subsection, where the pursuer alleges that the address of the defender is unknown to him, he shall satisfy the court that all reasonable steps have been taken to ascertain it.

(7) Any reference in this section to a settlement shall be construed as including a settlement by way of a policy of assurance to which section 2 of the Married Women's Policies of Assurance (Scotland) Act 1880 relates.

NOTE

1. Repealed by the Family Law (Scotland) Act 1985 (c.37), Sch.2 (but see *ibid.*, s.28(3)).
2. Saved by the Forfeiture Act 1982 (c.34), s.3.

6–8. [*Repealed by the Family Law (Scotland) Act 1985 (c.37), Sch.2.*]

Supplemental

Abolition of oath of calumny

9. [*Repealed by Family Law (Scotland) Act 2006 (asp 2), s.14.*]

Right of husband to cite paramour as a co-defender and to sue for damages abolished

10.—(1) After the commencement of this Act the following rights of a husband shall be abolished, that is to say—

(a) the right to cite a paramour of his wife as a co-defender in an action for divorce, and

(b) the right to claim or to obtain damages (including solatium) from a paramour by way of reparation.

(2) Nothing in the provisions of the foregoing subsection shall preclude the court from awarding the expenses of the action for or against the paramour or alleged paramour in accordance with the practice of the court.

(3) Section 7 of the Conjugal Rights (Scotland) Amendment Act 1861 (citation of a co-defender in an action for divorce and decree for expenses against him) shall cease to have effect.

Curator *ad litem* to be appointed in certain cases

11. Provision shall be made by act of sederunt for the purpose of securing that, where in an action for divorce the defender is suffering from mental illness, the court shall appoint a curator *ad litem* to the defender.

Amendments, repeals and transitional provisions

12.—(1) The enactments described in Schedule 1 to this Act shall have effect subject to the amendments specified therein in relation to them respectively.

(2) The enactments specified in columns 1 and 2 of Schedule 2 to this Act are hereby repealed to the extent specified in relation to them respectively in column 3 of that Schedule.

(3) Subject to the following provisions of this section and without prejudice to the operation of section 38 of the Interpretation Act 1889 (effect of repeals), nothing in this section shall affect any proceedings brought, anything done, or the operation of any order made, under any enactment repealed by this section; nor shall anything in this Act be taken to revive any rule of law superseded by any enactment repealed by this section.

(4) Anything which, prior to the commencement of this Act, could have been done under section 2 of the Divorce (Scotland) Act 1938 or section 26 or 27 of the Succession (Scotland) Act 1964 may, after the commencement of this Act, be done under the corresponding provision of section 5 or 6 of this Act.

(5) An order under section 2 of the Divorce (Scotland) Act 1938 for the payment of an annual or periodical allowance to or for the behoof of a child of the marriage may, after the commencement of this Act, be varied or recalled by a subsequent order under subsection (2) of that section as if that section had not been repealed by this Act.

(6) Subsection (5) of section 5 of this Act shall apply in relation to an order for the payment of an annual or periodical allowance under section 2 of the Divorce (Scotland) Act 1938 or of a periodical allowance under section 26 of the Succession (Scotland) Act 1964 as it applies in relation to an order for the payment of a periodical allowance under the said section 5.

Interpretation

13.—[1] (1) In this Act, unless the context otherwise requires—

"action for divorce" has the meaning assigned to it by section 1(1) of this Act;

"the court" means, in relation to any action, the Court of Session or the sheriff court, as the case may require.

(2) For the purposes of this Act, the parties to a marriage shall be held to cohabit with one another only when they are in fact living together as man and wife; and "cohabitation" shall be construed accordingly.

(3) References to this Act to any enactment are references to that enactment as amended, and include references thereto as applied, by any other enactment, including, except where the context otherwise requires, this Act.

NOTE
  1. As amended by the Divorce Jurisdiction, Court Fees and Legal Aid (Scotland) Act 1983 (c.12), Sch.1, para.22.

Citation, commencement and extent

14.—(1) This Act may be cited as the Divorce (Scotland) Act 1976.

(2) This Act except section 8 shall come into operation on 1st January 1977.

(3) So much of section 12 of, and Schedule 1 to, this Act as affects the operation of section 16 of the Maintenance Orders Act 1950 shall extend to England and Wales and to Northern Ireland as well as Scotland, but save as aforesaid this Act shall extend to Scotland only.

[1]DAMAGES (SCOTLAND) ACT 1976

(1976 c.13)

An Act to amend the law of Scotland relating to the damages recoverable in respect of deaths caused by personal injuries; to define the rights to damages in respect of personal injuries and death which are transmitted to an executor; to abolish rights to assythment; to make provision relating to the damages due to a pursuer for patrimonial loss caused by personal injuries whereby his expectation of life is diminished; and for purposes connected with the matters aforesaid.

[13th April 1976]

NOTE
  1. Applied by the Merchant Shipping Act 1995 (c.21), Sch.8, Pt. II, para.6(2) (effective 1st January 1996: s.316(2)). See the Consumer Protection Act 1987 (c.43), s.6(2), and the Income and Corporation Taxes Act 1988 (c.1), s.329A (inserted by the Finance Act 1995 (c.4), s.142) (structured settlements: sums received after 1st May 1995).

Rights of relatives of a deceased person

[1]**1.**—(1) Where a person dies in consequence of personal injuries sustained by him as a result of an act or omission of another person, being an act or omission giving rise to liability to pay damages to the injured person or his executor, then, subject to the following provisions of this Act, the person liable to pay those damages (in this section referred to as "the responsible person") shall also be liable to pay damages in accordance with this section to any relative of the deceased, being a relative within the meaning of Schedule 1 to this Act.

(2) No liability shall arise under this section if the liability to the deceased or his executor in respect of the act or omission has been excluded or discharged (whether by antecedent agreement or otherwise) by the deceased before his death, or is excluded by virtue of any enactment.

[2] (3) The damages which the responsible person shall be liable to pay to a relative of a deceased under this section shall (subject to the provisions of this Act) be such as will compensate the relative for any loss of support suffered by him since the date of the deceased's death or likely to be suffered by him as a result of the act or omission in question, together with any reasonable expense incurred by him in connection with the deceased's funeral.

[3] (4) Subject to subsection (4A), if the relative is a member of the deceased's immediate family (within the meaning of section 10(2) of this Act) there shall be awarded, without prejudice to any claim under subsection (3) above, such sum of damages, if any, as the court thinks just by way of compensation for all or any of the following—

(a) distress and anxiety endured by the relative in contemplation of the suffering of the deceased before his death;

(b) grief and sorrow of the relative caused by the deceased's death;

(c) the loss of such non-patrimonial benefit as the relative might have been expected to derive from the deceased's society and guidance if the deceased had not died,

and the court in making an award under this subsection shall not be required to ascribe specifically any part of the award to any of paragraphs (a), (b) and (c) above.

[4] (4A) Notwithstanding section 10(2) of, and Schedule 1 to, this Act, no award of damages under subsection (4) above shall be made to a person related by affinity to the deceased.

[4] (4B) In subsection (4A), a "person related by affinity to the deceased" includes—

(a) a stepchild, step-parent, stepbrother or stepsister of the deceased; and

(b) any person who was an ascendant or descendant of any of the step-relatives mentioned in paragraph (a).

[5] (5) Subject to subsection (5A) below, in assessing for the purposes of this section the amount of any loss of support suffered by a relative of a deceased no account shall be taken of—

(a) any patrimonial gain or advantage which has accrued or will or may accrue to the relative from the deceased or from any other person by way of succession or settlement;

(b) any insurance money, benefit, pension or gratuity which has been, or will be or may be, paid as a result of the deceased's death;

and in this subsection—

"benefit" means benefit under the Social Security Act 1975 or the Social Security (Northern Ireland) Act 1975, and any payment by a friendly society or trade union for the relief or maintenance of a member's dependants;

"insurance money" includes a return of premiums; and

"pension" includes a return of contributions and any payment of a lump sum in respect of a person's employment.

(5A) Where a deceased has been awarded a provisional award of damages under section 12(2) of the Administration of Justice Act 1982, the making of that award does not prevent liability from arising under this section but in assessing for the purposes of this section the amount of any loss of support suffered by a relative of the deceased the court shall take into account such part of the provisional award relating to future patrimonial loss as was intended to compensate the deceased for a period beyond the date on which he died.

(6) In order to establish loss of support for the purposes of this section it shall not be essential for a claimant to show that the deceased was, or might have become, subject to a duty in law to provide or contribute to the support of the claimant; but if any such fact is established it may be taken into account in determining whether, and if so to what extent, the

deceased, if he had not died, would have been likely to provide or contribute to such support.

[6](7) Except as provided in this section or in Part II of the Administration of Justice Act 1982 or under section 1 of the International Transport Conventions Act 1983 no person shall be entitled by reason of relationship to damages (including damages by way of solatium) in respect of the death of another person.

NOTE

1. As amended by the Damages (Scotland) Act 1993 (c.5), s.1 (effective 18th April 1993: s.8(3)). See the Consumer Protection Act 1987 (c.43), s.6(1)(c). Extended (*prosp.*): see the Antarctic Minerals Act 1989 (c.21), s.13(1). Excluded by the Social Security Act 1989, s.22(4)(d) and the Social Security Administration Act 1992 (c.5), s.81(3)(d) (effective 1st July 1992: s.192(4)). See also s.92.
2. Extended: see the Administration of Justice Act 1982 (c.14), s.9(2).
3. Saved by the International Transport Conventions Act 1983 (c.14), Sch.1, para.1. Amended by the Family Law (Scotland) Act 2006 (asp 2), s.35.
4. Inserted by the Family Law (Scotland) Act 2006 (asp 2), s.35.
5. Applied by the International Transport Conventions Act 1983 (c.14), Sch.1, para.2.
6. As amended by the Administration of Justice Act 1982 (c.53), s.14(1), and the International Transport Conventions Act 1983 (c.14), Sch.1, para.4(a).

Transmissibility to executor of rights of deceased relative

[1] **1A.** Any right to damages under any provision of section 1 of this Act which is vested in the relative concerned immediately before his death shall be transmitted to the relative's executor; but, in determining the amount of damages payable to an executor by virtue of this section, the court shall have regard only to the period ending immediately before the relative's death.

NOTE

1. Inserted by the Damages (Scotland) Act 1993 (c.5), s.2 (effective 18th April 1993: s.8(3)).

Rights transmitted to executor in respect of deceased person's injuries

[1] **2.**—(1) Subject to the following provisions of this section, there shall be transmitted to the executor of a deceased person the like rights to damages in respect of personal injuries (including a right to damages by way of solatium) sustained by the deceased as were vested in him immediately before his death.

(2) There shall not be transmitted to the executor under this section a right to damages by way of compensation for patrimonial loss attributable to any period after the deceased's death.

(3) In determining the amount of damages by way of solatium payable to an executor by virtue of this section, the court shall have regard only to the period ending immediately before the deceased's death.

(4) In so far as a right to damages vested in the deceased comprised a right to damages (other than for patrimonial loss) in respect of injury resulting from defamation or any other verbal injury or other injury to reputation sustained by the deceased, that right shall be transmitted to the deceased's executor only if an action to enforce that right had been brought by the deceased before his death and had not been concluded by then within the meaning of section 2A(2) of this Act.

NOTE

1. As substituted by the Damages (Scotland) Act 1993 (c.5), s.3 (effective 18th April 1993: s.8(3)).

Enforcement by executor of rights transmitted to him

¹ **2A.**—(1) For the purpose of enforcing any right transmitted to an executor under section 1A or 2 of this Act the executor shall be entitled—

(a) to bring an action; or

(b) if an action for that purpose had been brought by the deceased but had not been concluded before his death, to be sisted as pursuer in that action.

(2) For the purpose of subsection (1) above, an action shall not be taken to be concluded while any appeal is competent or before any appeal taken has been disposed of.

NOTE
1. As inserted by the Damages (Scotland) Act 1993 (c.5), s.4 (effective 18th April 1993: s.8(3)).

Certain rights arising on death of another not transmissible

3. [*Repealed by the Damages (Scotland) Act 1993 (c.5), s.7(3) (effective 18th April 1993: s.8(3)).*]

Executor's claim not to be excluded by relatives' claims: and vice versa

¹ **4.** A claim by the executor of a deceased person for damages under section 2 of this Act is not excluded by the making of a claim by a relative of the deceased for damages under section 1 of this Act; or by a deceased relative's executor under section 1A of this Act; nor is a claim by a relative of a deceased person or by a deceased relative's executor for damages under the said section 1 or (as the case may be) the said section 1A excluded by the making of a claim by the deceased's executor for damages under the said section 2.

NOTE
1. As amended by the Administration of Justice Act 1982 (c.53), s.14(2)(a), and the Damages (Scotland) Act 1993 (c.5), Sched., para.1 (effective 18th April 1993: s.8(3)).

5. [*Repealed by the Administration of Justice Act 1982 (c.53), s.14(2).*]

Limitation of total amount of liability

¹ **6.**—²(1) Where in any action to which this section applies, so far as directed against any defender, it is shown that by antecedent agreement, compromise or otherwise, the liability arising in relation to that defender from the personal injuries in question had, before the deceased's death, been limited to damages of a specified or ascertainable amount, or where that liability is so limited by virtue of any enactment, nothing in this Act shall make the defender liable to pay damages exceeding that amount; and accordingly where in such an action there are two or more pursuers any damages to which they would respectively be entitled under this Act apart from the said limitation shall, if necessary, be reduced *pro rata*.

(2) Where two or more such actions are conjoined, the conjoined actions shall be treated for the purposes of this section as if they were a single action.

³(3) This section applies to any action in which, following the death of any person from personal injuries, damages are claimed—

(a) by the executor of the deceased, in respect of the injuries from which the deceased died;

⁴(b) in respect of the death of the deceased, by any relative of his, or, if the relative has died, by the relative's executor.

NOTE
1. Excluded by the International Transport Conventions Act 1983 (c.14), Sch.1, para.2.
2. As amended by the Administration of Justice Act 1982 (c.53), s.14(2)(b)(i).
3. Added by the Administration of Justice Act 1982 (c.53), s.14(2)(b)(ii).
4. As amended by the Damages (Scotland) Act 1993 (c.5), Sched., para.2 (effective 18th April 1993: s.8(3)).

Amendment of references in other Acts

7. In any Act passed before this Act, unless the context otherwise requires, any reference to solatium in respect of the death of any person (however expressed) shall be construed as a reference to a loss of society award within the meaning of section 1 of this Act; and any reference to a dependant of a deceased person, in relation to an action claiming damages in respect of the deceased person's death, shall be construed as including a reference to a relative of the deceased person within the meaning of this Act.

Abolition of right of assythment

8. After the commencement of this Act no person shall in any circumstances have a right to assythment, and accordingly any action claiming that remedy shall (to the extent that it does so) be incompetent.

Damages due to injured person for patrimonial loss caused by personal injuries whereby expectation of life is diminished

9.—(1) This section applies to any action for damages in respect of personal injuries sustained by the pursuer where his expected date of death is earlier than it would have been if he had not sustained the injuries.

(2) In assessing, in any action to which this section applies, the amount of any patrimonial loss in respect of the period after the date of decree—
  (a) it shall be assumed that the pursuer will live until the date when he would have been expected to die if he had not sustained the injuries (hereinafter referred to as the "notional date of death");
  (b) the court may have regard to any amount, whether or not it is an amount related to earnings by the pursuer's own labour or other gainful activity, which in its opinion the pursuer, if he had not sustained the injuries in question, would have received in the period up to his notional date of death by way of benefits in money or money's worth, being benefits derived from sources other than the pursuer's own estate;
  (c) the court shall have regard to any diminution of any such amount as aforesaid by virtue of expenses which in the opinion of the court the pursuer, if he had not sustained the injuries in question, would reasonably have incurred in the said period by way of living expenses.

Solatium for loss of expectation of life

[1] **9A.**—(1) In assessing, in an action for damages in respect of personal injuries, the amount of damages by way of solatium, the court shall, if—
  (a) the injured person's expectation of life has been reduced by the injuries; and
  (b) the injured person is, was at any time or is likely to become, aware of that reduction,
have regard to the extent that, in consequence of that awareness, he has suffered or is likely to suffer.

(2) Subject to subsection (1) above, no damages by way of solatium shall be recoverable in respect of loss of expectation of life.

(3) The court in making an award of damages by way of solatium shall not be required to ascribe specifically any part of the award to loss of expectation of life.

NOTE
1. Inserted by the Damages (Scotland) Act 1993 (c.5), s.5.

Interpretation

10.—[1] (1) In this Act, unless the context otherwise requires—

[2] "personal injuries" includes any disease or any impairment of a person's physical or mental condition and injury resulting from defamation or any other verbal injury or injury to reputation, or injury resulting from harassment actionable under section 8 of the Protection from Harassment Act 1997;

"relative", in relation to a deceased person, has the meaning assigned to it by Schedule 1 to this Act.

[3] (2) References in this Act to a member of a deceased person's immediate family are references to any relative of his who falls within any of subparagraphs (a) to (c) of paragraph 1 of Schedule 1 to this Act.

(3) References in this Act to any other Act are references to that Act as amended, extended or applied by any other enactment, including this Act.

NOTE
1. As amended by the Damages (Scotland) Act 1993 (c.5), s.7(3).
2. As amended by the Damages (Scotland) Act 1993 (c.5), Sched., para.3, and the Protection from Harassment Act 1997 (c.40), s.8(8), (effective June 16, 1997: SI 1997/ 1418).
3. As amended by the Administration of Justice Act 1982 (c. 53), s.14(4) and the Family Law (Scotland) Act 2006 (asp 2), s.35.

Repeals

11. [*Repealed by the Damages (Scotland) Act 1993 (c.5), s.7(3).*]

Citation, application to Crown, commencement and extent

12.—(1) This Act may be cited as the Damages (Scotland) Act 1976.
(2) This Act binds the Crown.
(3),(4) [Repealed by the Damages (Scotland) Act 1993 (c.5), s.7(3).]
(5) This Act extends to Scotland only.

SCHEDULES

Section 1   SCHEDULE 1

DEFINITION OF "RELATIVE"

[1] 1. In this Act "relative" in relation to a deceased person includes—

[1,4] (a) any person who immediately before the deceased's death was the spouse or civil partner of the deceased or in a relationship which had the characteristics of the relationship between civil partners;

[2] (aa) any person, not being the spouse or civil partner of the deceased, who was, immediately before the deceased's death, living with the deceased as husband or wife or in a relationship which had the characteristics of the relationship between civil partners;

[1] (b) any person who was a parent or child of the deceased;

(c) any person not falling within sub-paragraph (b) above who was accepted by the deceased as a child of his family;

(ca) any person not falling within sub-paragraph (b) above who accepted the deceased as a child of the person's family;

(cb) any person who—

157

(i) was the brother or sister of the deceased; or

(ii) was brought up in the same household as the deceased and who was accepted as a child of the family in which the deceased was a child;

(cc) any person who was a grandparent or grandchild of the deceased;

[4](d) any person not falling within sub-paragraph (b) or (cc) above who was an ascendant or descendant of the deceased;

[1,4](e) any person not falling within sub-paragraph (cb)(i) above who was, or was the issue of, a brother, sister, uncle or aunt of the deceased;

[1](f) any person who, having been a spouse of the deceased, had ceased to be so by virtue of a divorce; and

[3](g) any person who, having been a civil partner of the deceased, had ceased to be so by virtue of the dissolution of the civil partnership

but does not include any other person.

NOTE

1. Amended by the Civil Partnership Act 2004 (c.33), Sch.28, para.42 and Sch.30.

2. Inserted by the Administration of Justice Act 1982, s.14(4) and amended by Family Law (Scotland) Act 2006 (asp 2), Sch.2.

3. Inserted by the Family Law (Scotland) Act 2006 (asp 2), s.35.

4. Amended by the Family Law (Scotland) Act 2006 (asp 2), s.35.

------

2. In deducing any relationship for the purposes of the foregoing paragraph—

(a) any relationship by affinity shall be treated as a relationship by consanguinity; any relationship of the half blood shall be treated as a relationship of the whole blood; and the stepchild of any person shall be treated as his child; and

[1](b) section 1(1) of the Law Reform (Parent and Child) (Scotland) Act 1986 shall apply; and any reference (however expressed) in this Act to a relative shall be construed accordingly.

NOTE

1. As amended by the Law Reform (Parent and Child) (Scotland) Act 1986, Sch.1, para.15, with effect from 8th December 1986.

INDEX

References are to sections of Family Law (Scotland) Act 2006